European Psychiatry on the Eve of War: Aubrey Lewis, the Maudsley Hospital, and the Rockefeller Foundation in the 1930s

(*Medical History*, Supplement No. 22)

European Psychiatry on the Eve of War: Aubrey Lewis, the Maudsley Hospital, and the Rockefeller Foundation in the 1930s

edited by

KATHERINE ANGEL, EDGAR JONES and MICHAEL NEVE

(*Medical History*, Supplement No. 22)

London
The Wellcome Trust Centre for the History of Medicine at UCL
2003

Introduction, essays, notes and biographical register
© The Trustee of the Wellcome Trust, 2003

Introduction and Report by Aubrey Lewis
© Institute of Psychiatry, 2003

All Rights Reserved. No part of this publication may be reproduced, stored in a retrieval system, or transmitted, in any form or by any means, electronic mechanical photocopying, recording or otherwise, without prior permission.

ISBN 0-85484-092-3

Supplements to *Medical History* may be obtained by post from Professional & Scientific Publications, BMA House, Tavistock Square, London WC1H 9JR, UK.

Contents

Illustrations	vi
Introduction MICHAEL NEVE	1
Aubrey Lewis, Edward Mapother and the Maudsley EDGAR JONES	3
Defining Psychiatry: Aubrey Lewis's 1938 Report and the Rockefeller Foundation KATHERINE ANGEL	39
Aubrey Lewis's Introduction to his Report	57
Aubrey Lewis's Report on his Visits to Psychiatric Centres in Europe in 1937	64
Biographical Register	148
Index	179

Illustrations

1. Edward Mapother (1881–1940) (Bethlem Royal Hospital Archives)   4

2. Frederick Mott (1853–1926) (Bethlem Royal Hospital Archives)   6

3. Aubrey Lewis (1900–1975) and others in Boston in 1927 (Dr Naomi Cream)   9

4. Frederick Lucien Golla (1878–1968) (Institute of Psychiatry)   19

5. Aubrey reading to his daughter, Naomi, August 1937 (Dr Naomi Cream)   22

6. Aubrey Lewis and J S Harris, July 1939 (Dr Naomi Cream)   26

7. Aubrey Lewis in 1942 at Mill Hill EMS Hospital (Dr Naomi Cream)   30

Introduction

The appearance of this 1938 report for the Rockefeller Foundation by Aubrey Lewis will – at last – satisfy a period of prolonged interest in the report and its contents among historians of medicine and psychiatry in particular. It will also open up a number of new perspectives on the European medical world in the years immediately before the Second World War.

The first of these is the centrality of the financial power and the policy decision making of the Rockefeller Foundation. The involvement of the Rockefeller in granting funds both to institutions – such as the Maudsley Hospital in south London – and to individuals within it are right at the heart of Lewis's journey and the report he made. He had to see for himself how things were going in European psychiatry and how the Maudsley compared. He also needed American patronage. What kinds of medicine and specifically what kinds of psychiatry would the Rockefeller Foundation approve? Did its policymakers have models in mind – Johns Hopkins in Baltimore for example – which it hoped grant applicants would imitate, thereby transplanting certain medical practices into different national contexts? And would one of the aims of that transplantation be the reduction of such national differences, thereby generating a world-wide medicine that was as close to homogeneity and uniformity as possible? And what would be the politics of those decisions? Might some approved medical systems – such as a full-scale social psychiatry – actually replace politics, substituting instead the politics of health, with the Rockefeller as a mighty global contender? Katherine Angel has a more specific task to perform in her essay in this *Medical History* supplement than answering these large questions, but she captures in fine detail the various debates and decisions that got under way and the participants in those events. Her essay also conveys something of the richness of the Rockefeller archive itself and the rewards to be gained by visiting it.

Secondly, the publication of this edition contributes to another story that has preoccupied medical historians, who have again been waiting for news that has been some time in coming: the history of the Maudsley Hospital. It would be an exaggeration to say that the history of the Maudsley has been shrouded in mystery but it is most striking how a place of such importance and influence, however small its beginnings and how relatively recent its full blossoming, has not received full historical attention. The essay by Edgar Jones is a notable attempt to begin the telling of the Maudsley story from the 1920s onwards, based on original research and providing an invaluable historical context.

A third and final perspective and a very illuminating one is to be able to see the *making* as well as the financing of a medical specialism in a world already on the edge of conflict (what had already happened in Germany guaranteed that Lewis, an

Australian born Jew, would not visit there while on his European tour). The question was straightforward and up for grabs: what was psychiatry of the kind that the Maudsley might want to represent actually to be? Somehow, as it turned out, a difficult path had to be trod. On the one side there were psychology and psychoanalysis; no doubt diverting in general educated culture but of no practical assistance in cases of serious mental illness. (Edward Mapother as well as Aubrey Lewis were both hostile to the Tavistock Clinic in London). But on the other side lay the lure of radical organicist interventions – insulin coma, ECT, leucotomy and the rest. Here, one of the prized goals of the Maudsley practitioners – the long case history – could be forfeit. There was a task to be done – get on with it. This clinical impatience (and its attendant dangers for the lives of patients) was equally dangerous. The early history of the hospital was entirely to do with negotiating this Scylla and Charybdis.

In the period covered in this report and in the essays provided with it, the actual sums granted by the Rockefeller were not large and were usually dependent on the arrival of approved (and émigré) individuals. But the journeys made across the Atlantic (Lewis had been at Hopkins in 1926 on a Rockefeller fellowship) and the endless correspondence that came with those are testimony enough. And what Lewis saw in Europe, what he approved and – more often than not – disapproved are all part of the negotiation as to the foundations of a proper medical specialism and medical practice. This is a truly international story.

The essayists have provided their own acknowledgements. We wish to recognise the generosity of the Lewis family, which was crucial to the project, and so thanks go to Dr Naomi Cream, Dr Gilbert Lewis and Dr Julian Lewis; thanks go to the Maudsley Hospital and to the Institute of Psychiatry library for providing facilities; to the Rockefeller Foundation Archive for helping Katherine Angel when she was there as well as giving permission to quote from the archive. No historian works in a vacuum and there are two individuals who were models of enthusiasm and practical assistance: Volker Roelcke and Peter Voswinckel then both at the University of Lübeck. When we were preparing the biographical register of as many European psychiatrists as possible, they gave a great deal of biographical information which they, especially Peter, had accumulated. Jean-Christope Coffin in Paris also helped with some of the dates. As readers will note, the biographical register does nonetheless contain some missing dates: we can only apologise for those. In the interests of time and after Herculean labours, it was decided to call a halt to searching and to send the edition to press.

I personally wish to thank Caroline Tonson-Rye for impeccable editorial suggestions and guidance, with the deadline always in sight. Through the good offices of Tony David and Edgar Jones, the Psychiatry Research Trust contributed generously to expense costs. And finally a most heartfelt vote of thanks goes to both Professor Hal Cook, director of the Wellcome Trust Centre at University College London and to the Centre's administrator Alan Shiel. Without their support and their financial wizardry, the outcome would have been simple: the Lewis report of 1938 would never have been properly historically contextualised, edited or published.

Michael Neve,
The Wellcome Trust Centre for the History of Medicine at UCL

Aubrey Lewis, Edward Mapother and the Maudsley

EDGAR JONES

Aubrey Lewis was the most influential post-war psychiatrist in the UK. As clinical director of the Maudsley Hospital in Denmark Hill, London, and professor of psychiatry from 1946 until his retirement in 1966, he exercised a profound influence on clinical practice, training and academic research. Many junior psychiatrists, whom he had supervised or taught, went on to become senior clinicians and academics in their own right. Although not a figure widely known to the public (indeed, Lewis shunned personal publicity), he commanded respect in other medical disciplines and among psychiatrists throughout the world. A formidable and sometimes intimidating figure, he had a passion for intellectual rigour and had little patience with imprecision or poorly thought-out ideas. More than any other individual, Lewis was responsible for raising the status of psychiatry in the UK such that it was considered fit for academic study and an appropriate career for able and ambitious junior doctors.

Comparatively little has been written of Aubrey Lewis's formative professional life, and, indeed, the Maudsley Hospital itself has been somewhat neglected by historians during the important interwar years. This essay is designed to address these subjects and to evaluate the importance of Edward Mapother not only in shaping the Maudsley but in influencing Lewis, his successor.

The Maudsley Hospital

The Maudsley Hospital was officially opened by the Minister of Health, Sir Arthur Griffith-Boscawen, on 31 January 1923.[1] The construction had, in fact, been completed

Edgar Jones, PhD, Institute of Psychiatry & Guy's King's and St Thomas' School of Medicine, Department of Psychological Medicine, 103 Denmark Hill, London SE5 8AZ.

Considerable help and time has been generously offered by Dr Naomi Cream, Dr Gilbert Lewis and Dr Julian Lewis in the preparation of this essay. The author also wishes to thank the following who kindly helped with the research of this essay: Dr James Birley, Dr J J Fleminger, Professor Neil Kessel, Professor Alwyn Lishman, Dr Malcolm Pines, Professor Gerald Russell, Dr Charles Rycroft, Dr Michael von Cranach and Dr Gerald Wooster. The proposal to publish Sir Aubrey Lewis's report on European psychiatry was originally suggested by Martin Guha, librarian of the Institute of Psychiatry, and was enthusiastically supported by Professor Tony David. They have both provided consistent support for the project's completion. Thanks are also due to the Rockefeller Archive Center, the staff of the Bethlem Royal Hospital Archives, Beckenham, and in particular to Colin S Gale and Patricia Allderidge. Combat Stress generously allowed me to consult the minute books of the Ex-Services Welfare Society. Dr Rhodri Hayward kindly commented on an earlier draft. Harriet Meteyard is owed a debt of gratitude for her care in transcribing the original typewritten report.

[1] Bethlem Royal Hospital Archives (hereafter BRHA), C12/4, Mapother Box 13, *Order of proceedings on the occasion of the opening of the Maudsley Hospital.*

in 1915 but, in view of the need to tackle the epidemic of servicemen diagnosed with shell shock and other psychiatric injuries, it had been taken over by the armed forces and run as a subsidiary of King's College Hospital. Designated as a "neurological clearing hospital", patients were first admitted to the Maudsley on 6 January 1916 and continued to be treated under the auspices of the Royal Army Medical Corps until August 1919, when responsibility passed to the Ministry of Pensions.[2] Faced with an epidemic of shell shock and uncertain how best to treat sufferers, the authorities gave the Maudsley a key diagnostic and investigative role. As Mapother recalled, it "received patients suffering from neuroses and psychoses of practically all types, and after a sufficient spell of trained observation, distributed each man to another hospital according to his particular type".[3] In addition, it was to undertake research into the causes of shell shock. Frederick Mott, director of the County of London Asylums Laboratory at Claybury, moved his scientific team to the Maudsley to investigate the pathology of this puzzling disorder.

When the hostilities came to an end and the Ministry of Pensions assumed responsibility for the treatment of soldiers hospitalised with so-called "war neuroses", it was necessary to recruit a medical superintendent to run the Maudsley. They chose Edward

Figure 1: A formal portrait of Edward Mapother (1881–1940) taken when he was part-time medical superintendent of the Maudsley Hospital (Bethlem Royal Hospital Archives).

[2] Patricia Allderidge, 'The foundation of the Maudsley Hospital', in German E Berrios and Hugh Freeman (eds), *150 years of British psychiatry, 1841–1991*, London, Gaskell, 1991, pp. 79–88, p. 87.

[3] E Mapother, 'Discussion on functional nervous disease in the fighting services', *Proceedings of the Royal Society of Medicine*, 1936, **29**: 855–68, p. 859.

Mapother (1881–1940), a former asylum doctor with military experience, whose tough and pragmatic policy at the army's neurological hospital in Stockport had impressed them.[4] Chronic or resistant cases of shell shock presented real treatment conundrums, while at the same time raising compelling questions of aetiology and pathological mechanisms. Mapother recalled how his service patients had been assembled in front of the Maudsley on 11 November 1919 to mark Armistice Day. The veterans, he wrote,

were lined up on the front drive awaiting the lorries which were to take them on a tour of the town. The end of the war was signalled by the maroons which had hitherto been the customary warning of an air-raid; "shell shockers" fell down in heaps on the ground.[5]

Although the Ministry intended that the Maudsley treat servicemen suffering from "severe neurasthenia", by December 1919 Mapother reported that "of the patients recently admitted about 90% are certifiable insane on admission" and were not voluntary. The restrictions and precautions that these psychotic veterans needed inhibited his ability to treat those with shell shock at a time when the waiting list numbered 67.[6] Facing spiralling costs for war pensions, the Ministry closed the hospital in November 1920, when Mapother returned to Long Grove Asylum as its deputy medical superintendent.[7]

Whilst the hospital operated under the auspices of the Ministry of Pensions, the London County Council (LCC) had been exploring the practicalities of opening the hospital for civilians in accordance with Henry Maudsley's original gift. Both Mapother and Mott provided staffing estimates and costs. In 1919, the Maudsley panel of the LCC's general purposes committee agreed that a part-time medical superintendent should be appointed for a period of six years. However, a general shortage of public funds compounded by a deep economic depression resulted in slow progress and it was not until March 1922 that Mapother was appointed as medical superintendent with a salary of £1,202 a year.[8] Aged forty-one, Mapother took on a role that was to consume his energy and interest until weakened health forced premature retirement.

Having experienced how difficult it had been to treat soldiers with psychological disorders and who had little motive to recover, Mapother made it a cardinal principle that no patient was to be admitted under section, nor would they be certified once in the hospital. All patients were voluntary and were free to leave on giving twenty-four hours' notice. Thus, a clear distinction was drawn between the Maudsley and the network of asylums that traditionally treated major mental illness in the UK. Mapother identified the following disorders as suitable for treatment:

Neuroses (hysteria of various forms, neurasthenia, anxiety and obsessional states), and certain varieties of psychoses, e.g. mild phases of the manic-depressive type, psychoses associated with exhaustion, with pregnancy and the puerperal period, with post-infective states, with syphilitic

---

[4] 'Obituary Edward Mapother', *Br. med. J.*, 1940, **i**: 552–3.

[5] E Mapother, 'War neurosis', *J. R. Army med. Corps*, 1937, **68**: 39–40.

[6] Public Record Office (hereafter PRO), PIN15/55 Treatment of Neurasthenia, E Mapother to Colonel Sheen, Ministry of Pensions, 29 December 1919, and 9 January 1920.

[7] BRHA, C12/4, Mapother Box 14, R H Curtis to E Mapother, letter, 5 October 1939.

[8] BRHA, C12/4, Mapother Box 14, H F Keene to E Mapother, letter, 3 March 1922.

brain disease of the interstitial types, with alcoholism and other drug habits, with endocrine disturbances, and generally cases exhibiting mental symptoms associated with all forms of definite bodily disease.[9]

Accommodation was provided for 157 patients in six wards each of twenty-four beds, divided equally between men and women, together with a further thirteen private rooms for women.[10] Mapother took great care over the appointment of the nursing staff: six general nurses, a matron with both general and mental training, and four ex-Voluntary Aid Detachments (VADs) whom he had known during the war.[11] With the help of Sir Frederick Mott, Mapother chose the original medical staff, recruiting three men (Drs A A W Petrie, the deputy medical superintendent, W S Dawson and William Moodie) from the LCC Service and one woman (Dr Mary Barkas). In its first year of operation, the Maudsley treated a total of 1,012 patients of whom 462 were admitted.[12]

Figure 2: Frederick Mott (1853–1926), wearing the uniform of a major in the Royal Army Medical Corps, seated at his laboratory bench in the Maudsley. As director of the London County Council's Central Pathological Laboratory at Claybury, he conducted extensive research into the physiology of the central nervous system in relation to mental illness. In 1916, when the military authorities found themselves faced with the apparently insoluble problem of shell shock, Mott transferred his laboratory to the Maudsley to study its physical effects on servicemen (Bethlem Royal Hospital Archives).

[9] 'The study of insanity: opening of Maudsley', *New Statesman*, 24 February 1923, p. 594.
[10] 'Opening of the Maudsley Hospital', *Hospital and Health Review*, March 1923, p. 142.
[11] A A W Petrie, 'The early days', *Bethlem Maudsley Hospital Gazette*, 1960, **3**: 8–10, p. 9.
[12] BRHA, C12/4, Mapother Box 14, Maudsley Hospital Medical Superintendent's annual report, year ended 31 January 1925.

Edward Mapother

The son of Dr Edward Dillon Mapother (1835–1908),[13] a professor of anatomy and former president of the Royal College of Surgeons of Ireland, Edward came from several generations of landed gentry.[14] Born in Merrion Square, Dublin, he was educated in England at University College School and University College Hospital. As house physician to Risien Russell, Mapother gained a lasting appreciation of neurology, which was later expressed in his plan to open a neurological wing at the Maudsley. Having completed his MD in 1908, Mapother then joined the staff of Long Grove Asylum, Epsom, as an assistant medical officer.[15] He had worked as a locum in various mental hospitals and found the work appealing despite its low status. Perhaps because psychiatry was not considered prestigious within the medical profession, Mapother then studied for a fellowship of the Royal College of Surgeons, achieving this in 1910. Curiously, he did not take his membership of the Royal College of Physicians until forty, describing it as his most difficult qualification. At Long Grove, Mapother found himself in distinguished company, including Hubert Bond, Bernard Hart and Henry Devine. Bernard Hart recalled that Mapother then had a reputation of being lazy;[16] this stood in stark contrast to his post-war career at the Maudsley when he over-worked to the extent of damaging his health.

Shortly after the outbreak of war in 1914, Mapother joined the Royal Army Medical Corps (RAMC) and served in France both as a surgeon and a medical officer attached to a field ambulance of the Lahore Division. In September 1915, deployed to an advanced dressing station during the battle of Loos, Mapother recalled seeing "something of the wholesale panic of large units, and a few cases of delirious shell shock".[17] After a posting to Mesopotamia where he caught dysentery, Mapother went to India to work as a surgeon but came home with sciatica in April 1917. He completed the three-month course in military psychiatry at the Red Cross Military Hospital, Maghull, before taking command of the neurological division of No. 2 Western General Hospital, Stockport.[18] Treating servicemen with a variety of post-combat disorders, including shell shock and disordered action of the heart (DAH), Mapother recalled taking a tough line:

Seven hundred men passed through the two hospitals of which I had charge ... So long as the war lasted, I set my face rigidly against discharge from the army and a pension, which was obviously what most of them wanted. After the armistice it was impossible to get support for this policy.[19]

---

[13] 'Obituary, Edward Dillon Mapother', *Lancet*, 1908, **i**: 823.
[14] Aubrey Lewis, 'Edward Mapother and the making of the Maudsley Hospital', *Br. J. Psychiatry*, 1969, **115**: 1349–66, p. 1350.
[15] 'Obituary, Edward Mapother', *Lancet*, 1940, **i**: 624–5.
[16] Lewis, 'Mapother', op. cit., note 14 above, p. 1365.
[17] BRHA, C12/4, Mapother Box 14, E Mapother to J R Rees, letter, 18 November 1938, p. 1.
[18] Ben Shephard, ' "The early treatment of mental disorders": R G Rows and Maghull 1914–1918', in Hugh Freeman and German Berrios (eds), *150 years of British psychiatry*, London, Athlone, 1996, pp. 434–64, on pp. 447–8.
[19] BRHA, C12/4, Mapother Box 14, E Mapother to J R Rees, letter, 18 November 1938, p. 2.

Mapother subsequently observed that one of the main difficulties preventing "the sane handling of war neuroses was the wave of sentimentality which swept the country – the disposition to regard as heroes all who joined the army".[20] This pragmatic approach endeared him to the Ministry of Pensions, which in August 1919, appointed him to run their special hospital for war neuroses in the buildings at Denmark Hill constructed to house the Maudsley.

Mapother had an enduring interest in war syndromes and the psychological problems of veterans. In March 1925, he was appointed psychiatric consultant to the Ex-Services Welfare Society (today called Combat Stress).[21] As such, he assessed veterans for their suitability for treatment in the Society's residential homes. From 1935 onwards, Mapother helped to organise annual conferences on "war neuroses", which drew together psychiatrists, senior members of the armed forces and pension officials.[22] His expertise in this area was acknowledged by the government in July 1939 when he was invited to join the Horder Committee – a select group of experts set up to debate the question of war neurosis, its treatment and any question of financial compensation.

Lewis and the Maudsley

On 29 June 1928, Aubrey Lewis began working at the Maudsley as a researcher, investigating sleep.[23] He had originally contacted Mapother when working at Queen Square and he applied for a position there because of the hospital's rising reputation. Lewis had not got far with this study when a vacancy for an assistant medical officer arose to which he was appointed.

Although Lewis spent the greater part of his professional career at the Maudsley, his route there had been a complicated one. An Australian, originally interested in anthropology, he had decided to apply in 1925 for a Rockefeller fellowship in psychology and psychiatry "with the special object of training the holder for studying the mental traits of the Australian aborigine". Thus, Lewis was initially drawn to psychiatry not for itself but as a way of enhancing his ability to undertake anthropological research.

Awarded a one-year Rockefeller fellowship in January 1926,[24] Lewis chose to study in the United States where a number of departments of psychiatry had been opened in the major medical schools.[25] In September 1926, he travelled to the Boston Psychopathic Hospital to work under Macfie Campbell. Between April and May 1927, Lewis was based at Dr William Healy's children's clinic at the Judge Baker Foundation. In June, Lewis went to the Phipps Psychiatric Clinic, Johns Hopkins University Medical School, Baltimore, to study under the Swiss neuropsychiatrist, Adolf Meyer, who was to exercise an important impact on his thinking.[26] Lewis attended Meyer's 9 a.m.

---

[20] Mapother, op. cit., note 3 above, pp. 862–3.

[21] Ex-Services Welfare Society Minute Book, 3, 31 March 1925; held by Combat Stress.

[22] Ex-Services Welfare Society Minute Book, 9, 3 June 1937, p. 61; 10, 7 September 1939, p. 78; held by Combat Stress.

[23] BRHA, C12/4, Mapother Box 14, Staff files.

[24] Norma S Thompson to Aubrey Lewis, letter, 12 January 1926; held by the Lewis family.

[25] Dr Clifford W Wells to Aubrey Lewis, letter, 8 January 1926; held by the Lewis family.

[26] Michael Gelder, 'Adolf Meyer and his influence on British psychiatry', in German E Berrios and Hugh Freeman (eds), *150 years of British psychiatry, 1841–1991*, London, Gaskell, 1991, pp. 419–35, pp. 431–2.

Figure 3: Aubrey Lewis (1900–1975) in Boston as part of his Rockefeller fellowship during 1927. From left to right: Professor Hartwell, unknown technician, A J Lewis, and Julia Denning (Dr Naomi Cream).

seminar and also treated patients (continuous narcosis, warm baths for anxiety states and even practised psychotherapy, which he judged not very successful). As a tutor, Meyer emphasised attention to detail, careful history taking and clarity of thought, though Lewis recalled that he was often difficult to follow perhaps because of language difficulties. Nevertheless, his grasp of the literature and intellectual honesty made Meyer an inspirational figure.

In August 1927, Lewis was awarded an extension to his fellowship so that he could spend three months at the National Hospital for Epilepsy and Nervous Diseases at Queen Square and a further three months in Germany. In London between October and December 1927, he worked with Gordon Holmes (1876–1965) as a clinical assistant. An aggressive and forceful personality, Holmes had built a reputation as consultant neurologist to the British Expeditionary Force during the war. With Henry Head, he had conducted pioneering research into the neurophysiology of sensory perception and the location of sensation. Although painstaking and a lucid thinker, Holmes soon became impatient with those who could not keep pace. Junior doctors who incurred his displeasure would be hit with a patellar hammer to the sound of his edict "Maybe I have to bang it into you".[27] Nevertheless, Lewis recalled that Holmes had been a conscientious tutor and he held his intellectual achievements in high esteem.

[27] John Howells interviewed by Hugh Freeman (1990), in Greg Wilkinson (ed.), *Talking about psychiatry*, London, Gaskell, 1993, pp. 207–29, on p. 213; J Purdon Martin, 'Reminiscences of Queen Square', *Br. med. J.*, 1981, **283**: 1640–2, p. 1641.

In Paris, en route for Berlin, Lewis obtained a letter of introduction to Professor Karl Bonhoeffer (1868–1948) in Berlin. When in Germany, he also studied under Karl Beringer and Mayer-Gross in Heidelberg. Lewis later recalled that Bonhoeffer's ideas had exercised the greatest influence on the development of his own philosophy of psychiatry. By proposing a fundamental distinction between endogenous and exogenous causes, Bonhoeffer proposed the existence of symptomatic psychoses. In contrast to schizophrenia or manic-depressive psychosis, these exogenous reaction disorders did not involve "a pathologic formation of certain functional systems" but were the result of "a reaction of inherently healthy brains to damages that have their onset during the course of life".[28] In the United States, similar ideas were explored by Adolf Meyer, who also had a significant influence over the Maudsley model of psychiatry.

Due to return to Adelaide in March 1928 to resume a career in academic psychiatry, Lewis met resistance. He was informed that it was unlikely such an opportunity would be created and that he should seek a position at the town's Parkside mental hospital.[29] While apparently remaining in London at the end of his fellowship, Lewis spent three months trying to find a more suitable post as it was a condition of his award that he return to Australia on its conclusion. In what must have been a low point in his life, Lewis then contacted the Rockefeller Foundation to request that they release him from this obligation. When it became clear that his training would not be used to great advantage if he were to return to Australia, it was agreed that he could remain in the UK. As a result, he decided to settle in his father's homeland. In London exploring his options, Lewis contacted Bernard Hart, consultant psychiatrist at University College Hospital. Over tea at the Royal Society of Medicine, Hart suggested that he apply to the Maudsley as the edge in training and research had moved there from the Bethlem.

Presumably to visit his parents, Lewis made a return visit to Australia in November 1930, working his passage on the *S S Otranto* as an assistant surgeon.[30] His merchant navy uniform subsequently found its way into his children's dressing-up box, though it had a final outing in the 1956 Christmas show at University College Hospital, which starred Jonathan Miller, son of the Maudsley psychiatrist, Emmanuel Miller.

Family and Education

Aubrey Lewis was the only son of George Solomon Lewis (1871–1931), a Jewish emigrant to Adelaide, South Australia.[31] George Lewis was the son of a carpenter and joiner formerly of Posen, Prussia, who had come to London by 1851 where he married the daughter of an established English Jewish family. One of eight children, George Lewis was orphaned at ten, and his relatives sent him to Australia in his mid teens where a married, older sister was living. He trained as a watchmaker and jeweller but never became wealthy. In Adelaide, he met Rachel Isaacs

---

[28] K-J Neumärker, 'Karl Bonhoeffer and the concept of symptomatic psychoses', *Hist. Psychiatry*, 2001, **12**: 213–26, p. 220.

[29] BRHA, C12/3, Lewis Box 10, C H Hacket, 'A few personal notes on the late Sir Aubrey Lewis' (typescript, 28 April 1975), p. 1.

[30] Certificate of Discharge, Aubrey J Lewis, 13 December 1930; held by the Lewis family.

[31] Information provided by Dr Naomi Cream, 14 December 2001.

(1866–1951), a prize-winning amateur elocutionist and teacher in the Hebrew school attached to the synagogue. She had been born in Tynemouth, though her parents also from Posen had emigrated to Australia when she was an infant. In August 1899, George Lewis married Rachel in the Adelaide Synagogue, and Aubrey was born on 8 November 1900.

Curiously for a person with a powerful academic bent, Aubrey Lewis did not learn to read until he was "six and a bit". Measles may have delayed his education as medical advice was then to avoid eyestrain. Being of modest means, George and Rachel Lewis tried to obtain financial assistance for their son's schooling at the prestigious Anglican St Peter's College in Adelaide on the grounds of a distant family connection with its Jewish benefactor, Benjamin Mendes da Costa.[32] Their application was turned down and Aubrey Lewis was sent to the Catholic Christian Brothers College, where he soon revealed a natural academic bent.[33] It is not certain when he decided on a medical career, though he had laid the foundations at school. In 1917, Lewis passed higher examinations in English literature, Latin, German, physics and inorganic chemistry; all were with credit apart from physics.

Lewis was a diligent and committed medical student. His passion for language was given expression as editor of the Medical Students Society's *Review* and as a regular participant in debates. Although the Adelaide Medical School did not have an outstanding reputation for medicine, it had appointed the distinguished anatomist and anthropologist, Frederick Wood Jones, who was to exercise a significant influence on Lewis's career.

After graduation in 1923, Lewis completed his house jobs at Adelaide Hospital, where a year later he was appointed as a medical registrar. His first ambition was to become a neurologist but having clinical contact with aborigines who came to the hospital for treatment, Lewis was drawn to anthropology. In 1925, under the influence of Wood Jones, together with T D Campbell he made detailed observations of twenty-six aborigines to record personality characteristics, colour of hair, eyes and skin, together with notes on ear formation and eyebrow ridges. The notebook kept by Lewis showed that he had recorded detailed accounts of people's dreams. While studying in the Adelaide public library as a schoolboy, Lewis had read the works of Freud. It is possible that this interest had been inspired either by Freud's *The interpretation of dreams* (1900), or *Totem and taboo* (1913),[34] which, in exploring the origins of the incest taboo, made reference to Australian aboriginals.

When Campbell and Lewis presented their findings at a meeting of the Royal Society of Australia in July 1926, they stressed that "it was impossible to perform valuable work among natives by hurried expeditions. Workers needed special training in research and must settle near the habitations of the aborigines and be patient and

---

[32] Naomi Cream, 'Revd Solomon Lyon of Cambridge, 1775–1820', *Jewish Historical Studies: Transactions of the Jewish Historical Society of England*, 1999–2001, **36**: 31–69, p. 68.

[33] Michael Shepherd, 'A representative psychiatrist: the career, contributions and legacies of Sir Aubrey Lewis', *Psychol. Med.*, 1986, supplement 10: 1–31, pp. 7–8.

[34] S Freud, *The interpretation of dreams*, vols 4 and 5 of *The standard edition of the complete psychological works of Sigmund Freud*, London, Hogarth Press, 1953; S Freud, *Totem and taboo*, vol. 13 of *The standard edition*, London, Hogarth Press, 1955.

painstaking".[35] Taking this message to heart, Lewis realised that he would need to study experimental psychology and applied to the Rockefeller Foundation to train in the United States.[36] However, a discussion with the Adelaide professor of psychology, whose interests lay in a philosophical direction, made it clear that if he were to pursue this training there would be no post for Lewis on his return. As a result, he decided to alter the focus of his study from psychology to psychiatry.

The Maudsley Model of Psychiatry

The first issue that Mapother sought to address was the low standing of psychiatry in medicine. Although a post-graduate qualification, the Diploma in Psychological Medicine (DPM), had been introduced, academic psychiatry had yet to emerge in the UK as a distinct discipline. There were so-called alienists who worked in large asylums treating major mental illness and small numbers of physicians with an interest in psychological questions who investigated functional somatic disorders such as railway spine and neurasthenia. Training and research remained ad hoc, proceeding according to the interests of particular consultants. Mapother believed that the only way to bring these diverse elements together and provide them with a structure, was to establish the Maudsley as a centre of clinical excellence.

Having recruited able and experienced doctors from the traditional asylums, Mapother insisted that permanent staff obtain their membership of the Royal College of Physicians to give the Maudsley medical credibility. Mildred Creak, the first child psychiatrist at the Maudsley, recalled that Mapother had urged her to obtain her MRCP. "Where I had come from", she recalled,

> They thought it quite good to get the DPM and I had no more thought of taking membership than of a degree in Greek history. He issued the idea as a firm ultimatum, and what a sound policy that proved, for we never lost sight (nor did he) of psychiatry as a branch of general medicine.[37]

Dr C P Blacker, who joined the Maudsley from Guy's Hospital in 1927, believed that he owed his appointment in part to his having obtained the MRCP. Both J S Harris, the deputy superintendent, and Lewis successfully sat the exam in 1929 at a time when the pass rate was rumoured to have been 10 per cent.

As regards doctrine, Mapother avoided a rigid adherence to any school of thought and firmly believed in advance through empirical research. The problem with psychiatry during the 1920s was that little hard evidence existed on which to build general theories. Because shell shock had been shown to be without neurological basis (despite Mott's earlier claim that the concussive and toxic effects of exploding gases caused microscopic haemorrhage),[38] the "organicists" had been forced to

---

[35] Press cutting 'Royal Society meets: Paper on Aborigines', 8 July 1926. These findings became Lewis first academic publication: T D Campbell and Aubrey J Lewis, 'The aborigines of South Australia: dental observations recorded at Ooldea', *Aust. J. Dent.*, 1926, **30**: 371–6.

[36] Institute of Psychiatry, Sir Aubrey Lewis interviewed by Michael Shepherd, c. 1970.

[37] Mildred Creak, 'The birth of child psychiatry', *Bethlem Maudsley Hospital Gazette*, 1961, **4**: 62–3, p. 62.

[38] Frederick W Mott, 'The effects of high explosives upon the central nervous system', *Lancet*, 1916, i: 331–8, 441–9.

retreat. Psychological explanations, sometimes distilled from psycho-analytic theory, had gained a little momentum from their apparent success in the treatment of so-called "war neurosis", though most of medicine remained unimpressed by these interpretations. The foundation of the Tavistock Clinic by Hugh Crichton-Miller (1877–1959) in 1920 reflected the small but growing interest in psycho-dynamic concepts.

It is far from certain that Mapother had a defined blueprint for academic psychiatry when he took command of the Maudsley in 1923. He was not aligned to any school of thought and had been educated in a spirit of sceptical empiricism. In essence, Mapother believed that the individual was a psychobiological unity to be dissected and classified at great risk. While Mapother recognised that schizophrenia and bi-polar effective disorder were different from neuroses and from organic brain disease, the distinction between neurosis and psychosis was not considered hard and fast and was regarded of limited diagnostic use. Mapother believed in the importance of hard facts, such as the precise amount of alcohol consumed by a patient. Although he encouraged a questioning attitude, Mapother disapproved of cross-discipline speculation about causation and the meaning of symptoms.[39] He was ambivalent about psychoanalysis.[40] Respectful of the writings of Freud and willing to employ a small number of psychoanalytically-orientated psychiatrists (such as W H de B Hubert), Mapother was highly critical of most psycho-dynamic hypotheses and regarded the Tavistock Clinic with disdain. He favoured organic factors in reaching clinical judgements.

Because of the difficulty in identifying hard clinical evidence to guide diagnosis and treatment and the need to demonstrate thoroughness, Mapother insisted that staff take scrupulous care over medical histories. As a trainee at the Maudsley, William Sargant recalled collecting over thirty pages of detailed information on one patient. In the absence of effective interventions, Sargant believed that such exercises gave "us a feeling that we were doing something for the patient by learning so much about him, even if we could not yet find any relief for his suffering".[41] Sargant also argued that the introduction of new treatments (insulin coma therapy, ECT, leucotomy and medication) removed the necessity for such history taking. Lewis, who was less impressed by some of these fashionable innovations, continued to insist that registrars gather extensive patient profiles during the 1950s and 1960s. Although he was certainly right to assume that the empirical justification for particular treatments was far from conclusive, it is less certain whether the meticulous detail that he demanded in the presentation of case histories was necessary. In part, Lewis may have used the procedure as a test to identify robust and motivated registrars.

As regards treatment, Mapother adopted a sceptical attitude to new interventions and followed the doctor's first dictum to do no harm. In the 1930s, for example, Sargant was keen to try cardiazol convulsions for resistant depression. Because cardiazol fits could produce anxiety and terror in the patient, clinical trials were not permitted at the Maudsley. Waiting for the absence of Mapother and his key deputy (presumably Lewis), Sargant recalled that he then persuaded Dr Sinclair, a visiting physician from

---

[39] Aldwyn Stokes, 'The teacher', *Bethlem Maudsley Hospital Gazette*, 1960, **3**: 10–15, pp. 12–13.

[40] Malcolm Pines, 'The development of the psychodynamic movement', in German E Berrios and Hugh Freeman (eds), *150 years of British psychiatry, 1841–1991*, London, Gaskell, 1991, pp. 206–31, p. 225.

[41] William Sargant, *The unquiet mind: the autobiography of a physician in psychological medicine* London, Heinemann, 1967, p. 36.

the Royal Melbourne Hospital, to administer the drug with apparent success. Insulin coma therapy was not introduced at the Maudsley until November 1938. The caution shown by Mapother in view of the serious medical risks to a patient undergoing such treatment was fully justified in 1957 by a controlled trial of coma induced by barbiturate compared with insulin.[42] Brian Ackner, Arthur Harris and A J Oldham found no significant differences in their efficacy for samples of schizophrenic and schizo-affective patients, and concluded that "insulin is not the specific therapeutic agent".[43] With the introduction of chlorpromazine and other neuroleptics, insulin coma therapy could no longer be justified.[44]

In wartime, when Maudsley staff were divided between Sutton and Mill Hill, the differences between the two schools of thought became apparent. In 1942, Louis Minski, medical superintendent at the former, also allowed Sargant and Eliot Slater to use ECT, insulin coma therapy and even to refer some servicemen suffering from post-combat disorders for leucotomies.[45] Lewis, as clinical director at Mill Hill, adopted Mapother's policy of critical restraint and commendably refused to allow any prefrontal leucotomies. Indeed, so incensed was he by the fashion of treating patients by this experimental method that Lewis wrote a stern editorial in the *Lancet* arguing that the efficacy of the operation should be the subject of thorough investigation by the therapeutic trials committee of the Medical Research Council.[46]

Because so many of Mapother's senior colleagues (Thomas Tennent, Lewis and Desmond Curran) had trained with Adolf Meyer (1866–1950), his ideas began to dominate during the 1930s. Swiss-born, Meyer had migrated to the United States in 1892, where as professor of psychiatry at Johns Hopkins University he proposed a unified vision of psychiatry that attempted to lift the study and treatment of mental illness to the level of all legitimate medical enterprise.[47] He argued for the full integration of mental institutions into the emerging university medical schools and hospitals. He offered a doctrine of psychobiology in which psyche and soma were considered different dimensions of the same entity. An individual's personality was to be the primary object of study. Meyer interpreted mental illness not as a structural defect of mind or body but as the lowering of a person's ability to function – a struggle that was bound up with his success in social relations. Instead of disease, Meyer, spoke in terms of maladaptation, or "maladjustment". Hence differences between normality and abnormality, between psychosis and neurosis were not absolute but shades of grey.

Meyer argued that the so-called functional psychoses (schizophrenia, manic-depression) were reaction patterns of the central nervous system and represented the interplay of three causal factors, heredity, physical disease and emotional development.

[42] Edward Shorter, *A history of psychiatry: from the era of the asylum to the age of Prozac*, New York, John Wiley & Sons, 1997, pp. 209–15.

[43] Brian Ackner, Arthur Harris, and A J Oldham, 'Insulin treatment of schizophrenia, a controlled study', *Lancet*, 1957, **i**: 607–11, on p. 611.

[44] M Fink, R Shaw, and F S Coleman, 'Comparative study of chlorpromazine and insulin coma in the therapy of psychosis', *JAMA*, 1958, **166**: 1846–50.

[45] Sargant, op. cit., note 41 above, pp. 54–5, 78, 97; William Sargant, and Eliot Slater, *An introduction to physical methods of treatment in psychiatry*, Edinburgh, E & S Livingstone, 1944.

[46] Editorial, 'Physical approach to the brain', *Lancet*, 1943, **i**: 404–5.

[47] Jack D Pressman, *The last resort: psychosurgery and the limits of medicine*, Cambridge University Press, 1998, p. 20.

Treatment was designed to ameliorate the patient's condition; guidance, re-education, occupational therapy and home visits by social workers were all encouraged in an attempt to improve the person's condition.[48]

Meyer found two significant allies in the implementation of his plan for psychiatry. The first was Thomas Salmon (1876–1927), chief medical officer of the National Committee for Mental Hygiene, and the second was Alan Gregg, the charismatic director of the medical sciences programme of the Rockefeller Foundation. Salmon, though a bacteriologist by training, had been recruited into the US Army to design a comprehensive system for the prevention and treatment of shell-shock cases following America's entry to the First World War.[49] Having studied British and French methods in detail, he set out to create a corps of neuropsychiatrists that would win the respect of other medical disciplines. After the war, he attempted to exploit the impetus given to the discipline by establishing or up-grading university psychiatric departments. In addition, Salmon strove to create a national system of medical facilities for veterans to treat war-related psychological injuries.[50]

In accord with its mission "to promote the well-being of mankind", the Rockefeller Foundation, the largest private charity of the day, had given medical science its highest priority. Within this strategy, psychiatry was identified as a primary target because it was regarded as "the most backward, the most needed, and the most probably fruitful field in medicine".[51] Under Gregg's direction, millions of dollars were invested in new departments of psychiatry and research institutes to create a new generation of neuropsychiatrists grounded in the latest science. Gregg was attracted to Meyer's paradigm of "maladjustment psychiatry" because it offered to alleviate human suffering, raise medical standards generally and even provide a vantage point from which to guide human affairs. Against a pre-war background of strikes and poor labour relations, the Rockefeller Foundation sought ways of building social stability. Concerned to yield tangible results, Gregg gave the laboratory centre stage, in the hope that research might generate the evidence required to bring Meyer's psychosomatic medicine to fruition. His goal was to break down, through the funds at his command, the institutional, professional and conceptual barriers that had hampered the scientific investigation of mental illness.[52]

It was in this context that Mapother travelled to the United States in 1929. He visited the leading departments of psychiatry that flourished with the influx of funds from the Rockefeller Foundation. The gap, in terms of resources and ideas, between the finest American institutes (at Pennsylvania Hospital, Harvard Medical School, McLean Hospital, and the Hartford Retreat) and facilities in the UK was apparent. However, Mapother believed that the crucial difference was one of attitude: "the medical spirit dominating [psychiatry], and consequent pre-occupation with treatment and

---

[48] Gelder, op. cit., note 26 above, p. 427.

[49] Thomas W Salmon, 'The care and treatment of mental diseases and war neuroses ("shell-shock") in the British army', *Mental Hygiene*, 1917, **1**: 509–47.

[50] Pressman, op. cit., note 47 above, pp. 25–6.

[51] Ibid., p. 30.

[52] Ibid., p. 34.

research".[53] Whilst in the United States, Mapother met Meyer and returned with a respect for his ideas.[54]

Mapother came closest to summarising his philosophy in a presentation to the Royal Society of Medicine in November 1933 entitled 'Tough or tender: a plea for nominalism in psychiatry'.[55] In this, he argued that the lack of progress evident in "scientific knowledge concerning psychology and psychiatry" was due "to distraction from painstaking factual studies of the sort which Kraepelin initiated by the facile charms of animist speculation".[56] In contrast to tough-minded nominalism, Mapother was critical of tender-minded "conceptualism", which included idealism, spiritualism and recent developments in psychoanalysis. He defined nominalism as the view that "universals or abstract concepts are mere names without any corresponding realities". He considered that phenomena, or "the immediate products of perception", were the only objects of knowledge. Hence, Mapother defined the goal of science as "the production of formulae summarising the maximum number of past phenomena in the simplest, most concise and most frugal manner possible, and enabling us to foretell the sequence of future phenomena with the maximum economy of thought".[57] Observation must be scrutinised for bias and must ultimately lend itself to quantitative results.

Subsequently, Eliot Slater argued that Mapother had been insufficiently ambitious in setting his goals for psychiatry and his proposals failed "to give a satisfying picture of the human mind at work in trying to understand the world around, and it fails to give that kind of foundation which feels firm enough to step off from the unknown".[58] Mapother was critical of the psychology advanced by William McDougall, Freudian psychoanalysis and Bernard Hart's attempts to make both relevant to psychiatry. Following the ideas of Meyer and Salmon, he believed that the way forward was to develop psychiatry in conjunction with neurology; that the science of the brain was the only legitimate way to understand psychosis and neurosis. He stood in the tradition of John Hughlings Jackson, C S Sherrington, Henry Head, and K S Lashley, seeking out the secrets of human nature by experiment. Yet, Mapother was not a visionary thinker. As a pragmatist who relied on empirical evidence, he had little on which to base a broad view of psychiatric endeavour. It was virtually impossible, in view of the absence of effective treatments and investigative tools, to devise an achievable strategy for academic psychiatry during the 1930s. Not until the invention of advanced scanning techniques and the design of sophisticated statistical instruments could researchers begin to gather robust scientific data.

Nevertheless, Mapother may have held an overly narrow view of psychiatry and too readily rejected interesting hypotheses because of their associations or the institutions from which they originated. His closely-defined goals for psychological medicine yielded little in the way of tangible discoveries during the interwar period. Rather, Mapother's significant contribution was to create an institution and environment in

---

[53] Edward Mapother, 'Impressions of psychiatry in America', *Lancet*, 1930, **i**: 848–52, p. 848.

[54] Eliot Slater, 'The psychiatrist', *Bethlem Maudsley Hospital Gazette*, 1960, **3**: 7–10, p. 7.

[55] E Mapother, 'Tough or tender: a plea for nominalism in psychiatry', *Proc. R. Soc. Med.*, 1934, **27**: 1687–712.

[56] Ibid., p. 1689.

[57] Ibid., p. 1693.

[58] Eliot Slater, 'Early thinkers at the Maudsley', *Br. J. Psychiatry*, 1972, **121**: 591–98.

which research could flourish from 1945 onwards. He is rightly remembered for his statesmanlike achievements in establishing the Maudsley as a centre of excellence, inspiring a generation of clinicians and defining an atmosphere of integrity and expertise.

Academic Endeavour: An Institute of Psychiatry

Although the Maudsley Hospital became part of the University of London in 1924, Mapother was painfully aware that British psychiatry lacked an authentic research and teaching base, often forcing postgraduates to travel abroad to complete their training. During the late twenties, Mapother had himself toured a number of European psychiatric clinics to discover more about their treatment methods and research projects. He was also concerned that most psychiatric research in the UK was undertaken by clinicians in their spare time. This, Mapother believed, led to an "unduly optimistic" outlook but also prevented "the laborious observation and experiment that forms the basis of every progressive science". Full-time scientists were needed in dedicated research institutes, "protected against overloading with elementary teaching".[59] He thought that key researchers should be scientists, rather than psychiatrists, as they alone would have the technical understanding to push back the limits of knowledge.

Having conceived the need for an "institute of psychiatry and psychopathology" at the Maudsley, Mapother set about the monumental task of raising funds for a low status discipline with little scientific grounding.[60] In summer 1929, at the invitation of the Commonwealth Fund of America, Mapother had visited the leading psychiatric departments in the United States and Canada. Whilst in New York, he obtained an introduction to Dr Richard M Pearce, director of medical education at the Rockefeller Foundation. He appears to have received some encouragement, though Pearce died in February 1930. Mapother then contacted his successor Dr Alan Gregg to request that the Foundation consider a significant endowment for "advanced research in psychiatry and allied subjects". In particular, he believed that there was a great need for scientists to work in biochemistry, the anatomy of the nervous system, psychology and genetics.[61] Gregg appeared sympathetic and in June 1930 visited the Maudsley while on the trip to the UK.[62]

In the following year, Mapother made a formal application to the Rockefeller Foundation for financial support. Although the charity recognised that the Maudsley was "easily [the] most important institution [of British psychiatry] and can hardly be omitted", Gregg opposed the grant of a large endowment, though he was sympathetic to the idea of funding "a series of men for five-year periods to develop its research and training".[63] As a result, Mapother's proposal was declined in April "in favour of further negotiation with you upon the subject with a view to a less extensive and more gradual

---

[59] Mapother, op. cit., note 55 above, p. 1711.

[60] BRHA, C12/4, Mapother Box 13, 'Appeal for the endowment of an institute of psychiatry and psychopathology at the Maudsley Hospital' (typescript, March 1931), p. 9.

[61] BRHA, C12/4, Mapother Box 13, E Mapother to A Gregg, letter, 21 February 1930.

[62] BRHA, C12/4, Mapother Box 13, A Gregg to E Mapother, letter, 4 June 1930.

[63] Staff conference excerpt, 16 March 1931, Record Group 1.1, series 401A, folder 247, box 18, Rockefeller Foundation Archive (hereafter RFA), Rockefeller Archive Center (hereafter RAC).

development of research activities at the Maudsley".[64] Although Gregg wrote that it was the "economic crisis" of 1931 that had prevented them from funding an institute of psychiatry,[65] it appears that he held reservations about the Maudsley's academic credentials and, indeed, about the progress that might be achieved in the discipline.

However, Gregg was not dismissive of the Maudsley and wrote in May 1932 to propose that the Rockefeller Foundation fund two junior and one senior fellowships at the hospital. "Behind such a project as this", he observed, "lies the conviction that not enough good minds are going into clinical psychiatry and the related and contributory sciences of psychology".[66] One of these fellowships was used to offer William Mayer-Gross a post in 1934 when he fled Germany to escape Nazi persecution.[67] In addition, Eric Guttman and Alfred Meyer were beneficiaries of Rockefeller monies during 1935.[68] The arrival of these distinguished scientists at the Maudsley gave Gregg the confidence he needed to finance this relatively junior and untried teaching hospital. Believing that German research was of a higher calibre than that in the UK, officials at the Foundation considered that the presence of these émigrés would encourage promising home talent.[69] As a result, the Rockefeller awarded the Maudsley £9,000 over three years from 1935 to fund research. In 1938, the Rockefeller Foundation agreed a further £5,000 per annum for five years to be divided equally between laboratory and clinical research.[70] Eliot Slater believed that the arrival of three distinguished German psychiatrists broadened the vision of their UK counterparts: "it gave a lot of people a lot more to think about. It taught them to pay close attention to their patients, to sift, to discriminate".[71] Whether or not it was the presence of émigré psychiatrists or the clinical and research efforts of Maudsley staff themselves, by March 1938 the hospital's reputation had been established. After a meeting with Daniel O'Brien, the Rockefeller Foundation's assistant director of medical services, Mapother wrote to Lewis to say that the charity regarded the Maudsley as "the cat's whiskers" and "would later be prepared to make a large capital endowment, e.g. a hundred thousand pounds".[72] Any doubts that had been held by O'Brien about Mapother's willingness to consider innovative research projects had also been dispelled.

Despite having launched an appeal in March 1931, Mapother never lived to see the Institute of Psychiatry become a reality. So committed to this project was Mapother that he left his entire income (with the exception of his home) to a trust fund set up to

---

[64] BRHA, C12/4, Mapother Box 13, A Gregg to E Mapother, letter, 13 April 1931.

[65] BRHA, C12/4, Mapother Box 13, A Gregg to E Mapother, letter, 11 December 1931.

[66] BRHA, C12/4, Mapother Box 13, A Gregg to E Mapother, letter, 13 May 1932.

[67] Aubrey Lewis, 'Edward Mapother and the making of the Maudsley Hospital', *Br. J. Psychiatry*, 1969, **115**: 1358.

[68] Aubrey Lewis, 'William Mayer-Gross: an appreciation', in *The later papers of Sir Aubrey Lewis*, Oxford University Press for the Institute of Psychiatry, 1979, p. 220.

[69] Lambert to O'Brien, letter, 8 January 1935, RG 1.1, series 401A, folder 251, box 19, RFA, RAC.

[70] BRHA, C12/4, Mapother Box 14, *Opening of the new buildings, forming the second extension of the hospital... 14 July 1939*, p. 3.

[71] Eliot Slater interviewed by Brian Barraclough (1981), in Wilkinson (ed.), op. cit., note 27 above, pp. 1–12, on p. 8.

[72] E Mapother to A J Lewis, letter, 15 March 1938; held by the Lewis family.

Figure 4: Frederick Lucien Golla (1878–1968), who succeeded Mott as director of the Central Pathology Laboratory at the Maudsley in 1923. Educated at Magdalen College, Oxford, Golla had completed his medical studies at St George's Hospital and undertaken research in neurology at the West End Hospital for Diseases of the Nervous System. In August 1914, he volunteered for military service, serving in the Royal Army Medical Corps. On demobilisation, Golla returned to St George's as a consultant physician, and gave the 1921 Croonian lectures on the physiology of neurosis. When the Maudsley closed in 1939, Golla became the first director of the Burden Neurological Institute in Bristol (Institute of Psychiatry).

finance psychiatric research and contribute towards the construction of a neurological wing at the Maudsley.[73]

In 1936, Mapother was appointed the first professor of psychiatry at London University, and at the same time a chair was created in the pathology of mental disease for Frederick Lucien Golla, who had succeeded Mott as director of the Central Pathological Laboratory of the London County Mental Hospitals in 1923. Golla had trained at St George's Hospital and undertaken research in neurology at the West End Hospital for Diseases of the Nervous System before volunteering for military service in August 1914. Posted to France with the Royal Army Medical Corps, Golla appears to have worked at the Maudsley in the latter stages of the conflict and certainly experimented

[73] BRHA, C12/4, Mapother Box 14, The will of Edward Mapother, 17 December 1935.

in Mott's laboratory where he became a disciple of his outlook and methods. In the immediate post-war period, Golla was appointed a consultant physician at St George's Hospital, then at Hyde Park Corner.

Despite undertaking important work on the location of cerebral tumours by electro-encephalography, the Maudsley laboratories did not win international acclaim during the interwar period. In part, this reflected the limited resources available to Golla; he had a staff of only four assistants, though he was able to call on the pathology laboratories set up in the various mental hospitals surrounding London. However, this outcome was also a product of the uneasy relationship that existed between Golla and the rest of the hospital. He operated a separate fiefdom and did not interact dynamically with his clinical colleagues. Indeed, according to Slater, Golla regarded Mapother's attempt to found psychiatry on neurophysiology and mental mechanisms as "doomed to frustration but also a kind of barbarism".[74] In his Croonian Lectures of 1921, Golla had attempted to establish that neurosis, far from being a psychogenic phenomenon, should be understood as a physical disability, a failure of organic equilibrium, which could be assessed by physiological methods.[75] In the way that Mott had sought to find objective signs for hypothyroidism and dementia praecox, he attempted to show that the psychogalvanic reflex, or electrical activity of the skin, could serve as a reliable indicator of neurosis. Once at the Maudsley, he embarked on a programme of research into the physiology and biochemistry of what were then termed the "functional psychoses" (schizophrenia and manic-depression). In one experiment, Golla found that a group of psychotic patients, including some diagnosed with schizophrenia, hardly responded to inhalation of an atmosphere containing 2 per cent carbon dioxide, while almost all the controls showed increased ventilation. This appeared to show a disturbance of respiratory regulation, which Golla believed might be connected with a defect of oxidative processes.[76]

It is uncertain what subjects Mapother considered to be the appropriate targets for the Maudsley to research. While in Oslo on his European tour, Lewis met Professor Gjessing who suggested that Mapother believed that schizophrenia was best studied in chronic patients confined to mental hospitals. Lewis thought that the acute forms of psychosis treated at the Maudsley were also worthy of study. Certainly to abandon them would not leave "much ... for the Maudsley on the somatic side since of the non organic conditions, the neuroses are not likely to show much on the metabolic side but more on the social side".[77]

Mapother was concerned by the failure to exploit the full potential of the hospital's laboratories, and wrote to Sargant in April 1939:

There are a number of schemes which I am anxious to put through before I go ... The chief of these are the reorganisation of the medical staff, the acquisition of a really suitable successor to the post of director of the laboratory, and reform of the relations between clinical and laboratory

---

[74] Slater, op. cit., note 58 above.

[75] Alfred Meyer, 'Frederick Mott, founder of the Maudsley laboratories', *Br. J. Psychiatry*, 1973, **122**: 497–516.

[76] A Spencer Paterson, 'A personal memoir: 1931–32', *Bethlem Maudsley Hospital Gazette*, 1961, **4**: 65–9, p. 67.

[77] Aubrey Lewis to Hilda Lewis, letter, September 1937; held by the Lewis family.

staff, the agreement of the [London County] Council to the provision of a neuro-psychiatric wing and definite agreement by the Rockefeller Foundation to provide a large endowment (£100,000 or £200,000) for salaries for research personnel.[78]

Golla had retired in 1938 but the threat of war delayed the appointment of a successor and it was not until 1945 that Dr S Nevin took over as laboratory director.[79]

Mapother and Lewis

When Lewis arrived at the Maudsley in 1929, it remained relatively small-scale. Indeed, the entire medical and scientific staff could sit around a single table for lunch. By 1931, there were only seven full-time psychiatrists, together with two part-time doctors for out-patients, while Mapother himself was never fully employed at the hospital.[80] The doctors, including J S Harris (who had succeeded Petrie as deputy superintendent in January 1926), were relatively young.[81] Only Mapother and Blacker had seen military service during the First World War. Harris was said to have possessed great tact and took care not to provoke Mapother, while shielding junior colleagues. However, he could not protect them from the mid-morning case conferences when juniors were expected to present new admissions. Invariably, Mapother was delayed and many believed that much time was wasted having to wait and then listen to the presentations of others. Both Lewis and Blacker found these meetings irksome. Mapother would earlier have discussed new or problematic patients with Miss Walker, the matron, whom he met as soon as he arrived. It was thought that she exercised too great an influence, having the first opportunity to brief him.

Mapother was impressed by the youthful Lewis and appointed him a consultant in 1932 at the age of thirty-two. Because of his obvious intellectual talent and commitment to academic research, Mapother made him clinical director four years later. Although Lewis and his fellow consultants had little formal time for research, they succeeded in generating a growing number of papers during the 1930s. These publications gave the Maudsley a measure of international credibility, and two papers by Lewis were later regarded as classic accounts of depression.[82] By 1939, Lewis was regarded as Mapother's most likely successor as professor of psychiatry, though, given the fact that the LCC suspended the post for six years after Mapother's resignation, there could have been a suspicion that Lewis was not yet sufficiently experienced.

Lewis, in turn, had a great respect for Mapother, and subsequently wrote about him with affection. Mapother became an important role model for a number of young psychiatrists, including Sargant. Something of the post-war animosity between Lewis and Sargant may have been influenced by the latter's overt admiration for Mapother

[78] BRHA, C12/4, Mapother Box 14, E Mapother to W Sargant, letter, 14 April 1939.
[79] *Institute of Psychiatry 1924–1974*, London, Bethlem Royal and the Maudsley Hospital, 1974, p. 1.
[80] BRHA, C12/4, Mapother Box 13, 'Staff of the Maudsley Hospital from 1931'.
[81] BRHA, C12/4, Mapother Box 14, Maudsley Hospital Medical Superintendent's Report, 1 January 1927 to 31 December 1931, p. 1.
[82] A J Lewis, 'Melancholia: a clinical survey of depressive states', *J. ment. Sci.*, 1934, **80**: 277–8; A J Lewis, 'Melancholia: prognostic study and case material', *J. ment. Sci.*, 1936, **82**: 488–558.

Figure 5: Aubrey Lewis reading to his daughter, Naomi, while on holiday in August 1937, possibly at Frinton-on-Sea (Dr Naomi Cream).

and wish to be his true intellectual successor. Yet Mapother's shyness and the fact that he had no children of his own made him uneasy with the paternal aspect of the teacher-pupil relationship.[83] Although addressing his junior staff, he found teaching the DPM course stressful and was usually on edge before a lecture. Before major presentations, his nerves sometimes made him physically sick.

By 1931, when the Maudsley had 207 beds, its total staff had risen to 152, including 17 permanent doctors. In addition, a large number of trainee psychiatrists were employed, such that between September 1932 and May 1939 91 doctors had worked there. Many of the famous names of post-war British psychiatry had learned their clinical skills at the Maudsley under Mapother, including Harold Palmer, William Sargant, Eliot Slater, Maxwell Jones, John Bowlby, Dennis Hill,[84] together with a number of prominent psychoanalysts such as John Sutherland, later director of the Tavistock Clinic, and Wilfrid Bion.[85] One of the clinical assistants had been Dr Hilda Stoessiger, whom Lewis married in February 1934.

[83] Stokes, op. cit., note 39 above, p. 14.
[84] BRHA, C12/4, Mapother Box 14, List of staff of the Maudsley Hospital, September 1932 to May 1939.
[85] BRHA, C12/4, Mapother Box 14, Clinical Assistants, 1923–1937.

Table 1:
The patient population of the Maudsley Hospital (1923–30)

	Out-patients		In-patients			Total treated
	Adults	Children	Adults	Children	Private patients	
1923	850	44	418	8	36	1,012
1924	989	56	500	34	56	1,304
1925	1,252	57	598	42	48	1,566
1926*	1,147	61	581	45	71	1,505
1927	1,285	105	707	24	66	1,730
1928	1,605	144	693	39	64	2,225
1929	1,613	143	663	34	50	2,208
1930	1,746	165	671	40	58	2,394

Note: The total number treated is less than the sum of total out-patients and in-patients because some subjects initially seen in out-patients were subsequently admitted to the wards.
*Eleven months only.
Source: BRHA, C/12/4 Mapother Box 13.

North London Clinics

From the outset, the Maudsley was able to attract considerable numbers of patients (Table 1), suggesting that a substantial gap existed in the provision of mental health services. Although the in-patient population grew slowly (limited by the accommodation available), the number of out-patients more than doubled between 1923 and 1930. An analysis conducted in 1926 showed that the majority of patients (54%) had been referred by private doctors and only 15% had come from other hospitals with a further 3% from asylums.[86]

In addition, it was demonstrated how few of the Maudsley's out-patients lived in North London. Located in Denmark Hill, the hospital was regarded as inaccessible by many. In order to attract these patients, clinics were opened at Mile End Hospital, Bancroft Road, St Mary's in Highgate and at St Charles' Hospital in Ladbroke Grove. At first, Maudsley psychiatrists were sent to each of three clinics for one session a week, though demand saw this increased to two. Their chief role was assessment to select those suitable for admission to the Maudsley. Aubrey Lewis ran the Mile End clinic, Dr E W Anderson that at St Mary's and Dr Louis Minski worked at St Charles.[87]

Maudsley and the Tavistock

Although Mapother was prepared to consider psychoanalytical ideas, he was less tolerant of its institutions. In particular, he exhibited hostility to the Tavistock Clinic while remaining on reasonable personal terms with its medical director, J R Rees. It is said that Mapother, as London University's professor of psychiatry, resisted all attempts by Rees to gain academic recognition for the Tavistock as a post-graduate

---

[86] BRHA, C12/4, Mapother Box 13, Appeal for the endowment of an institute of psychiatry, p. 9.

[87] BRHA, C12/4, Mapother Box 14, Medical Superintendent's Report 1927–1931, p. 10.

institution.[88] Mapother appears to have held contradictory views about the Tavistock. When setting up his own psychotherapy department, for example, he had sent his clerk of works to the Malet Place premises of the Tavistock to find out how treatment rooms should be laid out and furnished. Yet Mapother is reported to have told Rees that he would rather see another "Maudsley" set up on the north side of the Thames than that the Tavistock's conceptual framework should flourish. He did little to conceal his disdain of much psycho-analytical theory, commenting on one psychiatric report with an interpretive slant that it was "damned Tavistockery".[89]

In April 1930, perhaps as a way of taking the sting out of Mapother's criticisms, Rees persuaded him to join the advisory board of the Tavistock Clinic. Yet a year later Mapother was to propose his resignation. The Tavistock had launched a major appeal to set up an Institute of Medical Psychology and some of the promotional publicity had upset him. As Mapother wrote to Rees:

We are both trying to tap the same financial resources, and in so far as the supply forthcoming from these sources is necessarily limited, we are rivals ... I would much rather have my hands free and have no sense of any conflicting obligations.[90]

Rees maintained friendly personal relations with Mapother and visited him during his last illness. Mapother is said to have apologised "as a good Catholic" for his opposition and stated that he now regretted not having supported their university recognition. Rees believed that "Mapother, another 'principled' introvert, had felt lacking in medical support and was deeply envious of the numbers of post-graduates and various overseas visitors that flocked to see the Tavistock at work and to join our training courses".[91] This explanation seems implausible as the Maudsley was far larger than the Tavistock, had secure funding from the London County Council, and by the early 1930s was the UK's leading postgraduate psychiatric institute, attracting distinguished refugees from the Continent. By comparison, the Tavistock struggled to survive financially and its very future remained in doubt.

Mapother had genuine intellectual doubts about the validity of psycho-analysis as a theoretical system and effective clinical intervention. In a presentation to the Royal Society of Medicine in November 1939, Mapother criticised the

tendency to universal statements and the absence of any attempt to produce statistical or quantitative evidence. [The] adoption of the observational method which from the start disqualifies its findings from consideration as science on account of the privacy of their collection and the impossibility of any verification.[92]

Lewis shared Mapother's mistrust of the Tavistock. During the Second World War when appointed consultant psychiatrist to the army with the rank of brigadier, Rees was able to appoint Tavistock staff and trainees to key posts within the military. Lewis was concerned lest the kudos and influence they gained should undermine the Maudsley's

---

[88] H V Dicks, *Fifty years of the Tavistock Clinic*, London, Routledge & Kegan Paul, 1970, p. 60.
[89] Desmond Curran, 'Mapother the man', *Bethlem Maudsley Hospital Gazette*, 1960, **3**: 4–5, p. 4.
[90] BRHA, C12/4, Mapother Box 14, E Mapother to J R Rees, letter, 18 May 1931.
[91] Dicks, op. cit., note 88 above, p. 62.
[92] BRHA, C12/4, Mapother Box 14, 'An appreciation of Freud', speech delivered to the Royal Society of Medicine, November 1939.

leading role for research and teaching. For the future, it was important that Maudsley psychiatrists not only perform creditably within the civilian health service but also take prominent roles in the armed forces. Desmond Curran, Harold Palmer, R F Barbour and W H de B Hubert, amongst others, held senior posts in the army or navy. Gordon Holmes proved to be a powerful ally and supporter of the Maudsley cause. He had little sympathy for or understanding of psychotherapy, and profoundly disagreed with Rees over the treatment of servicemen suffering from so-called "war neuroses".

In the post-1945 period, Alan Gregg approached Lewis as professor of psychiatry to ask him to assist the Tavistock secure formal recognition from the University of London. Gregg considered it had developed a livelier intellectual agenda than the Maudsley and was keen to support its claim. Lewis found himself caught between not wishing to alienate one of his most important benefactors and having to promote an institution whose intellectual basis he questioned.[93]

Horder Committee: War Pensions

On 3 July 1939, when war again threatened, the Ministry of Pensions convened a conference under Lord Horder (1871–1955), honorary consultant physician to the Ministry of Pensions. Concerned that another epidemic of shell shock would deprive the military of manpower and cost the exchequer dear in pensions, a group of experts was gathered together. They included Sir Farquhar Buzzard, Sir Hubert Bond, Gordon Holmes, Bernard Hart, Mapother and various senior officials, including Dr J F E Prideaux (1880–1952), director of medical services to the Ministry of Pensions. Little agreement was reached at the first meeting. The neurologists had come to the German point of view that war neurosis did not exist and that symptoms were simply an expression of constitutional weakness. Prideaux, Hart, Holmes and Buzzard all argued that there should be no financial compensation for "war neurosis".[94] With his broad experience of treating servicemen and veterans, Mapother countered this view forcefully, arguing that exposure to intense or prolonged stress played an important role. "There were a number of cases", he declared,

which arose solely from war service and showed no indication of previous abnormality. Justice required that adequate provision be made for such men ... To label a man as a constitutional neurotic though you could trace no evidence of it in his past history was unjustifiable.[95]

When Mapother refused to bow to the majority view, Horder decided to refer the question of war pensions to a second, smaller committee. Gathered in Mapother's rooms in Queen Anne Street, under the chairmanship of Buzzard, it consisted of Hart, Prideaux, Air Vice-Marshal Richardson, Dr Bolus of the Ministry of Pensions and Mapother. The debate continued and Mapother argued that "eventually most [cases of war neurosis] recover" and some patients did not even apply for a pension.[96] As a result, he proposed that all servicemen diagnosed as neurasthenic should be retained

---

[93] Institute of Psychiatry, Sir Aubrey Lewis interviewed by D L Davies, *c*. 1970.

[94] Ben Shephard, '"Pitiless psychology": the role of prevention in British military psychiatry in the Second World War', *Hist. Psychiatry*, 1999, **10**: 506–7.

[95] PRO, PIN15/2401, 1B, Minutes of the Horder Conference, 3 July 1939.

[96] Ibid., 14A, Report of the meeting of 31 July 1939.

in the armed forces until the end of the hostilities when they could be assessed.[97] The small minority that deserved a pension could be compensated, while allowing time to treat promising or mild cases. Mapother was not uncritical of ex-servicemen and their representatives. He had observed how financial compensation tended to hinder natural recovery processes and was not always in the best interest of the veteran. Mapother succeeded in persuading the Ministry to adopt a pragmatic policy, which allowed an opportunity for treatment and postponed the pension issue without offering undue encouragement to claimants. After the administration and development of the Maudsley, this was perhaps Mapother's second greatest achievement.

Closure of the Maudsley and Death of Mapother

In August 1939, shortly after the completion of the private patients' wing and children's department (it is uncertain whether they were occupied until after the hostilities), the Maudsley closed.[98] Because London was assumed to be the target of an intense bombing campaign, the staff were divided between two hospitals located in the

Figure 6: Aubrey Lewis (left) and J S Harris, deputy medical superintendent of the Maudsley Hospital. They are standing in front of the newly-constructed private patients' wing, possibly at the reception on 14 July 1939 to mark its completion (Dr Naomi Cream).

[97] Ex-Services Welfare Society Minute Book, 6 (7 September 1939), p. 86; held by Combat Stress.
[98] BRHA, C12/4, Mapother Box 13, E Mapother to D P O'Brien, letter, 29 December 1939.

outer suburbs of London. One party under Louis Minski, and including Eliot Slater and William Sargant, went to Belmont Hospital, Sutton. The other group, under W S Maclay as medical superintendent and including Aubrey Lewis, A B Stokes, W H Gillespie, Mildred Creak, Eric Guttman and Maxwell Jones were sent to the converted public school at Mill Hill. They were joined by Emilio Mira, formerly professor of psychiatry at Barcelona University, whose accounts of the effects of air-raids during the Spanish Civil War had proved timely. Mira and Lewis occasionally played chess until the former's departure for Argentina. Designed to treat civilian psychological casualties of aerial bombing, both hospitals were deliberately located close to the action but in positions of relative safety.

Mapother suffered increasingly with asthma and pulmonary fibrosis of the lungs. He had often tried to go abroad during the winter months to escape respiratory infections. Following the closure of the Maudsley, he resigned as medical superintendent on 31 December 1939. With his impending retirement and health concerns in mind, Mapother had explored the possibility of leaving the UK to work for the Rockefeller Foundation.[99] Ironically, Mapother's death in March 1940 came at a time when he was at the height of his professional power. He had exercised a significant influence on the policy for dealing with soldiers, their treatment and eligibility for war pensions. The expertise of the Maudsley appeared to have been recognised by the authorities, and members of staff were given key appointments.

Despite his forbidding exterior, Mapother inspired considerable affection amongst his colleagues. Two psychiatrists, recruited into the Royal Navy, wrote spontaneously to the *Lancet* in April 1940 to express their appreciation of their former "chief":

No-one can think of Mapother's teaching without thinking also of his quick Irish wit ... "What did you think of that presidential address, sir?" one of us asked him. "Pontifical superficiality", he replied. He gave great credit to Freud, but his over-enthusiastic followers sometimes got short shrift ... He had too an endearing absent-mindedness as when he joined in the clapping of his own speech on sitting down at a medical meeting.[100]

Lewis contrasted Mapother's "slight build, restless movements, and sometimes his troubled breathing" with his sharp intellect, characterised by "a touch of legal inquisition" and his wit, which "served as an astringent partner to his zest for controversy".[101] According to Desmond Curran, Mapother was "a very serious person, quite incapable of relaxing". As a result, "his general tension", Curran wrote,

made him appear somewhat forbidding. He was certainly not a man with whom anyone would have dreamt of taking liberties. This may all sound rather unattractive, but I do not think anybody who worked at the Maudsley with Mapother did not regard him with deep admiration ... He was a man of invincible courage and complete integrity.[102]

Mapother had a combative side, though apparently without malice. Blacker recalled a quarrel, which led to his giving a month's notice. Shortly afterwards, the two were reconciled. "It was when we were both apologising", Blacker recalled,

[99] O'Brien to Gregg, letter, 19 April 1939, RFA, RAC, RG 1.1, series 401A, folder 216, box 19.

[100] 'Dr Mapother', *Lancet*, 1940, **i**: 671. The authors were apparently Desmond Curran and Denis Williams.

[101] Lewis, 'Mapother', op. cit., note 14 above, p. 1365.

[102] Curran, op. cit., note 89 above, p. 4.

that I first beheld the thaw. He looked straight, searchingly and half humorously at me and smiled most engagingly – as if he were thinking what fools we both were, but that nevertheless we should make allowances for each other. Suddenly I found myself much drawn to him.[103]

According to Sargant, who visited him shortly before his death, Mapother believed that the war had destroyed his life's work at the Maudsley. The hospital stood empty and the new private patients' block had never been occupied. His ashes were scattered in the hospital gardens where he had often walked with colleagues.

What, then, had Mapother achieved? He had succeeded in establishing a specialist psychiatric hospital with a growing international reputation for treatment and teaching. Golla argued that a lack of funds and an intransigent university had deflected Mapother from the original aim of Maudsley and Mott that the hospital should be a centre for the intensive study of mental illness. This, he believed, had led Mapother to follow "a more therapeutically dramatic and assertive career that in the view of many somewhat detracted from its utility as a home for research".[104] Certainly, the Maudsley's research record was not impressive but, as Lewis discovered on his tour of the Continent, this was a reflection of the general state of psychiatric knowledge. Nevertheless, constrained by limited finances, the Maudsley remained small-scale in comparison with the leading American and European institutes. More, perhaps, could have been done to promote the institution, particularly overseas. When in Stockholm, Lewis met Dr Wigert who had the idea that the Maudsley was simply a "clearing house". Lewis thought that visitors had not been given sufficient attention and remarked that wherever he went in Europe, the "heads of clinic, quite often famous or busy men, would give up two or three hours to show me around or talk to me".[105] Mapother was only part-time at the Maudsley and probably gave public-relations activities a low priority.

Wartime: Mill Hill

Under Maclay and Lewis, occupational and social psychiatry was the goal of Mill Hill EMS Hospital. Aerial bombardment was a serious concern in the approach to war as large numbers of civilian casualties were expected. Some psychiatrists predicted that psychological cases would outnumber physical injuries by two or three times.[106] As a result, the government planned to open a number of specialist hospitals in the outskirts of London, located within the sound of air-raids to prevent the development of evacuation syndromes. When the mass civilian psychiatric casualties failed to materialise, Mill Hill found a new role treating servicemen. Lewis outlined the strategy in a letter to Daniel O'Brien of the Rockefeller Foundation:

The concentration of all effort syndrome cases here with Paul Wood from the Post-Graduate Hospital, Boyd from the Surgical Unit at Bart's and of course Guttmann, Maxwell Jones, Stokes, Fraser and other Maudsley people (including two psycho-analysts) on the staff, gives us an extraordinary good chance for careful investigation of an important psycho-somatic problem

---

[103] C P Blacker, 'Mapother memorial', *Bethlem and Maudsley Hospital Gazette*, 1960, **3**: 5–7, p. 5.
[104] F Golla, 'An appreciation', *Lancet*, 1940; **i**: 625–6.
[105] Aubrey Lewis to Hilda Lewis, letter, September 1937; held by the Lewis family.
[106] Richard M Titmuss, *Problems of social policy*, London, HMSO, 1950, pp. 338–9.

from many angles; the other Maudsley people at Sutton will probably have similar chances with concussion cases.[107]

An "effort syndrome unit" of 150 beds was set up at Mill Hill under the joint directorship of Paul Wood, a cardiologist, and Maxwell Jones, a psychiatrist.[108] At first, the unit was run along conventional hospital lines but Jones soon began to appreciate the value of educating patients with functional somatic disorders and then moved towards creating a therapeutic community.[109] The lecture approach was abandoned in favour of discussion and the traditional barriers between doctors, nursing staff and patients were lowered, though not eliminated.[110] Groups, largely of an educational character, were held three times a week and average admissions were six to eight weeks. In addition, programmes of physical exercise and occupational therapy were provided.

Four psychologists were employed, including Hans Eysenck, funded by the Rockefeller Foundation, and J C Raven who attempted to screen psychologically vulnerable soldiers. Using Penrose–Raven Progressive Matrices, a pre-war test designed to measure innate intelligence, he sought to identify unsuitable recruits on the basis that neurotic men had less consistent scores over time.

By early 1941, it had become apparent that many servicemen diagnosed as psychoneurotic, who had responded well to treatment, relapsed on return to their original units and duties. As a result, they were discharged into civilian life where, if their symptoms endured, they would be a burden on the state. At the suggestion of Lewis, the so-called "annexure scheme" was introduced by the War Office in May 1941.[111] This involved making an assessment of a soldier's abilities and skills so that he could be assigned to a suitable job thereby preventing further breakdown or discharge from the armed forces. As part of their occupational therapy, service personnel assigned to the annexure system were sent to Hendon Technical College for instruction in four-week courses. These were either clerical (typewriting, book-keeping, records management) or in mechanical and electrical engineering.[112] A follow-up investigation in 1943 found that 60% of men who had been treated for psychoneurosis and who otherwise would have been invalided were retained under the annexure scheme and of these 83% had performed satisfactorily in their new military roles. Rees observed of the scheme that it had "helped to maintain the man-power of the army and to ensure that certain jobs are well done by men whose employability is limited, so releasing other fitter men, but also it should be of some value to us in planning for the treatment and disposal of the chronically neurotic men and women in civilian life".[113] Around 10,000 servicemen were retained in the forces under the scheme, which was ended in August 1945.

---

[107] A Lewis to D P O'Brien, letter, 20 January 1940; held by the Lewis family.

[108] BRHA, C12/4, Mapother Box 14, 'The Medical Superintendent's report on the organization and work of Mill Hill Emergency Hospital to December 31 1940', p. 2.

[109] D W Millard, 'Maxwell Jones and the therapeutic community', in Hugh Freeman, and German Berrios (eds), *150 years of British psychiatry: 1841–1991*, London, Gaskell, 1996, pp. 581–603, pp. 583–5.

[110] Maxwell Jones, et al., *Social psychiatry: a study of therapeutic communities*, London, Tavistock Publications, 1952, pp. 2–3.

[111] Robert H Ahrenfeldt, *Psychiatry in the British Army in the Second World War*, London, Routledge and Kegan Paul, 1958, pp. 155–9.

[112] Aubrey Lewis and K Goodyear, 'Vocational aspects of neurosis in soldiers', *Lancet*, 1944, **ii**: 105–8.

[113] J R Rees, *The shaping of psychiatry by war*, London, Chapman & Hall, 1945, p. 41.

Figure 7: A formal portrait of Aubrey Lewis dating from 1942 when he was clinical director at Mill Hill EMS Hospital (Dr Naomi Cream).

Aubrey Lewis, as clinical director at Mill Hill, repeatedly urged the careful collection of statistics so that clinical work could be properly evaluated. Maclay, supported by his deputy Stokes, was reluctant to alter established routines and was generally mistrustful of anything which involved the military. In July 1943, for example, Lewis expressed dissatisfaction "with the energy and pertinacity shown in respect to getting follow-up returns, particularly those after one year".[114] Similarly, in February 1944, Lewis raised the question of the inadequate filing and retrieval systems for patient records, which limited the ability to undertake representative research.[115] Although Jones occasionally supported Lewis in committee debates, he made little attempt to employ statistical methods. A paper he co-authored with Lewis, published in the *Lancet* in June 1941, compared the symptoms and behaviour of 35 patients returned to full duty with 35 discharged from the forces. As the authors noted, "comparison of small groups in respect of individual symptoms and features is not the most satisfactory way of discovering what chiefly decides the outcome of an illness such as this".[116] In

---

[114] BRHA, Mill Hill EMS Hospital, Medical Committee Minutes, 8 July 1943, p. 28.
[115] Ibid., 10 February 1944, pp. 66–7.
[116] Maxwell Jones and Aubrey Lewis, 'Effort syndrome', *Lancet*, 1941, **i**: 813–18, p. 818.

subsequent papers, however, Jones simply quoted individual case studies to support his claims with no objective measures.[117]

Despite the difficulties he had encountered with the record system, Lewis was able to conduct one of the few follow-up studies of the war. During 1942, in an attempt to discover the lasting effects of treatment at Mill Hill, he led a team of psychiatric social workers who visited 120 servicemen between four and twelve months after they had been discharged from the forces. Lewis described the results as "disturbing" as the men had gone downhill as a group: "they were less usefully employed than before, earning less, less contented, less tolerable to live with, less healthy".[118] He discovered that fifteen were unemployed and a further seven in the ARP [Air Raid Precautions] so that 18% were not in gainful work. Only 50% could be classed as "socially satisfactory in respect of work and otherwise". These findings led Lewis to the pessimistic conclusion that "some neurotic soldiers, discharged from the army when they are no longer of any use to it, are not in civilian life as useful or as healthy as they were before they joined the army".[119] This evidence also suggested that the psychological problems experienced by servicemen were not as amenable to therapy as many contemporaries had claimed.

Because Mill Hill had been set up to treat promising but well-established cases of "neurosis", the number of referrals fell towards the end of the war and by September 1944 they had 200 empty beds. Cases of acute combat stress were treated in the field (and if referred to the UK went to Northfield) so Mill Hill found itself looking for a new role. The hospital's treatment expertise was considered suitable for British prisoners-of-war who were slowly being liberated as the Allies advanced through northwest Europe and Italy. In May 1945, the decision had been taken to close Mill Hill and transfer patients to Dartford Hospital, which would then operate as a POW rehabilitation centre, treating the most psychologically disturbed.[120] Under Maxwell Jones, it operated for a year and admitted 1,400 servicemen. By July 1945, most of Mill Hill had closed and plans were well advanced for the re-opening of the Maudsley on 1 September. As clinical director, Lewis did not transfer to Dartford but returned to the Maudsley, which had remained unoccupied throughout the war, to take up his former post.

The war also provided Lewis with the opportunity to write one of his most influential publications. In 1937, he and Mapother had co-authored the section on 'Psychological Medicine' in Price's *Textbook of the practice of medicine* and four years later a new edition allowed Lewis to make it his own.[121] Aware that he could influence a generation of medical students, Lewis took great care over its presentation and his lucid and inspirational account attracted the interest of many young doctors. Revised and updated, it remained a classic summary of the parameters of clinical psychiatry and

---

[117] Maxwell Jones, 'Emotional catharsis and re-education in the neuroses with the help of group methods', *Br. J. med. Psychol.*, 1948, **21**: 104–10.

[118] Aubrey Lewis, 'Social effects of neurosis', *Lancet*, 1943, **i**: 167–70, pp. 168–9.

[119] PRO, AIR2/5998, A Lewis, 'An enquiry into some social effects of neurosis' (typescript, 16 January 1943), p. 3.

[120] BRHA, Medical Committee Minutes, 3 May 1945, pp. 136–7; 17 May 1945, p. 142.

[121] Aubrey Lewis, 'Psychological medicine', in Frederick W Price (ed.), *A textbook of the practice of medicine*, Oxford University Press, 1941.

was, in effect, a statement of Lewis's own philosophy. "A biological foundation may be assumed for the syndromes with which psychiatry works", he wrote, while diversity

can be due to a combination of single hereditary causes and to the effect of each individual's special environment throughout his life upon his development and behaviour ... Part of the psychiatrist's business is to discover how this interplay has led to the present illness. The interplay, moreover, is sufficiently varied in the course of each patient's life to make prognosis and the effect of treatment a matter of individual study, rather than of summary inference from the diagnosis, once made.[122]

In retrospect, Lewis believed the war had exercised a damaging influence on the development of the Maudsley. Although it had stimulated interest in the treatment of neuroses, rather than psychosis, he thought the creation of two schools of thought (social and occupational psychiatry versus aggressive physical methods) hindered post-war unity. In addition, the professorship of psychiatry had lain unoccupied for six years, creating a vacuum in research and training.[123]

At the beginning of 1942, encouraged by Lord Horder, Churchill had expressed his suspicion of the growing role of psychiatrists and psychologists in the armed forces. To forestall any precipitate action by the prime minister, the War Cabinet set up a ministerial committee under the chairmanship of Sir Stafford Cripps, the Lord Privy Seal, to investigate their role. Cripps' conclusion that "there was no substance in the criticisms made of the psychologists and psychiatrists in the Army" prompted the setting up of an advisory committee to co-ordinate the work of the three services and "to study its methods with a view to their post-war application".[124] In September 1942, an expert committee under the chairmanship of Sir William Wilson Jameson (1885–1962), was set up and its members included D K Henderson, F C Bartlett, A W P Wolters and Aubrey Lewis.[125] In July 1945, with the war drawing to a close, Brigadier H A Sandiford, director of army psychiatry, was concerned about the dramatic loss of psychiatric expertise that would follow the return to peace. As a result, he proposed the creation of an "Advisory Committee on Army Psychiatry".[126] With the support of Major-General Alex Hood, its first members comprised D K Henderson, G W B James, Aubrey Lewis and J R Rees, chaired by the director of army psychiatry. Functioning over the next twenty years, Lewis remained an influential member of the committee.

Lewis: Psychiatric Perspective

The interwar period had been a difficult time to practice as a psychiatrist. Little was understood about the relationship between neurophysiology and mental illness, there was no really effective anti-psychotic or anti-depressant medication. Treatment included restraint, sedation and occupational therapy together with a limited range of dynamic psychotherapies.

---

[122] Ibid., p. 1835.

[123] Institute of Psychiatry, Sir Aubrey Lewis interviewed by D L Davies, c. 1970.

[124] PRO, PREM4/15/2, December 1942.

[125] PRO, AIR2/5998, Minutes of the Expert Committee on the Work of Psychiatrists and Psychologists in the Services.

[126] PRO, WO32/13462, H A Sandiford, Army Psychiatry Advisory Committee Minutes, 5 July 1945.

During the early 1930s, it looked as though eugenics might hold the solution for psychiatry. Faced with crippling and chronic mental illnesses, such as schizophrenia for which both cause and cure were unknown, Lewis was attracted to prevention through the voluntary sterilisation of families with an established history of major mental illness. When Germany passed legislation in 1933–4 compelling the sterilisation of people with a range of mental illnesses, Lewis offered measured criticism of the proposals.[127] Concerned by the compulsory nature of the programme and the fact that carriers of certain diseases had to be "reported for sterilization, even though his illness is past and he has for many years been quite healthy", Lewis also questioned how accurately certain disorders could be diagnosed.

When it subsequently became clear that eugenic ideas had been hi-jacked by the Nazi party to pursue overt racial discrimination, Lewis was forthright in his condemnation. In an editorial published in the *Lancet* in 1933, he argued that a number of distinguished physicians and geneticists had allowed political beliefs to cloud their medical judgement, thereby showing "a disregard for the individual human being, and a willingness to act upon racial prejudice". "Upon these misstatements and exaggerations ...", Lewis wrote, "there is being constructed a system of compulsory interference with the liberty to propagate, the total effects of which ... can scarcely be other than bad".[128]

During the 1930s, a number of radical solutions were proposed for the treatment of major mental illness, including epileptiform convulsions induced by pentetrazol and later by electric shock, surgery (prefrontal leucotomy), and hypoglycaemic shock induced with insulin. Although most of these novel, physical treatments were pioneered abroad, one of their most enthusiastic advocates was William Sargant, subsequently a stern critic of Lewis's approach. Sargant had come to the Maudsley having himself suffered from a mental collapse. Dr G W B James, consultant psychiatrist at St Mary's, had recommended Sargant to Mapother.[129] At the Maudsley, Sargant became a devotee of Mapother and argued that the appointment of Lewis as his successor "profoundly changed the hospital's character". Sargant claimed to be the true inheritor of the Mapother legacy, though, as this essay has shown, this was far from the case. In 1936, Sargant began to use amphetamines for depression, insulin treatment for schizophrenia two years later, and while in Harvard on a Rockefeller fellowship was introduced to leucotomy,[130] a technique he subsequently employed on servicemen suffering from resistant post-combat disorders. Having returned to the Maudsley after wartime work at Sutton, Sargant resigned in 1948 to take charge of the department of psychological medicine at St Thomas' Hospital. Although Sargant wrote that the cause was over access to beds at the Maudsley, the matter remains obscure, as Lewis never discussed the matter in public.

In sharp contrast to these physical remedies was psychoanalysis, which required patients to lie on the couch for five sessions a week. Lewis, disillusioned by the

---

[127] Aubrey Lewis, 'German eugenic legislation: an examination of fact and theory', *Eugenics Review*, 1934, **26**: 183–91.

[128] Editorial, 'Eugenics in Germany', *Lancet*, 1933, **ii**: 297–98, p. 298.

[129] 'Obituary, W W Sargant', *Br. med. J.*, 1988, **297**: 789–90, p. 789.

[130] 'Obituary, William Walters Sargant', *Lancet*, 1988; **ii**: 695–6, p. 695.

worst excesses of eugenics, was not impressed by either extreme physical or psychological approaches. Felix Post observed that "Lewis didn't believe much in treatment" largely because most at that time were ineffective. "He was not enamoured of ECT and certainly not of insulin coma. Lithium, he, and Shepherd too, thought dangerous nonsense".[131] Nevertheless, because there was so little empirical evidence on which to build, Lewis believed that it was important to advance on a broad front. Consequently, Lewis encouraged clinical initiatives, such as psychotherapy, in which he had little personal faith. As a social psychiatrist, he favoured the gathering of information and less damaging interventions (such as continuous warm baths, occupational therapy and vocational training) until such time as more effective interventions were discovered. As his *Times* obituary stated, Lewis "had less sympathy with those who dedicated themselves to relieve the plight of sick individuals than with those who, standing back from the clinical struggle as he did, tried to advance knowledge of the subject".[132]

As regards diagnosis and clinical training, Lewis was strongly influenced by Meyer. He emphasised extensive history-taking, leading first to a diagnosis and then to an understanding of the patient as a unique individual. Life charts were used to show relationships with social or psychological events and episodes of mental disorder. Cases were formulated in a way that reflected Meyer's psychobiological approach with its emphasis on multiple causes combined with Emil Kraepelin's nosological system.[133] Thus, a diagnostic formulation was made first, followed by an aetiological statement in which the evolution of the personality and that of the illness were traced along psychobiological lines.

Lewis never attempted to state a general theory of psychiatry. When asked by Eliot Slater why he had avoided such an enterprise, Lewis replied that "there was such an abundance of theories that it was not necessary to find a new one or adopt one of the old".[134] Although Slater regarded this as "his greatest weakness as a scientific worker", time has perhaps proved Lewis right. In the absence of conclusive evidence about causation and even treatment, it would have been premature to have made unequivocal statements about the nature of mental illness. Lewis knew only too well how previous movements, such as eugenics, or charismatic figures, such as Freud, Egas Moniz or John F Fulton, had fallen from grace.

Lewis: Personal Style

Although he rarely showed anger, Lewis could intimidate trainee psychiatrists and even senior colleagues. D L Davies recalled the "awe and sometimes the fright he seemed to induce" in junior doctors. A registrar at a case conference who had not learned by heart the family history of a patient would soon find himself exposed. Lewis would question him until it had become clear that his knowledge was lacking.

---

[131] Felix Post interviewed by Brian Barraclough (1988), in Wilkinson (ed.), op. cit., note 27 above, pp. 157–77, on p. 167.

[132] *The Times*, obituary of Sir Aubrey Lewis, 22 January 1975, p. 14.

[133] Gelder, op. cit., note 26 above, p. 432.

[134] Quoted from Michael Gelder, 'Sir Aubrey Lewis's contributions to psychiatry', *Br. J. Psychiatry*, 1976, **128**: 33.

"Are you sure that you asked the right question?" Lewis would remark. If he began to drum his fingers on the desk then it was a sure sign that the presentation was not going well. Anthony Storr, who was Lewis's first senior registrar on the newly-created professorial unit, recalled of his two years there: "Once you had suffered the experience of presenting a case at one of his Monday morning conferences, no other public appearance, whether on radio, TV or the lecture platform, could hold any terrors for you".[135]

Lewis was a scholar of considerable erudition and encyclopaedic breadth. He read widely and could, for example, distinguish between different editions of German textbooks. In fact, he read psychiatric literature not only in its original German but also in French and Italian. When he took the London MRCP examination there was a requirement to translate a passage either from Greek, Latin, French or German and Lewis was proud to have completed all four.[136] Lewis was also scrupulous in the use of language, about which he cared greatly.[137] As a result, he developed a formidable skill in detecting errors of thought. For Lewis case material was an intellectual challenge and an opportunity to improve the academic capacities of others. Throughout his career Lewis wrote for academic journals, though the character of his output changed.[138] During the 1930s and the war years, he undertook original research in epidemiological and social psychiatry. When the teaching and administrative demands of his professorship imposed limitations on his ability to study large patient groups, Lewis focused on re-evaluating and synthesising the work of others, continuing to write in his retirement.

Some thought him unfeeling in his Socratic pursuit of information. In fact, Lewis was driven by a desire to get things right and an almost obsessional need for accuracy and detail. He was genuinely surprised by the effect his questioning had on doctors. He was equally puzzled why juniors rarely gave him drafts of their work to read and did not seem to appreciate that his criticism could undermine self-confidence. Although some colleagues believed that he lacked empathy, Hilda Lewis, his wife, wrote that he did not "bear grudges and he accepts people as he finds them without any moralising or crusading spirit, but only a desire where professional duties lie to help them think clearly".[139]

Once appointed professor with its heavy teaching commitment, Lewis reduced his patient caseload, though he continued to conduct weekly ward rounds on the metabolic unit until retirement. Most of his clinical work was conducted through the supervision of his registrars. During the 1930s, when he was responsible for a ward and the Mile End out-patient clinic, Lewis had extensive patient contact. Slater recalled his work with a Jesuit priest who was tormented by obsessions: "Aubrey spent hours and hours and hours talking to this priest. They shared a common fund of arcane knowledge,

---

[135] 'Obituary, Anthony Storr', *Psychiatric Bull.*, 2001, **25**: 365.
[136] Shepherd, op. cit., note 33 above, p. 10.
[137] Gerald Russell, 'Obituary of Michael Shepherd', *Psychiatric Bull.*, 1996, **20**: 632–7.
[138] Aubrey Lewis, *The state of psychiatry: essays and addresses*, London, Routledge and Kegan Paul, 1967; Aubrey Lewis, *Inquiries in psychiatry: clinical and social investigations*, London, Routledge and Kegan Paul, 1967; *The later Papers of Sir Aubrey Lewis*, Oxford University Press for the Institute of Psychiatry, 1979.
[139] Lady Hilda Lewis to Dr C P Blacker, letter, 5 July 1966; held by the Lewis family.

because Aubrey himself had been brought up in a Jesuit school; he knew all the Jesuitical ways of looking at things, and he could talk to this Jesuit fine".[140]

Lewis had a small group of trusted colleagues, including Dr C P Blacker (1895–1975), who also became a family friend. An Etonian, Blacker had been decorated while serving in the Coldstream Guards during the First World War.[141] He subsequently studied medicine at Oxford and Guy's Hospital, qualifying in 1925. Blacker was briefly a post-graduate student at the Tavistock where he took an interest in psychoanalysis before joining the staff of the Maudsley in 1927.[142] With responsibility for the two acute wards, Blacker had an argument with Mapother over the quality of a case history written in haste, and offered his resignation.[143] Although the two resolved their differences, Blacker left the Maudsley. Nevertheless, he and Mapother often went to boxing and all-in wrestling competitions where they vied to predict the winner. When the smoky atmosphere began to aggravate Mapother's asthma, they went to out-of-door promotions.

As secretary of the Population Investigation Committee, Blacker wrote several papers on eugenics and shared the general fear of the declining birth rate.[144] He strongly advocated a policy of encouraging families identified as healthy, intelligent, socially-useful and free from "genetic taints" to have large numbers of children.[145] Yet, in the absence of effective treatments for major mental illnesses, Blacker also advocated voluntary sterilisation for "a small group of antisocial, backward, and highly fertile people who form about 10% of the population – the so-called social-problem group".[146] During the Second World War, at Lewis's suggestion, Blacker conducted a detailed survey of out-patient referrals to assess the epidemiology and nature of "neurosis" in England and Wales. Designed to inform the shape of post-war psychiatric services, it provided Lewis with some of the data he needed when setting up training and patient facilities.[147] Blacker returned to the Maudsley in 1946 at Lewis's invitation where he worked exclusively as an out-patient consultant.

Apart from their genuine friendship, Blacker seems to have provided Lewis with support and a sense of comradeship in the competitive and highly-charged atmosphere of the Maudsley. Because of Blacker's friendship with Mapother, Lewis may also have valued him as a link with his former mentor. Perhaps he provided an outsider with a sense of Englishness as Blacker was "Eton, Oxford and the Guards", a heroic soldier and something of an eccentric, who would occasionally offer his patients peppermint humbugs. Apocryphally, Lewis was once asked whether he would choose to

---

[140] Slater, see note 71 above, p. 8.

[141] John Blacker (ed.), *Have you forgotten yet? The First World War memoirs of C P Blacker MC, GM*, Barnsely, Leo Cooper, 2000.

[142] Dicks, op. cit., note 88 above, p. 36.

[143] Institute of Psychiatry, C P Blacker interviewed by Sir Aubrey Lewis, *c.* 1970.

[144] C P Blacker and D V Glass, *Future of our population*, London, Population Investigation Committee, 1938, pp. 19–25; C P Blacker, 'The medical causes of infertility. How can they be investigated?' *Medical Press and Circular*, 1937, **195**: 1–14.

[145] C P Blacker, *Eugenics in prospect and retrospect*, Glasgow, Hamish Hamilton, 1945, pp. 24–5.

[146] C P Blacker, 'Neurosis and the mental-health service', *Lancet*, 1946, **i**: 279–81, p. 281.

[147] C P Blacker, *Neurosis and the mental health services*, London and New York, Humphrey Milford, Oxford University Press, 1946.

spend an evening at dinner with a distinguished Nobel laureate or an earl of indifferent intelligence. He is said to have replied that the company of the aristocrat was preferable.[148]

Lewis shunned personal publicity.[149] As D L Davies recalled, Lewis was an "unassuming man as no one could doubt when meeting him any morning in well worn hat and raincoat, hurrying up Denmark Hill from the tram – later the bus – which had dropped him at Camberwell Green".[150] Some argued that Lewis might have adopted a higher public profile during the 1950s and early 1960s when psychiatry met hostile criticism from the press and patient groups. As his *Times* obituary commented, "he had great determination and courage, but he rarely defended his position".[151]

Lewis took little interest in sartorial smartness. He had a stock of pale blue, utility shirts, which some took to be airforce issue on account of his appointment as civilian consultant in psychiatry to the RAF. Lewis lived modestly in Barnes where he would do his own carpentry, building bookcases for his extensive library. He did not covet the trappings of greatness but presumably believed that his writings and teaching would speak for themselves.

The Post-War Years

In 1946 Lewis was appointed professor of psychiatry at the University of London, only the second person to hold the post. It was decided not to combine the chair with the post of medical superintendent as in the days of Mapother. It was probably judged that the teaching, research and administrative demands on the professor were too great to allow him to manage the clinical aspects of the hospital as well. Accordingly, Lewis set up the professorial unit with its own ward and out-patient clinics so that he and his juniors would have a steady supply of cases for research and training.

Some have seen 1948 as a turning point in the fortunes of the Maudsley. First, it became part of the newly created National Health Service. Secondly, the merger with the prestigious Bethlem Royal Hospital was concluded, providing the Maudsley with access to a generous endowment fund and substantial in-patient facility. Thirdly, Aubrey Lewis succeeded in persuading the British Postgraduate Medical Federation, a school of the University of London, to take financial responsibility for the Maudsley Hospital Medical School, renamed as the Institute of Psychiatry; Mapother's dream had become a reality.[152] Finally, Lewis also obtained finance from the Medical Research Council to set up the Unit for Research in Occupational Adaption, later known as the Social Psychiatry Research Unit.[153] He served as its honorary director while Morris Carstairs, the assistant director, was responsible for its daily running.

The achievements of Lewis in building up the clinical, teaching and research reputation of the Maudsley in post-war Britain lie beyond the scope of this essay. Suffice

[148] Dr Charles Rycroft interviewed by Edgar Jones, 7 May 1998.
[149] Lady Hilda Lewis to Dr C P Blacker, letter, 5 July 1966; held by the Lewis family.
[150] D L Davies, 'Memorial address for Sir Aubrey Lewis given at the Liberal Jewish Synagogue, St John's Wood' (typescript, 17 April 1975), p. 2.
[151] *The Times*, obituary of Sir Aubrey Lewis, 22 January 1975, 14.
[152] *Institute of Psychiatry 1924–1974*, op. cit., note 79 above, p. 2.
[153] Kenneth Rawnsley interviewed by Brian Barraclough (1987), in Wilkinson (ed.), op. cit., note 27 above, pp. 98–133, on p. 107.

it to say, that he succeeded in raising its status to international excellence and in turn lifted the standing of psychiatry within the UK medical profession. The survey he had conducted of Continental psychiatry during 1937 and his experience of treating and researching servicemen during the Second World War were crucial in forming his strategy for the Maudsley. They provided him with an intellectual framework and a clinical perspective that were to serve well into the 1950s. Thereafter, increasing specialisation and the flowering of internationally renowned department heads resulted in the institution developing a momentum of its own.[154]

Lewis had much in common with Mapother and indeed wrote about him with affection and regard. As heads of the Maudsley, they both had

a contempt for humbug and pretension and ... a zest for controversy about matters of principle. Both were rationalists, distrustful of orthodoxy and appeals to authority; and to both the reification of universals was like a red rag to a bull. They both had a remarkable capacity for work ... [were devoted to] the healthy growth of the hospital and medical school, and the furtherance of psychiatry as a reputable branch of medicine, founded on sure evidence and equally regardful of the well-being of the individual and well-being of society.[155]

The quotation is in fact by Lewis and written of Maudsley and Mapother; it applied perhaps even more accurately to Mapother and Lewis themselves.

When asked to summarise what he believed was "Maudsley psychiatry", Lewis observed that the term had both positive and negative connotations. It could be used pejoratively to imply a lack of psycho-dynamic understanding, but he believed that it also represented practices that were empirically based, that avoided extremes but which were assessed critically using statistically validated research. Lewis thought that the particular strengths of the hospital and institute lay in social and epidemiological psychiatry.[156]

Lewis retired in 1966. He died on 21 January 1975 having suffered from Parkinson's disease for a number of years. Dennis Hill, his successor at the Maudsley, wrote the following appreciation:

Lewis will be remembered above all for his educational achievements, but his philosophical essays and studies will be read for a long time ... He had absolute integrity of character. The exercise of his formidable intellectual powers sometimes left an aggressive impression, but this belied his humanity. His friendship was sparingly given, but many were devoted to him. His shyness hid his real concern for others, but not always his mischievous sense of humour ... The debt which psychiatry owes him is immense.[157]

---

[154] Maarten Derksen, 'Science in the clinic: clinical psychology at the Maudsley', and Michael Rutter, 'The emergence of developmental psychopathology', in G C Bunn, A D Lovie and G D Richards (eds), *Psychology in Britain: historical essays and personal reflections*, Leicester, BPS Books, 2001, pp. 267–89, 422–32.

[155] Aubrey Lewis, 'Mapother memorial, a final word', *Bethlem Maudsley Hospital Gazette*, 1961, **4**: 155–6.

[156] Institute of Psychiatry, Sir Aubrey Lewis interviewed by D L Davies *c.* 1970.

[157] 'Obituary, Aubrey Julian Lewis', *Lancet*, 1975, **i**: 288–9, p. 288.

Defining Psychiatry: Aubrey Lewis's 1938 Report and the Rockefeller Foundation

KATHERINE ANGEL

Introduction

Aubrey Lewis finished his report on psychiatry in Europe in 1938, having travelled to centres of psychiatry and allied fields on the Continent between March and September 1937. He had been at the Maudsley Hospital for nine years, with five years as a consultant and one as clinical director. While Lewis stated that the aim of the trip to the Continent was "to learn what is being done in neuropsychiatry and related fields", saying that it was "at the suggestion and with the support of the Rockefeller Foundation",[1] it is worth dwelling on the question of the wider aims it may have served.

The trip can be located in the context of Edward Mapother's desire to create an outstanding institution which would foster research, raise teaching and training standards, and thereby raise the quality and status of psychiatry in England.[2] Mapother, keen to groom individuals who would pursue the same goals of institutional, disciplinary and scientific excellence which he admired in American psychiatry, and having Lewis in

---

Katherine Angel, MA, MPhil. (Cantab), Department of History and Philosophy of Science, Cambridge University, Free School Lane, Cambridge CB2 3RH.

This paper has come out of research I undertook while Research Assistant to Michael Neve and Edgar Jones. I would like to thank Professor Hal Cook and Alan Shiel at the Wellcome Trust Centre for the History of Medicine at University College London for encouraging me to visit both the Institute for the History of Science and Medicine at the University of Lübeck and the Rockefeller Archive Centre in Sleepy Hollow, New York. Thanks are also due to Thomas Rosenbaum and Dr Erwin Levold at the Rockefeller Archive Center; Dr Naomi Cream for providing valuable background material; and Professor John Forrester for helpful comments on the earlier drafts of my essay. Warm thanks in particular to Michael Neve for insightful discussion throughout.

[1] Bethlem Royal Hospital Archives, C/12/3, Aubrey Lewis Box 9, p. 1.

[2] A refashioning of the notion of Englishness in the late nineteenth and early twentieth centuries was a key element in negotiating concepts of liberalism, democracy and civilisation. According to Robert Colls and Philip Dodd, the new cultural understanding of "Englishness" was crucial to the stabilisation of British life; a significant factor in the dominant version of Englishness in the last two decades of the nineteenth century and the early years of the twentieth century was its ability to represent itself to others and others to themselves; so Englishness also defined the Scottish, the Welsh and the Irish. While at one level it would seem that Lewis uses the term "English" to denote psychiatry in England, it is worth thinking about the ways in which usage of this term might embody certain debates about the concept of Englishness. See Christopher Lawrence and Anna-K Mayer, 'Regenerating England: an introduction', in *idem* (eds), *Regenerating England: science, medicine and culture in inter-war Britain*, Clio Medica 60, Amsterdam, Rodopi, 2000, pp. 5–9. See also Robert Colls and Philip Dodds (eds), *Englishness: politics and culture 1880–1920*, London, Croom Helm, 1986.

mind as his potential successor,[3] may have perceived the trip as a means for Lewis to gain the knowledge of techniques, new developments and theoretical perspectives in other countries that Mapother felt was necessary for such a position.[4]

What complicates the reading of Lewis's tour as a means to acquire the expertise of seasoned institutions (expertise in research and clinical methods as well as in the organisation of institutions) is the wealth of negative impressions he records from his visits[5] – a fact made more interesting by the negotiations that Mapother was holding with the Rockefeller Foundation on possible increased financial support for the Maudsley. When in June 1930, Alan Gregg, director of the Rockefeller Foundation's Medical Services Division, first visited the Maudsley Hospital and Mapother, he said that he could not undertake a commitment regarding funding until he had visited similar institutions in England and on the Continent.[6] Mapother must have felt keenly the negative comparison the Maudsley might suffer with other European institutions. At the time of Lewis's trip, psychiatry in Europe was not a coherent or unified enterprise, nor was there agreement over uncomplicatedly successful therapeutics, or a persuasive theoretical framework intersecting with therapies. Several countries, however – most obviously Switzerland, Austria and France[7] – boasted individuals in prestigious institutions producing significant findings, as well as people practising the relatively young but increasingly influential psychoanalysis, the relation of which to psychiatry was not yet clear. These features of European psychiatry must have highlighted only too sharply the relative inertia of the field in England.

While in 1934 and 1935 the Rockefeller funded three German émigrés at the Maudsley, and in 1935 awarded the hospital £9,000 over three years, with in 1938 a further £5,000 per year for five years, Mapother had initially asked for more substantial sums from the Foundation, which had dragged its feet.[8] While in his introduction Lewis acknowledges the superior training and experience in research in continental institutions, he emphasises the increasing renown of the Maudsley, and claims that England and the USA are supplanting Germany in medical and psychiatric progress.[9] Although he invokes political reasons for the demise of German psychiatry, he does seem to

---

[3] Mapother had admired the "medical spirit dominating psychiatry" when he visited America. Edward Mapother, 'Impressions of psychiatry in America', *Lancet*, 1930, **i**: 848.

[4] Mapother, writing to Alan Gregg, described Lewis's trip as "just the sort of thing he needs to fit him to take over the lead of the teaching side from me presently", adding that "he will be of very real advantage for the future of the hospital". Mapother to Gregg, 12 December 1936, series 401A, Record Group (RG) 1.1, Rockefeller Foundation Archive (hereafter RFA), Rockefeller Archive Center (hereafter RAC), Sleepy Hollow, New York. Rockefeller documents recording Lewis's fellowships state that the 1937 trip was felt to "be of particular importance to L. and to his colleagues in London, and will bring about greater familiarity with work in other countries and a better correlation of research activities. Because of L's qualifications and critical abilities, his trip should be of unusual profit; and the full reports which he consented to write on his visits should be of value to the Paris Office". Fellowship cards, RG 10, series MS Great Britain, RFA, RAC.

[5] See Report, especially the concluding 'General Impressions', pp. 143–7.

[6] Alan Gregg officer's diary, 11 June 1930, RG 12.1, RFA, RAC.

[7] The political situation in Germany made a journey there fraught with difficulties (as was a trip to civil war-torn Spain). Lewis was therefore unable to visit the country where successfully institutionalised, scientific and research-based medicine and psychiatry had originated and excelled until the 1930s.

[8] The significance of the presence of the German émigrés is addressed in the conclusion. See also Edgar Jones's essay, p. 18.

[9] See Introduction to the Report, p. 57.

want this claim to signify something positive about English psychiatry *per se*. While Lewis was sent to the Continent to gain the perspectives and knowledge that would help to make the Maudsley a more impressive candidate for Rockefeller patronage,[10] his disappointments and criticisms perhaps indicate a desire on his part, and possibly that of Mapother, to take continental psychiatry down a peg or two and dispel what certainly Lewis deemed was a myth of excellence. Of course, it may simply be that Lewis's criticisms reflect the character traits which later led to his reputation as someone who spoke the truth, regardless of the views of others or the inconvenience it might cause.[11]

In this essay I propose to study Lewis's report with the presence of the Rockefeller Foundation in mind. I shall first consider briefly the state of psychiatry in Europe at the time, and then look at American psychiatry. Common to both was a desire to make psychiatry a scientific discipline on a par with the rest of medicine, with all the trappings and the connotations that such an achievement would confer. Within this context I shall consider the engagement of the Rockefeller with the question of what psychiatry was – what it included, and therefore what its status was. Worries about this still rather inchoate field were foremost in the thinking of the Rockefeller, forming a crucial backdrop both to Lewis's trip to the Continent and to the question of Maudsley funding. To the extent that Lewis's trip was heavily influenced, if not designed, by the Rockefeller, that Lewis echoed the Rockefeller's feelings regarding the boundaries of a respectable, scientific psychiatry, and that the Rockefeller played a crucial role in the development of the Maudsley Hospital and therefore of English psychiatry, such a consideration of the dynamics between the Foundation and Lewis's early career is instructive. Although a thorough examination of the question lies beyond the scope of this essay, it is clear that Rockefeller influence was of great importance to his career in, and ideas about, psychiatry, especially given the extent to which these would shape English post-war psychiatry.

A Note on Terminology

The term "psychiatry" is useful but potentially misleading. What would gradually *become* psychiatry over the course of the first few decades of the twentieth century was, at the time of Lewis's trip, still a fragmented domain of mental health, which embraced asylum-based doctors (*aliénistes*), private-practice neurologists, general practitioners, and, increasingly, psychoanalysts. Although the term "psychiatry" was widely used in the thirties, its meaning was slippery. By the turn of the twentieth

---

[10] While the Rockefeller Foundation aimed to fund institutions in need of help, it also had a long-standing policy of "building on strength rather than on weakness". Raymond B Fosdick, *The story of the Rockefeller Foundation*, London, Odhams Press, 1952, p. 119.

[11] It is not clear from the sources available what happened to Lewis's report; we know that the Rockefeller Foundation read it and found it useful, but not whether they read a more official version than the one we have here, or what the reaction to some of its quite critical content may have been. O'Brien wrote to Gregg on the possibility of a visit to the US by Mapother that "[w]hat I had in mind was something analogous to the survey made by Aubrey Lewis in Europe, which I found useful." O'Brien to Gregg, 11 March 1939, RG 1.1, series 401A, folder 256, box 19, RFA, RAC. Gregg replied that the "difference between Mapother's visit to the United States and the survey made by Aubrey Lewis in Europe lies more in the usefulness of such a visit to the future than in its immediate value to us." Gregg to O'Brien, 30 March 1939, RG 1.1, series 401A, folder 256 box 19, RFA, RAC.

century, psychiatry's status was problematic (given the overcrowded asylums), and the increasing (and increasingly laboratory-based) focus in the nineteenth century on the brain as underlying mental illness, along with the practice of casting psychiatric illness as "nervous illness",[12] had led to a situation where the distinctions between psychiatry and neurology were by no means clear.[13] While in the early twentieth century in Britain and America psychiatrists were still mostly asylum-based, with "nerve specialists" becoming part of general medicine's élite, in central Europe psychiatry and neurology were kept together. Thus many of Lewis's contemporaries on the Continent were professors of mental and nervous diseases, or of psychiatry and neurology, terminology which reflects the legacy of (mostly German) nineteenth-century biological and anatomical psychiatry.

Psychiatry in the 1930s

As Edgar Jones indicates in his essay, psychiatry in Britain was highly fragmented in the interwar period; it remained in the asylums virtually until the Second World War, and there were almost no laboratories or research institutes. The Maudsley was to fill a real gap, and its creation was part of a larger trend that had been unfolding in psychiatry: the foundation of institutions often linked to universities, with clinics providing the link between laboratory science and clinical practice.

More generally, psychiatry in Western Europe in the first decades of the twentieth century had seen the nineteenth century's biological and anatomical focus wane. Despite the rise of neurology, and eminent figures such as Pavlov, Alzheimer, Pick and Sherrington doing lasting neuropathological work, what would come to be called "brain mythology" had yielded relatively little in terms of concrete aetiological, diagnostic and therapeutic findings. And although popular forms of treatment included rest and diet cures, barbiturates, baths, massages and surgery in cases of focal sepsis, there was little consensus about how they worked and no unifying framework for them.

By the beginning of the century in many European countries (even before any consistent dissemination of Freud's ideas), psychodynamic approaches and an already robust notion of the unconscious were fairly widely used by figures such as Eugen Bleuler and Auguste-Henri Forel in their theoretical and clinical work. By the 1930s, psychoanalysis had a significant presence in Europe. However, there was no compulsion to

---

[12] Edward Shorter argues that the association of psychiatry with degeneration and insanity led to an endorsement of notions of "nervous illness", which both fostered office-based "neurology" and reassured patients fearful of psychiatry's implications. Edward Shorter, *History of psychiatry: from the era of the asylum to the age of Prozac*, New York, John Wiley, 1997, pp. 113–44. "Psychiatrists" were originally alienists, based in asylums, while "neurologists" were originally trained in pathology and internal medicine; the latter, however, had come under pressure to focus on psychoneuroses in addition to their primary interest in neurological implications of all sorts of disease. Neurologists thus became office-based practitioners of psychotherapy, catering to the middle- and upper-classes; such comforts would play a role in the later move towards psychotherapy and psychoanalysis amongst psychiatrists.

[13] As Shorter writes of the ultimately unsuccessful laboratory-focused psychiatry at the end of the nineteenth century, "What Nissl and Alzheimer could find under their microscopes they declared 'neurology'. What they couldn't find was psychiatry." (Shorter, op. cit., note 12 above, p. 109.) Nissl himself wrote that without clarification of the relationships between brain anatomy and brain function, the search for relationships between the findings of brain anatomy and psychiatric findings was difficult and ultimately pointless. (Franz Nissl, 'Über die Entwicklung der Psychiatrie in den letzten 50 Jahren', *Verhandlungen des Naturhistorisch-Medizinischen Vereins,* 1908, N.F. **8**: pp. 510–25.)

choose between it and organic, or biological, psychiatry; many practitioners, such as Max Müller in Switzerland – as Lewis notes with interest – fostered analysis as well as the new physical treatments. Psychoanalysis and psychotherapy received renewed scrutiny and respect after the First World War, and became increasingly attractive to psychiatrists eager to have an office-based specialty. By the 1920s both these fields had begun to have a strong presence in continental universities and education generally, influencing a growing number of disciplines. To the hysterical and neurotic disorders under the gaze of psychoanalysis had been added problems such as schizophrenia, although this widening of the remit of analysis led to debate within the movement which partly contributed to various splits. By the time of Lewis's visit, however, the future presence of psychoanalysis in the UK, and its pre-eminence in the US, had been guaranteed by the emigration of several key analysts.

While the biological thinking of the nineteenth century had begun to disintegrate, psychiatry, in the fifteen years or so before Lewis's trip, had stumbled upon some highly organic interventions, largely unconnected to particular theoretical frameworks, which raised new hopes of therapeutic success. These discoveries, however, yielded multiple complications, and failed to deliver their initial promise of dramatic cure. So while Wagner-Jauregg's fever therapy for neurosyphilitic psychosis had been producing results from the early twentieth century, and brought the therapeutic nihilism often attributed to the epoch to an abrupt halt, it turned out to be highly dangerous.[14] Moreover, neurosyphilis had a distinctive and specific cause; other causes of major mental illness (the "functional" psychoses such as schizophrenia, or manic-depressive illness), were, however, of unknown aetiology, which made searching for treatments far less successful.

Jakob Klaesi's prolonged narcosis to treat psychosis was widely adopted in the twenties, but it too turned out to be dangerous. In 1927 Max Müller exposed the death rate associated with Somnifen,[15] the drug Klaesi used (the technique was later modified with other drugs).[16] At the time of Lewis's trip, Manfred Sakel's publications on insulin coma therapy were very recent,[17] and, despite enthusiasm for the treatment,

---

[14] Paul Ehrlich's proposals in 1910 to use Salvarsan for neurosyphilis had also seemed promising, but in order to be effective the compound had to be administered early, and, by the time symptoms were clinically evident, it was often too late.

[15] Max Müller, 'Die Dauernarkose mit flüssigem Dial bei Psychosen, speziell bei manisch-depressivem Irresein', *Zeitschrift für die gesamte Neurologie und Psychiatrie*, 1927, **107**: 522–43.

[16] Klaesi saw the use of prolonged narcosis as a means of making patients more accessible to psychotherapy – not necessarily to effect an outright cure by physical means. It was used in this way for quite some time.

[17] Manfred Sakel published his initial findings on the beneficial effects that inadvertently going into an insulin coma had on the restlessness and agitation of morphine addicts in 'Neue Behandlung der Morphinsucht', *Zeitschrift für die gesamte Neurologie und Psychiatrie*, 1933, **143**: 506–34, and then the results of the application of this finding to schizophrenia in a 13-part series, 'Schizophreniebehandlung mittles Insulin-Hypoglykämie sowie hypoglykämischer Shocks', *Wiener Medizinische Wochenschrift*, 3 November 1934, **84**: 1211–13, to 9 February 1935, **85**: 179–80. Lewis, in his Report (p. 85), writes that Steck in Lausanne had suggested this use of insulin previously, and it seems that Sakel was unaware of previous attempts to use it as a treatment for psychosis. (See F E James, 'Insulin treatment in psychiatry', *Hist. Psychiatry*, 1992, **3**: 221–35.)

it was soon shown to be equally beset by complications.[18] 1935 saw the publication of Ladislas von Meduna's experiments with camphor-induced convulsions on psychosis, and later with cardiazol; but these were unreliable and produced too great anxiety and pain in patients.[19] Lewis refers in his report to the risks of insulin and cardiazol use, distinguishing immediate from long-term outcome, and noting that much depends on what is meant by "good results" of insulin.[20] Recovery without insight, he says, is "a dubious kind of recovery",[21] and he is critical of Ugo Cerletti's claims regarding "cured" patients.[22]

At the time, these were exciting breakthroughs in the treatment of psychiatric illness. But, although they provoked results undreamed of thirty years previously, it soon became clear they were primarily useful in sedating agitated patients, rather than curing them. Moreover, psychiatrists struggled with the problems they raised, lacking in systematic theoretical understanding of the phenomena with which they were confronted. These discoveries appeared while psychiatry was on the cusp of the new hope that electroshock therapy would offer, as well as a few years away from the successful use of penicillin in primary syphilis. These new beacons of light for intractable conditions seemed merely to highlight the frustrating aetiological and therapeutic quandaries besetting the field.

Psychiatry was thus unsettled, exciting and perplexing, with representatives from its various specialties tussling to define its nature. It seemed to many, however, that great success could be found within it, if only an institutional and scientific context for it could be fostered. Mapother's project at the Maudsley Hospital was part of such a process, and Lewis and the Rockefeller Foundation, both so crucial to the Maudsley's development, were subject to the puzzles and anxieties which went hand in hand with such a task.

Political Contexts

One cannot think of Europe in 1937 without a grim awareness of the very recent developments preventing Lewis from visiting the very country whose institutions were the prototype for Mapother's project, as well as for most psychiatric institutions in Europe and the United States in the early twentieth century. Germany's position in psychiatry was pre-eminent until 1933, but by 1937 the field had been unrecognisably altered by political incursions. The Law for the Prevention of Offspring with Hereditary Diseases, enforcing compulsory sterilisation, was introduced only a few months after Hitler seized power in 1933. Many of the diseases considered hereditary – schizophrenia, cyclothymia, hereditary epilepsy, Huntington's chorea, severe

---

[18] Although it soon became clear that real cure was not achieved, temporary improvement and the comparative gentleness of insulin therapy ensured that it was still used in many countries until relatively recently.

[19] Cardiazol was none the less widely used, especially in the United States until the end of the 1940s.

[20] The quote is in the report, p. 89. Lewis discusses the issues also on pp. 85–6, 89–90.

[21] Report, p. 89.

[22] Report, page 101. See also pp. 108–9 where Lewis records scepticism about Sakel's insulin treatment and Otto Pötzl's involvement in Sakel's work. Shorter writes that "beyond the university clinic, Sakel's results were considered a joke, the man himself a charlatan, and Pötzl's patronage of him a mystery." Shorter, op. cit., note 12 above, p. 210.

Defining Psychiatry

alcoholism, and congenital mental deficiency – fell under psychiatry's remit. The killing of psychiatric patients had been planned since 1935 at least, and was to be undertaken in earnest in 1939, when Nazism revealed the full brutality of its psychiatric and medical programmes.

The Soviet Union was also beginning to hold psychiatry hostage to politics. Stalin's extraordinary repressive purges had been going on in earnest from 1936, although the Academy of Sciences of the USSR, like many other organisations, had been a target of purges from as early as 1929.[23] Transferred in 1934 from Leningrad to Moscow and made directly subordinate to the government, the Academy of Sciences was merged in 1936 with the Communist Academy in order to increase its political orientation. It became at this time the most important scientific institution in the nation.[24] All of the thirteen successive secretaries of the Kiev Academy of Sciences between 1921 and 1938 were arrested,[25] and Sidney Bloch and Peter Reddaway state that between 1936 and 1938 Andrei Vyshinsky, subordinate of the head of secret police, initiated the confinement of dissenters in prison psychiatric hospitals.[26] Robert Conquest estimates that between 1933 and 1935, 5 million people were imprisoned in labour camps, and this number rose slightly between 1935 and 1937.[27] Whether Lewis would have been aware of these particular developments at the time of his trip is unclear; he certainly seems frustrated in Russia by the grandiose (and he thinks false) claims made for Russian psychiatric work, as well as by the impenetrability of institutions and individuals. He may well have been unaware of the magnitude of the pressures on, and potential risk to, the individuals he met.[28]

The Rockefeller Foundation and Psychiatry

The 1930s saw the Rockefeller Foundation injecting significant funds into scientific research in, and the institutional organisation of, psychiatry, in much the same way that it had previously done in medicine.[29] In 1933 in the United States, "teaching

---

[23] Zhores A Medvedev, *Soviet science*, New York, W W Norton, 1978, p. 27.

[24] Ibid., p. 38.

[25] Robert Conquest, *The great terror: a reassessment*, London, Hutchinson, 1990, p. 293.

[26] Sidney Bloch and Peter Reddaway, 'Psychiatrists and dissenters in the Soviet Union', in Eric Stover and Elena O Nightingale (eds), *The breaking of bodies and minds: torture, psychiatric abuse and the health professions*, New York, W H Freeman, 1985, pp. 132–63, on p. 133. Bloch and Reddaway state that the little evidence there is suggests that the policy of systematically interning dissenters in mental hospitals began during Stalin's rule in the late 1930s. (Ibid., p. 133.)

[27] Conquest, op. cit., note 25 above, p. 311.

[28] His introduction, which appears to have been written after the trip, reveals a greater awareness of the political repression at work. He mentions Italy as well as the Soviet Union (Introduction to the Report, pp. 57–8, 60); for details on the Italian situation, see the Italy section in the report.

[29] It was only relatively recently that medicine had attained scientific status, with the laboratory as a defining component in that status. Again, the models for this were mostly German institutes. The role of the Rockefeller in encouraging the scientisation of medicine stemmed from the joint initiative of John D Rockefeller Sr and Frederick T Gates, principal adviser in business and philanthropy to Rockefeller. The story goes that Gates was impressed with the retarded development of American medicine as he read about it in W Osler's *Principles and practice of medicine*, and he and Rockefeller put in motion their plans to foster scientific inquiry and medical research. This led to the creation, between 1901 and 1913, of the Rockefeller Institute of Medical Research, the General Education Board, the Rockefeller Sanitary Commission, and the Rockefeller Foundation. See Fosdick, op. cit., note 10 above, pp. 16–28. For a non-insider view of the strategies and philosophies of the Rockefeller, see Ilana Löwy and Patrick Zylberman, 'Medicine as

in psychiatry was poor, research fragmentary, application feeble", the presence of psychology and neurology departments in medical schools was sporadic, and those that did exist were isolated and badly integrated with their neighbouring disciplines.[30] The practice of psychiatry was often still largely custodial, in unwieldy mental hospitals. Dr David L Edsall, Dean of the Harvard Medical School and a trustee of the Rockefeller Foundation, wrote a report in 1930 on the state of psychiatry which helped to launch the new Rockefeller psychiatry programme. In it he commented, "[p]sychiatry has been distinctly separated from general medical interests and thought, to such a degree that, to very many medical men, it seems a wholly distinct thing with which they have little relation".[31]

Adolf Meyer became professor at the new psychiatric unit of the Johns Hopkins Medical School in 1908, where he developed a university psychiatric research and teaching hospital of the kind it was felt the United States needed, and upon which later schools were based. He played a key role in establishing university training for psychiatrists and fostering a more integrated relationship between mental institutions and the growing university medical schools and hospitals.[32] In so doing, he helped to create a new professional role for psychiatrists, one which would ensure membership of the scientific and medical establishment. These changes in the organisation of a previously splintered field brought together the interests of the *aliénistes*, trying to shake off the negative associations still conjured up by the asylum, and the neurologists and the internists in the laboratory and the clinic, all of whom were seeking renewed medical authority in the shape of a bona fide, unified professional structure.[33] Meyer's psychobiology, with its concepts of maladaptation – not a structural defect of mind or body but rather the lowering of a person's ability to function – both increased the client base for psychiatry and potentially afforded different kinds of practitioners equal legitimacy in a pragmatic approach towards environmentally mediated conditions.

This new drive to place psychiatry on a par with scientific medicine was accompanied by a more general change in society's conception of mental illness and psychiatry, especially after the First World War.[34] These movements are reflected in a changing orientation within the Rockefeller Foundation which had, in the early 1920s, focused on medicine in relation to university teaching, steering clear of basic research.[35] It had

---

a social instrument: the Rockefeller Foundation, 1913–1945', in *Studies in the History and Philosophy of Biological and Biomedical Sciences* (*Special Issue: The Rockefeller Foundation and Biomedical Sciences*) September 2000, **31c** (3): 365–79.

[30] Fosdick, op. cit., note 10 above, p. 148.

[31] David L Edsall, 'Memorandum regarding possible psychiatric developments', 3 October 1930, Rockefeller Foundation, cited in Fosdick, op. cit., note 10 above, p. 147.

[32] Theodore Lidz, 'Adolf Meyer and the development of American psychiatry', *Am. J. Psychiatry*, 1966, **123**: 320–32; Mathew Thomson, 'Mental hygiene as an international movement', in Paul Weindling (ed.), *International health organisations and movements, 1918–1939*, Cambridge University Press, 1995. pp. 283–305; Theodore M Brown, 'Alan Gregg and the Rockefeller Foundation's support of Franz Alexander's psychosomatic research', *Bull. Hist. Med.*, 1987, **61**: 155–82; Jack Pressman, *Last resort: psychosurgery and the limits of medicine*, Cambridge University Press, pp. 18–47.

[33] The concern besetting the diffuse field of mental illness in the first decades of the twentieth century was precisely that of whether, and how, to contain within one speciality practices as diverse as asylum psychiatry, neurology, neuropathology, brain anatomy, psychology, and psychotherapy.

[34] See Pressman, op. cit., note 32 above, pp. 18–30, for details on the initiatives of the National Committee for Mental Hygiene chief medical officer Thomas Salmon.

[35] Fosdick, op. cit., note 10 above, p. 142.

Defining Psychiatry

had little involvement with psychiatry, although during his directorship of the Division of Medical Education (1919–1930), Richard M Pearce had ruminated on a possible new programme in psychiatry, and taken an interest in Emil Kraepelin's Institute in Munich, the Kaiser Wilhelm Institute for Brain Research in Berlin, and the Pasteur Institute at the Collège de France in Paris.[36] In 1929 the Rockefeller Foundation was reorganised, and the Division of Medical Education became the Division of Medical Sciences, reflecting a new policy of extending knowledge through support of scientific research, and eventually with a new focus on psychiatry, encouraged by Pearce's successor Alan Gregg.[37]

When Gregg succeeded Pearce in 1930, he had to persuade the Foundation, presided over by the sceptical Max Mason, a former physicist, of the wisdom of a significant endorsement of psychiatry. Edsall's memorandum in 1930 had articulated the worries of many in the Rockefeller: he described psychiatry as a "field dominated by elusive and inexact methods of study and speculative thought"; he urged cautious investigation via exclusive pursuit of "real scientific studies" in "forcible laboratories or institutes, prepared to study such matters related to psychiatry as are subject to attack by the methods of more or less exact sciences". He urged that psychoanalysis should be bypassed because it could not at that time be "accurately studied from a scientific viewpoint".[38] In a discussion in 1930 of a possible psychiatry programme, there was uncertainty as to the methods psychiatry should employ, and as to its fit within a scientific medicine: a representative comment was that the subject "requires fresh thinking; the experimental method of medicine does not apply; there must be new techniques".[39] In the same discussion, Edsall is recorded as contrasting the changes which had come about in thirty years in medicine – through physiology and nutritional studies – with the state of psychiatry, in which practitioners "have not produced the kind of advance upon which to build".[40] While the Rockefeller's mission was to "improve the well-being of mankind", and its activities were not confined to pure science, it was a dogged advocate of the merits of science, especially within medicine, and was highly preoccupied by the risk of undertaking projects which might undermine this ideal.

In April 1933 the Trustees agreed to "the plans of the Division of Medical Sciences to concentrate on psychiatry",[41] the justification being that psychiatry was one of the most backward, but "also one of the most probably fruitful",[42] fields. A sense of optimism with regard to medicine also fostered a growing involvement in psychiatry: "With increasing control over organic diseases, functional diseases will more and more be

[36] Ibid., p. 142.

[37] Mathew Thomson writes that the Rockefeller Foundation's failure to make progress in the field of mental hygiene, which it had supported between 1919 and 1939, may have encouraged the Foundation to concentrate on a more scientific approach (op. cit., note 32 above, p. 290).

[38] David Edsall, 'Memorandum regarding possible psychiatric developments', 3 October 1930, RG 3, series 906, folder 19, box 2, RFA, RAC.

[39] Excerpt from Rockefeller Foundation Conference Report, 12 October 1930, RG 3, series 906, folder 19, box 2, RFA, RAC.

[40] Ibid.

[41] Report of Appraisal Committee, 11 December 1934, RG 3, series 906, folder 19, box 2, RFA, RAC.

[42] Excerpt from the Agenda for Rockefeller Foundation meeting, 11 April 1933, RG 3, series 906, folder 19, box 2, RFA, RAC.

presented as the problem", a member in a staff conference claimed.[43] (Gregg, in 1941, praising the advances in medicine from 1880, also wrote that "there has been, for the past fifty years, however, something approaching neglect of the patient as a person".[44]) The annual report for 1934 argued that, in addition to research and maintenance grants to help train already established men, able persons had to be found, trained and allowed to conduct research in psychiatry through scholarships, fellowships and decently-paid posts. The best young talent would then be attracted to a solid and eminent field.[45]

Thus the number of projects funded by the Medical Science Division under the Psychiatry Program of Specific Concentration in 1934 rose from a modest four in 1933 (costing $234,900) to eleven (costing $255,000), with another $49,100 spent on five projects in neurology and $45,900 spent on other medical fields.[46] Until the war at least, money from the Medical Sciences Division went primarily to psychiatry.[47] The director's Report on the Program in Psychiatry in 1935 states that "[p]sychiatry here comprises clinical psychiatry; clinical neurology; the anatomy, physiology, chemistry, pharmacology and pathology of the nervous system; some phases of psychology; and those phases of other branches of medicine which bear directly on the understanding of human behaviour".[48] While the range of subjects encouraged were sometimes oddly diverse – neurosurgery alongside anthropometric studies of handwriting, for instance[49] – there was from the outset, and increasingly, a heavy emphasis placed on those fields of endeavour which were physical and laboratory-based; or at least experimentally-based. The annual report of 1936 urges that a factual foundation be found "for what is often called psychobiology".[50] The aim was a psychiatry whose methods and tools resembled most closely the medicine which had flowered in the previous half-century or so, with pathology, anatomy and physiology the models to which psychiatry should aspire. Edsall's memorandum had, after all, emphasised the need to develop "real scientific studies of psychiatric problems".[51]

---

[43] Staff Conference documents, 7 October 1930, RG 3, series 906, folder 17, box 2, RFA, RAC.

[44] 'What is psychiatry?' by Alan Gregg, 3 December 1941, RG 3, series 906, folder 19, box 2, RFA, RAC.

[45] Rockefeller Foundation Annual Report 1934, New York, p. 79.

[46] Ibid., pp. 111–13.

[47] In 1935, the Division allocated $2,733,050 for medical sciences, of which $1,459,450 went to psychiatry (Rockefeller Foundation Annual Report 1935, New York, p. 69). In 1936, the total for the medical sciences was $1,623,750, of which $702,050 went to "psychiatry and allied subjects", $112,000 to public health and preventive medicine teaching, and the rest to fellowships and small grants in aid (Rockefeller Foundation Annual Report 1936, New York, p. 133). In 1937, the Medical Sciences spent $2,392,100 of which $1,392,100 went to psychiatry (Rockefeller Foundation Annual Report 1937, New York, pp. 132–3). In 1938, psychiatry and allied fields received $873,300 out of the $5,344,700 spent by the Medical Sciences (Rockefeller Foundation Annual Report 1938, New York, p. 154). In 1939, the Medical Sciences allocated $1,927,180, with psychiatry, neurology and allied fields getting $699,330 (Rockefeller Foundation Annual Report 1939, New York, p. 160).

[48] Excerpt from the Medical Sciences Director's Report on the Program in Psychiatry, 11 December 1935, RG 3, series 906, folder 19, box 2, RFA, RAC.

[49] Excerpt from Staff Conference, 7 October 1930, RG 3, series 906, folder 17, box 2.

[50] Rockefeller Foundation Annual Report 1936, New York, p. 24.

[51] David Edsall, 'Memorandum regarding possible psychiatric developments', 3 October 1930, RG 3, series 906, folder 19, box 2, RFA, RAC.

Alan Gregg and the Definition of Psychiatry

Alan Gregg was in control of a huge financial resource for the development of psychiatry; through his choices, the Rockefeller Foundation was contributing to the shaping of the field of psychiatry and defining what to exclude and what to include. Gregg's role and certain aspects of his biography and career encourage a portrayal of him as an enthusiastic champion of Meyer's psychobiology, of an all-embracing philosophy of mental illness, of an eclectic therapeutic and clinical approach and of Freudian psychoanalysis and psychoanalytically-infused psychosomatic medicine.[52] Thus, Pressman writes of "Gregg's plan to remake psychiatry through a commitment to a program of psychobiology", claiming that Gregg refabricated "Meyer's doctrine of psychobiology in such a way that the laboratory was given center stage, resulting in a new framework that he made famous in America as *psychosomatic* medicine".[53] While it is true that Gregg directed an ultimately quite visionary programme in psychiatry and was keenly influenced by Meyer's psychobiology, these statements of a straightforwardly positive commitment to a particular kind of psychiatry obscure his uncertainty, throughout his career, about the domain of psychiatry. Brown may be right that the philanthropy of a large foundation crystallised a movement towards a notion of psychosomatic medicine,[54] but this emphasis threatens to underplay the difficulties of delimiting the boundaries of psychiatry and attempting to resolve fundamental questions about its nature.

Gregg had become interested in psychology and psychoanalysis while at Harvard.[55] At the Boston Psychopathic Hospital during the clinical years of his medical training, he became increasingly focused on physiology and infused with the scientific ideals dominating there. He then won a place at Massachusetts General Hospital, working in the highly physiologically and biochemically oriented scientific medicine recently introduced by David Edsall, Harvard's Jackson professor of medicine since 1912. Gregg's diaries at this time reveal that he was unsure about the adequacy of science as the sole basis for the practice of medicine.[56] Gregg started working at the Rockefeller Foundation in 1919, and in 1922 Richard Pearce offered him a job as his assistant in the Division of Medical Education (created in 1919). Pearce had trained under Simon Flexner (who became director of the Rockefeller Institute for Medical Research in 1902) and had worked with Edsall in the struggle for "scientific medicine" at Pennsylvania University. Pearce, when Gregg joined him, organised the Division in line with the expectations of Flexner, who was highly sceptical about psychiatry. In 1924 Gregg became associate director of Medical Education in charge of European operations; his work embodied Pearce's concerns with science and rigorous experimentation

---

[52] For accounts which tend to endorse this view, see Pressman, op. cit., note 32 above; Brown, op. cit., note 32 above; and Theodore M Brown, 'The rise and fall of psychosomatic medicine', read at the New York Academy of Medicine 29 November 2000, also published online in *Human Nature*, 8 November 2001, which tends slightly this way, although to a much lesser extent. See note 85 below.

[53] Pressman, op. cit., note 32 above, p. 33, italics in original.

[54] Brown, op. cit., note 52 above.

[55] The following account of Gregg's life is derived from Wilder Penfield, *The difficult art of giving: the epic of Alan Gregg*, Boston, Little Brown, 1967; Brown, op. cit., note 32 above; and 'The reminiscences of Alan Gregg', a partial oral history memoir prepared by Dr Saul Benison for the Columbia Oral History Research Office, cited in Brown, op. cit., p. 157.

[56] Penfield, op. cit., note 55 above, p. 95.

in medical research, and he expressed little interest in psychiatry or nervous and mental diseases. From the mid-twenties onwards, when the importance of psychiatry was becoming increasingly acknowledged, the Division of Medical Education began to encourage a predominantly biological approach to psychiatry – although at this time Gregg began to rediscover his interest in psychoanalysis.

After becoming director upon Pearce's death, Gregg succeeded, a few years later, in persuading the Foundation of the validity of the newly-proposed psychiatry programme. But behind the confident rhetoric concerning psychiatry in Gregg's and the Foundation's official publications and correspondence with outsiders, internal correspondence points to a considerable confusion as to what psychiatry included and excluded – a confusion which sat alongside an insistence on a psychiatry akin to scientific medicine. Thus in 1935, when the Foundation's psychiatry programme was well under way, Gregg reported at a staff conference "Kappel's suggestion that several organizations in and around New York interested in mental hygiene hold a conference for *mutual information*".[57] And as late as 1940, Raymond Fosdick (President of the Foundation from 1936 to 1948) wrote to Gregg that he had lunched with "Walter Steward, and he said he thought the lay members of the Board of Trustees didn't really understand what psychiatry was. He said he thought that some of them, at least, confused it with psychoanalysis, and thought it was primarily concerned with Freud and Jung. ... His suggestion was that at some future Board meeting ... you take half an hour to explain what modern psychiatry means and what you are trying to do with your program".[58]

The Chicago Institute for Psychoanalysis

Gregg's involvement with the Chicago Institute for Psychoanalysis, set up in 1932 and headed by Franz Alexander,[59] is sometimes invoked as an example of his own personal commitment to a vision of psychiatry that is Meyerian in its breadth, as well as to psychoanalysis in particular (about which Meyer himself had reservations).[60] Thus Pressman writes that "Gregg underwrote the cost of one of the first psychoanalytic training institutes in America precisely because its director aggressively promoted a distinct psychosomatic orientation".[61] Several Rockefeller sources reveal, however, that Gregg experienced considerable doubts about the merits of the Institute and increasingly of psychoanalysis.

In the early years of the psychiatry programme, the Foundation excluded psychoanalysis as a potential recipient of funding;[62] a staff conference document in 1930 stated that "psychoanalysis is in a stage of development where it cannot be attacked philosophically and can be left to its own devices – it does not need money but needs

---

[57] Staff Conference, 14 November 1935, RG 3, series 906, folder 18, box 2, RFA, RAC. (Italics added.)
[58] Fosdick to Gregg, 28 November 1940, RG 3, series 906, folder 18, box 2, RFA, RAC.
[59] Franz Alexander (1891–1964) was a Hungarian who, after studying physiology, became a leading European analyst, moving to Chicago in the early 1930s. He developed psychoanalytic theories of somatic and psychological disorders.
[60] See Pressman, op. cit., note 32 above.
[61] Ibid, p. 35.
[62] See the annual reports of the Foundation in the early 1930s.

Defining Psychiatry

maturity and needs defeat in places where it does not stand up".[63] Gregg rejected the Chicago Institute's initial overtures regarding funding on the grounds that it was a non-university institute, while Chicago University still had no department of psychiatry.[64] He was, however, willing to correspond with and visit the Institute.

Dr Daniel O'Brien, assistant director of the Medical Sciences Division who advised Lewis prior to his trip, was not very impressed with the Institute or its doctors in 1933. He did not feel that they were "exceptional investigators or were presenting original ideas".[65] O'Brien's tone is more dismissive than that of Gregg, who, in the same year, was "interested in the future of the Institute but did not think that this was the time for any action by the RF",[66] and who, according to Alfred K Stern (President of the Chicago Institute), had "recommended analysis to young psychiatrists in several cases".[67] But Gregg was very cautious, and quick to quell the enthusiasm Stern sometimes misleadingly attributed to him while corresponding with Institute figures.[68] Gregg thought that the Institute's members had "plenty of winnowing to do before they know enough to have something definitely to contribute to the study of somatic diseases"; he also stated that he had not "yet seen included what makes the simplest and to me the best case for psychoanalysis".[69]

In 1935, however, a grant of $100,000 for three years was awarded to the Chicago Institute. The rationale was that "[p]sychoanalysis occupies an important part of the training of psychiatrists and is under present conditions costly and unsatisfactory, partly due to the fact that it is on a non-institutional basis". The Institute trained only medically qualified individuals, and emphasised the "correlation of medical and physiological problems with the findings of psychoanalysis". The aid would "afford an opportunity to psychoanalysis" and "protect and foster its relationship to medicine and psychiatry".[70] Though "handicapped by the enthusiasms of some of its extreme adherents and the excited resentment of its opponents", psychoanalysis "deserves a fair opportunity to prove its ability and to be stripped of its false or useless phases".[71] Testing psychoanalysis in an institution "would favour comparison, exchange of opinion, verification and a correlation with the findings of internal medicine, surgery and the more orthodox views of psychiatry".[72] Funding would thus temper the unscientific

---

[63] Excerpt from Staff Conference, 7 October 1930, RG 3, series 906, folder 17, box 2, RFA, RAC. See also Edsall's 'Memorandum regarding possible psychiatric developments', cited in note 38 above.

[64] Alan Gregg officer's diary, 4 April 1932, RG 12.1, RFA, RAC.

[65] Daniel P O'Brien officer's diary, 13 January 1933, RG 12.1, RFA, RAC.

[66] Alan Gregg officer's diary, 18 May 1933, RG 12.1, RFA, RAC.

[67] Stern to Gregg, 2 June 1933, RG 1.1, series 216A, folder 26, box 3, RFA, RAC.

[68] Stern forwarded to Gregg a document for the Board of Trustees at the Chicago Institute; in it Stern claimed that the Foundation was ready to consider fellowships for exceptional candidates and that if after a few years, "when subscriptions were no longer adequate to carry on the Institute's program and a university has not yet taken over the Institute, [Gregg] would be willing to recommend a direct appropriation from the RF." Next to this Gregg wrote in the column of his copy: "Conditions may change so that I would not be willing to do this." Moreover, he requested Stern not to send this document to his Trustees; Gregg would himself make a statement on his position. Stern to Gregg, 2 June 1933, RG 1.1, series 216A, folder 26, box 3, RFA, RAC.

[69] Alan Gregg officer's diary, 14 February 1933, RG 12.1, RFA, RAC.

[70] 'Program in Medical Sciences', June 1935, RG 1.1, series 216A, folder 25, box 3, RFA, RAC.

[71] 'Program in Medical Sciences' 3 April 1935, RG 1.1, series 216A, folder 28, box 3, RFA, RAC.

[72] Ibid.

tendencies of psychoanalysis and bring it under the control of a scientific psychiatry. The Foundation's involvement was generous, but controlling; support and supervision went hand in hand, in the hope that the Rockefeller could help shape the Institute's activities and encourage the shedding of any speculative elements.[73]

The Chicago Institute was the only such institution funded by the Rockefeller at the time.[74] The annual report of 1935 shows that the bulk of funds for the development of teaching and research went largely to subjects such as genetics, obstetrics and gynaecology, surgery, dementia praecox, neuroanatomy, experimental neurology, physiological optics, reflex behaviour, living tissue growth, and infantile paralysis.[75] (These same priorities are evident in the annual reports of the following years.) Fosdick, giving an overview of Gregg's psychiatry programme, lists brain chemistry, epilepsy, neurophysiology, carbohydrate metabolism, schizophrenia, genetic factors in mental and nervous disease and heredity as the subjects given grants.[76] While some of these projects may have incorporated psychoanalytic, psychosomatic or psychodynamic elements, claims that the Rockefeller's programme derived from a positive vision of psychiatry as all-embracing, environment-focused and psychosomatic, seem misrepresentative.[77]

By 1937, Gregg indicated that, despite progress in teaching, there were problems emerging with the Chicago Institute. There would "probably not be a case for further RF aid beyond a three-to-five year period beyond 1937", and any action taken by the RF "must be made with a clear understanding of termination at the end of the period".[78] Gregg and his colleagues became irritable and exasperated with Alexander and Stern,[79] experiencing difficulties in persuading Alexander to steer clear of speculative work and focus on sound experimental work on psychogenic and somatic factors. In 1939, R A Lambert, associate director of the Medical Sciences Division, while discussing a

---

[73] Gregg also employed this strategy with Stanley Cobb's psychoanalytic projects at Massachusetts General. See Brown, op. cit., note 52 above.

[74] Brown writes that Alexander was the only psychoanalyst to receive large direct grants from the Rockefeller Foundation; Brown, op. cit., note 52 above. The Division later funded, however, psychoanalytic projects at Massachusetts General, Cornell Medical School and Washington University, and, after the war, Gregg tried to help the Tavistock Clinic obtain university recognition. See note 85 below.

[75] Rockefeller Foundation Annual Report 1935, New York, pp. 69–117. Of 25 grants-in-aid paid to American physician post-doctoral students, 8 went to psychiatry, 4 to neuropathology, 4 to neurophysiology, 3 to neurology, 2 each to advanced psychiatry and neuroanatomy, and 1 each to clinical psychiatry, public health administration, neurosurgery, psychoanalysis, endocrinology, biochemistry and educational psychology. Ibid, p. 98.

[76] Fosdick, op. cit., note 10 above, p. 150.

[77] While Brown tends to argue this view (see op. cit., note 52 above), he also captures the overall philosophy of Gregg's programme by describing it as an "interdisciplinary amalgam" in neuropsychiatry "dominated by the biological sciences but interspersed with psychoanalysis". Brown, op. cit., note 32 above, p. 167.

[78] Alan Gregg officer's diary, 2 November 1937, RG 12.1, RFA, RAC.

[79] Gregg recommended to Alexander and Stern that they "avoid getting a martyr complex on the subject of the position of psychoanalysis in medicine", and that they should avoid alienating the sympathies of interested observers with "flare-ups of ambition". (Alan Gregg officer's diary, 8 February 1934, RG 12.1, RFA, RAC). He repeatedly stalled the ambition of Alexander, for example over the project for a Journal of Psychosomatic Medicine. (Alan Gregg officer's diary, 15 October 1935, RG 12.1, RFA, RAC.) And Alexander and Stern made requests Gregg and his colleagues found presumptuous; after Stern wrote to Max Mason in 1934 (President of the Rockefeller 1929–1936 and Director of the Natural Sciences Division 1928–9) about an apparent pledge of $20,000 a year, Mason wrote in the column: "Too strong by 1000%. I said I would mention their present need to AG, but Stern knew our attitude, which was highly conservative". Stern to Mason, 1 February 1934, RG 1.1, series 216 A, folder 21, box 3, RFA, RAC.

Defining Psychiatry

possible appointment at the Institute, wondered whether an applicant is "just a pseudo-scientist, as most others in his field", adding, "I still don't think much of the Chicago Institute crowd. Maybe Alexander has contributed a little something towards making psychoanalysis respectable, but he certainly has not brought it into the scientific fold. I shall feel a relief when the RF grant terminates – and is not renewed".[80] In his reply, O'Brien concurred.[81] While these men may have been more hostile than Gregg to the Institute, the latter nevertheless recorded that "the lack of the service of a first-rate physiologist with the equipment of a physiological lab" constituted a "defect in realizing the present program of the Institute and its investigations of psychosomatic medicine".[82] Pressman's statement (see page 50 above) regarding the rationale for Gregg's funding of the Chicago Institute can now be seen as misleading, obscuring as it does Gregg's constant and increasing uncertainty as to the merits of the institution.

Gregg's psychiatry programme had to be seen to address satisfactorily worries over any projects whose scientific status was questionable. The Chicago Institute was the main project risking criticism on this front, and it was not entirely successful.[83] In Gregg's career – which saw a move from a straightforward enthusiasm for psychoanalysis to an endorsement of the merits of a scientific approach – his position at the Rockefeller involved a concrete attempt to define the boundaries of psychiatry; that is, to answer a pressing philosophical question about the nature of the scientific study of the mind. The success – in his view and the Rockefeller's – of the decisions he would take over whom to fund would no doubt have represented to Gregg the extent of the judiciousness of his answer to this question, and that of his own professional and personal choices.

Gregg was not, then, a lone pioneer seeking to convince sceptics; he was sympathetic to psychoanalysis and psychosomatic medicine, but he favoured an interdisciplinary matrix dominated by experimentally grounded sciences. Gregg was operating within a hugely powerful institution with a robust ideology about its role within the development of science and about the methods of science. It was trying to work out just how psychiatry fitted into this scheme. As psychiatry grew into a medical specialty it would have to commit to certain criteria of medical science, such as the importance of controlled experiments, rather than the judgement of individual clinicians. While the Rockefeller helped to establish a field where clinical and research opportunities were significantly widened and the boundaries between self and society were increasingly dissolved, medicalising psychiatry presented difficult challenges. Pressman, writing about the pressures that emerged once this movement was well under way and achieving some success, notes that in order for a unified professional and disciplinary identity to be forged, notions of what constituted valid scientific and medical knowledge had

---

[80] Lambert to O'Brien, 22 August 1939, RG 1.1, series 216 A, folder 37, box 3, RFA, RAC.

[81] O'Brien to Lambert, 30 August 1939, RG 1.1, series 216 A, folder 37, box 3, RFA, RAC.

[82] Alan Gregg officer's diary, 18 September 1939, RG 12.1, RFA, RAC.

[83] Gregg was involved in other, more rigorous and fruitful, experimental work being conducted on psychosomatic interactions by Stanley Cobb's department at Massachusetts General and by Harold Wolff at Cornell Medical Center. In 1938 Gregg launched a new, and ultimately more successful, project at Washington University in St Louis, with the aim of bringing together neurological, psychiatric and psychoanalytic elements. By this time psychoanalysis was slowly gaining an increasing presence in university psychiatric departments, and the enterprise may not have been so much of a risk, partly due to the nature of this later work and also to the length of time the psychiatry programme had been running.

to be large enough to allow diverse groups to work together under the same banner, and that this created anxiety amongst established scientists by potentially enabling non-medically trained professionals to encroach on the field and dilute the scientific credentials of a hard-won respectability.[84] But he omits the significance of this anxiety about the boundaries of psychiatry at the outset of the field's consolidation[85] – an anxiety that was clearly besetting both the Rockefeller as a whole and Gregg in particular, shaping the lens through which they perceived institutions and projects and thus their choices of which to fund and develop.

The Rockefeller and Aubrey Lewis

The Rockefeller was initially hesitant when approached by Mapother for funding of the Maudsley; its concerns were not so much with any particular activity of the hospital, but rather with the general backwardness of (scientific) psychiatry in England.[86] Lambert commented, "there are not enough scientific papers being turned out in England to fill one small journal whereas lesser countries like Belgium and Italy support several such journals of comparable quality.... Outside London there is hardly a place where any research in psychiatry is being done.... I feel a little disappointed myself at the Maudsley show. The laboratory facilities are limited, and there is hardly any provision for animal experimentation".[87]

These concerns may go some way towards explaining the Foundation's caution regarding the Maudsley, although the reason given for holding back was the economic crisis facing the US.[88] Its initial decision to fund training fellowships would support this, especially as the influx of German émigrés after 1933 provided an opportunity, as Mapother himself phrased it, "of securing a bargain group of first-rate men".[89] The presence of German scientists was felt to have injected valuable scientific work and methods to the hospital, encouraging the Rockefeller Foundation to consider more substantial funding.[90] More funding from the Rockefeller Foundation would depend

[84] Pressman, op. cit., note 32 above, pp. 41–6.

[85] Although Brown gives a detailed account of the increasing scepticism Gregg experienced with respect to the Chicago Institute, he too somewhat obscures both Gregg's worries at the inception of the psychiatry programme and in the early stages of the Chicago project. (Brown op. cit., note 32 above, pp. 167–82, and *idem*, op. cit., note 52 above.)

[86] "Eventually, even if successful, the program will not involve anything like half of what Mapother is now visualising", from Staff Conference, 16 March 1931, RG 1.1, series 401A, folder 247, box 18, RFA, RAC.

[87] R A Lambert officer's diary, 5 December 1933, RG 1.1, series 401A, folder 248, box 18, RFA, RAC. It is interesting that in the report Lewis notes (p. 99) that although there is a proliferation of Italian research literature in journals, the standard is quite low.

[88] Gregg to Mapother, 11 December 1931, series 401A, folder 247, box 18, RFA, RAC. Also Gregg to Mapother, 31 May 1932, RG 1.1, series 401A, folder 248, box 18.

[89] R A Lambert officer's diary, 5 December 1933, RG 1.1, series 401A, folder 248, box 18, RFA, RAC.

[90] Gregg to Mapother, 21 December 1933, RG 1.1, series 401A, folder 248, box 18, RFA, RAC. O'Brien writes that the "scheme for aid at the Maudsley is to benefit by the presence of the deposed Germans there". O'Brien to Gregg, 5 November 1934, RG 1.1, series 401A, box 19, folder 250, RFA, RAC. In Lambert's view "[it] is clear that psychiatry in England needs a real center of research, and that an opportunity for setting up such a center presents itself at the Maudsley through the fortuitous presence of an exceptionally able group of German workers.... It might be hoped that in a year or two a supply of British [*sic*] might be coming on to take the places of foreigners who drop out for one reason or another. The reason for using foreigners now is simply that there are practically no natives of equal calibre to be had." Lambert to O'Brien, 8 January 1935, RG 1.1, series 401A, folder 251, box 19, RFA, RAC.

on its perceiving the Maudsley as pursuing a scientific orientation, and having the resources and personnel to do this. The Maudsley's long-term status would be best fostered by British workers themselves steeped in expertise of the kind the German émigrés had brought; and thus Lewis's trip can be seen as a step towards this end.

The report, however, can also be seen as one element in a wider dialogue during the 1930s concerning the definition of psychiatry and as part of the dynamics between philanthropic foundation and possible beneficiary. One of the report's most interesting features is the extent to which it is shaped by the Rockefeller and mirrors its concerns and attitudes. Lewis met and exchanged letters with Daniel O'Brien, Alan Gregg's deputy, who sent him a list of key people to meet – which Lewis pretty much adhered to – as well as letters of introduction. O'Brien's list favoured highly experimental, physiological and laboratory-based workers and institutes; writing about Vienna he noted – briefly and possibly dismissively – the "Freudian group (Herr Geheimrat and daughter Anna)", who "hardly need be mentioned", as well as the Bühlers, but emphasised physiological and scientific figures.[91] In his introduction, Lewis describes psychiatry as an enormous field straddling innumerable disciplines and activities and urges collaboration amongst these;[92] in his concluding comments he notes that "almost everywhere I found a greater interest and activity on the physical than on the psychological or sociological side of psychiatric inquiry" and that psychological investigations tended to "follow safe rather than speculative lines",[93] suggesting that the dominance of "physical" psychiatry represented in his report is to some extent just a feature of the field. His attitude, however, echoes O'Brien's; he is sceptical of individuals with psychoanalytic backgrounds and interests, being pleasantly surprised when they reveal scientific knowledge and common sense;[94] he gives the Freudians short shrift while in Vienna; and consistently displays irritation with "speculative" developments and a preference for elements representative of a scientific and medical psychiatry. What is evident throughout the report is his concern with clarifying the boundaries of psychiatry;[95] with the dispassionate study of psychotherapy's merits;[96] and with the pruning of extravagances which "delay the development of the social and psychological side of psychiatry".[97]

Both Mapother and Lewis considered scrupulous fact-gathering and rigorous quantitative evaluation methods crucial to grounding psychiatry as a reputable branch of medicine. Mapother favoured neurology as psychiatry's ideal partner and both urged experiment as the means to determine therapeutic efficacy. The individual may be a psychobiological entity to be approached with a range of methods, but the scientific nature of these methods would determine the discipline's legitimacy. Both Lewis and Mapother would have keenly felt the need to continue courting the Rockefeller Foundation in order to prolong and enlarge its funding of the Maudsley, and the funding

---

[91] Letter from D P O'Brien to Aubrey Lewis, 23 February 1937, p. 6; held by the Lewis family.
[92] Introduction to the Report, pp. 57–9.
[93] Report, p. 146.
[94] For example: "Lagache is a Freudian, but fairly well equipped also on the somatic side", Report, p. 81.
[95] For example, Introduction to the Report, p. 59.
[96] Introduction to the Report, p. 60.
[97] Introduction to the Report, p. 60.

question was inextricably linked to the question of the nature and status of psychiatry. What Lewis's report very neatly reflects is a discipline in flux, whose membership was being worked out, both by psychiatrists and by the Foundation, in a way that would shape the field's development. It was lucky that Lewis, a notoriously frank man (who indeed risked coming across as arrogant and dismissive in his criticisms of continental psychiatry) shared the Foundation's fundamental orientation and scepticism over certain branches of the field. His report, which endorses an ideal held by the Rockefeller and Alan Gregg in particular – the ideal of science as a criterion to weed out speculative and descriptive elements – was one factor in a protracted negotiation between benefactor and beneficiary that could ultimately only bear fruit given a shared vision of psychiatry. The Maudsley-Rockefeller marriage was a relatively happy one, with both parties longing to delineate – as Mapother put it – "the objective facts of psychiatry omitting the spookery".[98]

---

[98] Mapother to Gregg, 12 December 1936, RG 1.1, folder 253, box 19, series 401 A, RFA, RAC.

Aubrey Lewis's Introduction to his Report

At the suggestion and with the support of the Rockefeller Foundation I visited in 1937 all the European countries except the Balkans, Spain and Portugal, and Germany. As I had already seen something of the psychiatric work in Spain before the Civil War, and had studied in Germany some years ago, when the level of medical work there was higher than it is at present, these omissions did not appreciably affect the purpose of my journey, which was to learn what is being done in neuropsychiatry and related fields. The net was cast fairly wide, in that I was provided by the foundation with letters of introduction not only to those active in teaching and research in neurology or psychiatry, but also to the physiologists, psychologists, geneticists, and others who were pursuing in these fundamental sciences studies which would throw light on our clinical problems and methods of investigation; I was also able to see administrators who controlled organization and development.

Such a round of visits (formidable in many respects, and quite impracticable if one had not already from the literature and from personal contacts some knowledge of the work being done) was a reminder of the enormous field psychiatry now straddles over or touches; from social legislation, psychotherapy, or statistics, to neurology, internal medicine, and the minutiae of laboratory research.

I have put down in order the men and places I visited, and stated at the beginning some general impressions. It would be possible to avoid so bald a catalogue of an immensely informative and stimulating journey by giving a much more detailed account, which would be to a large extent technical, and by expressing freely the opinions I formed about what I saw in each place, but these, in the circumstances, might sound patronising when appreciative, and hasty or ill-mannered when critical. Moreover, it was impossible not to see the close influence which the political and social situation in each country had upon psychiatry, whether as a branch of public health, medical practice, or research (this, however, goes rather beyond what were my immediate "terms of reference"). It was evident – perhaps as a by-product of this state of affairs – that in many places where Germany had long been regarded as the European seat of authority and progress in medical, and especially psychiatric, matters, its place was being taken by England and USA. Many people, I found, were eager to turn to our journals and to get into contact with the men in our centres of activity. Their familiarity with the teaching and research institutions here was far greater than used to be the case. The National Hospital at Queen Square has, of course, long been famous, but I found that the Maudsley Hospital, too, was known in a way that seemed, in view of the recency of its foundation, remarkable.

So comprehensive a round of visits naturally yielded much that is difficult to summarize; its fruits were mainly of two kinds – those more immediately applicable to one's work, e.g. fresh knowledge and ideas for treatment, research, etc.; and less precise general impressions, chiefly about trends and methods which might be compared with those at home.

It was everywhere being recognised that psychiatry was a far more important branch of medicine than had generally been realised and that its two great needs were research and better organisation (the latter in the largest sense). In all the places I visited, the main or only centre for research and teaching was the university clinic, but at Dikemark and some other mental hospitals important research or treatment was being done independently; nearly always this was due either to one enterprising and able doctor who had sufficient control of the administration of a hospital to carry through his plans, or to the influence of someone at the university. The problems of the mental hospitals were necessarily of a different order from those of the university clinics; in many places where they were represented as largely economic it seemed that, even if this were true, better training of nurses and use of occupational measures might have disposed of some of the difficulties in the proper care and treatment of the patients. In some countries the institutional and extra-mural treatment of the insane was on an admirably high a level, so far as I could observe or learn of it. The standards of selection, recruitment, and training of nurses varied widely, and, like those of medical and social worker personnel, of course depended to a considerable extent on the general economic and cultural conditions of the country, but to this there were some striking exceptions.

In the university clinics neurology and psychiatry were, as a rule, a combined discipline under the one professor. Sometimes this had tended to disproportionate emphasis being laid on one or the other, according to the professor's special interests. Even those who, on account of this, advocated separate departments conceded, however, that a purely psychiatric or purely neurological clinic led to an artificial, regrettable limitation of interest and outlook.

The concentration of research and teaching in the university clinics – to which it is true, there is an occasional outstanding exception, as at Dikemark – is so much the rule abroad that the professor in charge usually has his hands full of this work, and consequently exercises a general rather than a detailed supervision over administrative routine, much as in American clinics. In principle he is in charge of all such matters, though the extent to which he has actually the final say within the clinic sometimes depends on whether immediate political influence is brought to bear on the internal work of the clinic, as was evident in Russia, for instance, and Austria. One cannot generalise about it. Usually, however, the day-to-day administration is delegated to the Oberarzt, Chef de Clinic, or similarly named position, by the professor, so that he can himself devote his time to teaching and research. Economic necessity, moreover, may lead to encroachments on his time in the form of private practice. Conditions cannot very well be compared with those prevailing in England, since in nearly all these countries no one who is unconnected with the university clinic is likely to have much standing as a consultant in private practice, and on the other hand the clinic cannot pay an appropriate living wage to its doctors. Consequently the senior staff of the university clinics is mostly on a part-time basis and is made up of the active leaders of the speciality. Moreover, the prestige attaching to a position in the clinic is

Introduction to Report

so advantageous in private practice that there is great inducement for people to work in the out-patient departments and elsewhere for a small salary. Entirely honorary work is, however, rare because of the exigencies of earning a living. In all these respects psychiatry is organised in the university clinics on the same lines as are followed in other departments of medicine. The effort is everywhere to make these clinics a part of the single university hospital, (the mental hospitals being seen as the future field of work for those trainees of the university clinics who do not propose to go into private practice). Thus, in Denmark all appointments to a mental hospital superintendency go to the staff of the university clinic: this has the apparent disadvantage that the Professor is almost the only permanent member of the senior staff there, and the continuity of research is in danger. The links between the other medical clinics and the psychiatric one are strengthened by the growing practice of seconding men from the latter to work for a year in laboratories of physiology or internal medicine, and, on the other hand, as in Amsterdam, putting men trained in internal medicine into the psychiatric hospitals, not so much to learn psychiatry as to deal expertly with the physical problems, and promote research and treatment along these lines.

A great deal of the most promising research that was being done consisted in the application to clinical psychiatry of methods that had been worked out in other fields, for example, sociology, biochemistry, internal medicine, physiology, genetics. It followed that the best research of this kind was done by collaboration rather than by psychiatrists alone attempting to employ the methods and ideas with which they had become acquainted only by reading, instead of by training. Occasionally, of course, brilliant work was being done by men who had set themselves to acquire an adequate training in both psychiatry and the relevant science. On the whole, it was in places where collaboration between the various departments of the university and the psychiatrists was best developed that the most valuable psychiatric research was being done. The more isolated the psychiatrists, the more likely was their research to be humdrum or unreliable. On the other hand, in a few places research and psychiatry was being done, mainly on laboratory lines, by men who had not any thorough acquaintance with clinical psychiatry; in such cases their research seemed often to be departing from rather than approaching problems of psychiatry, sometimes confusing issues or leading them in deeper shadow through ignorance of the many sided phenomena of mental disorder and the fallacies and real questions they may give rise to. Where research was being directed by a half-time psychiatrist who was engaged in private practice it tended to be hand to mouth, uncritical, or unduly influenced by fashions of the moment and practical exigencies; in short, bulky rather than valuable.

The need for specialization within the psychiatric field is well recognised. Where it can be afforded, there are men separately concerned with the psychological, social, physiological, biochemical, psychotherapeutic, and other divisions of the work. The Professor and some other senior men serve to co-ordinate all this, whether in treatment, research, or teaching. In different countries or different centres the emphasis falls on this or that department, naturally, according to prevailing interests. It was noteworthy that hardly anywhere had psychoanalysis established itself as an acceptable theory or practice, incorporated in the general body of psychiatry. Its influence in stimulating the development of psychological treatment and dynamic psychological modes of approach had obviously been great, but general acceptance of the fundamentals of psychoanalytic doctrine seemed now to be less likely than it was, perhaps, some years ago, and its use as a mode of treatment seemed very restricted.

In nearly all countries the financial deterrents to entering on a career of research seemed to be a hindrance in the development of psychiatry. Those who go into private practice, as the majority must, are forced in the richer countries to direct their interests largely into psychotherapy, without being able to study its problems dispassionately, and in the poorer ones to aim at some prestige-giving academic status which may be less of a by-product of ability and enthusiasm than a means towards earning a living. Nevertheless, academic status (e.g. having spent some years in a university clinic, teaching) and a record of having done conscientious research have so much more to do with any advancement in a psychiatric or other medical a career abroad than they have in England that the general level of training and experience in what may recall the hack-work of research – making a prescribed investigation painstakingly or at any rate industriously, working through the literature of a problem and summarising it with discrimination, using advice and criticism and learning one's limitations – was higher among the general run of psychiatric aspirants than it is with us. Particularly in Scandinavian countries the rigorous demands of the MD qualification raised the standard of work in the university clinics and institutes, and indirectly throughout the country. I find it difficult to generalise, however, because of the enormous differences between countries, e.g. between Hungary and Holland; Sweden and Czechoslovakia; or even adjacent ones like Russia, Poland, and Finland. Political factors and jobbery were, however, rapidly altering the state of affairs in the dictator or semi-dictator ruled countries: clearly the future professors and hospital directors were going to "get by" with less to their scientific credit than their predecessors had to show.

In some countries there was a contrast between their impressive buildings and laboratory equipment on the one hand, and, on the other, the low standard of hospital care and of social concern or provision for the patients who were outside an institution. In short, all that in England or the United States is linked up with the psychiatric nurse and the social worker seemed to call for much improvement in some of the countries I visited. In some places the predominance of neurology and the extravagances of some psychotherapists seem to have had almost an equal share in delaying the development of the social and psychological side of psychiatry. There were, in addition, political and economic factors to which I have already referred. There was, in part, the tendency in totalitarian countries to reward spectacular work, whether sound and not, also to promote party men, to damp down scientific criticism, and to hamper or exclude some able people who should have had influential positions and good opportunities to work; even, sometimes, to modify a theory for irrelevant reasons (e.g. in genetics of insanity and defect, value of psychological measurements, aetiology of neuroses). An indirect and less obvious effect, though a real one, was the personal distress and unhappiness, apart from any material difficulties of their own, that some of the best productive workers feel while living under tyranny or a threat, so that they cannot pursue their work with a free and single mind. In all countries individual economic problems, of course, troubled research workers and practitioners.

Introduction to Report

One of the commonest developments in psychiatry in the various countries was the establishment of clinics for children. In the less advanced places there were the very simple beginnings of a special out-patient department at which abnormalities of behaviour in children could be hastily investigated and treated: in a few places, it is true, they went no further than still unrealised plans, but hardly any university clinic had failed to recognise the necessity for having such a department. In the most advanced centres there was a thoroughly organised, well staffed out-patient department, run on much the same lines as those established in Great Britain and the United States; moreover, in some instances, a separate residential block had been provided for the observation and treatment of a small number of children for a limited period. These residential blocks were almost exclusively to be found in Switzerland, where in spite of such disadvantages as, in some cases, that of being situated in the grounds of the mental hospital, their value was recognised not only by the psychiatrists but by the administrators and the public of the canton. The importance of research, as apart from treatment, in the social, psychological, and somatic aspects of children's behaviour and maladaptations was everywhere strongly felt, but the investigators were also well aware of the limits set to their work by the necessarily unsatisfactory and incomplete opportunities that purely out-patient work can offer. Even in the few places where this deficiency was being supplied by an in-patient block the arrangements and the work done were so influenced by immediate practical needs (e.g. for the supervision of delinquent children) that the full possibilities and requirements for sound continuous work were scarcely anywhere being met. Certainly there was nothing being done for children that compared with what is available for adults whose behaviour is abnormal.

The work with children had partly arisen out of social needs: juvenile courts, for example, wanted the psychiatrist's advice. In some countries the more extensive social side of psychiatry, with adults as well as children, had received much attention. Thus, in Belgium the Law of Social Defence has stimulated, or perhaps one should say is evidence of, the great concern in that country with social problems where they touch on medicine, and particularly on psychiatry: the control of delinquency, alcoholism, etc., is recognised to be a field in which psychiatry has much to say. In Switzerland much of the social psychiatric work that would be done only sporadically in England is in some cantons regularly referred to the psychiatrist: in Zürich, for example, he writes regular reports on all women whom the gynaecologists at the general hospital are considering for abortion or sterilisation. In Scandinavian countries, France, Russia, and elsewhere, the social side of psychiatry is being increasingly organised, though there is obviously still much to be done. There was also a good deal of anxiety, I found, lest over-enthusiastic or half-baked work in this field should prejudice sound development. Consequently, independent efforts at dealing with the psychiatric side of delinquency, feeble-mindedness, prostitution, incapacity for employment, etc., were thought far less satisfactory than the referral of such matters to the psychiatric clinic or to reliable and well-trained psychiatrists who had been on the staff of the clinic. In Sweden Prof Kinberg had his own department for examining criminals, working directly under the Ministry of Justice: Dr Schiff similarly in Paris, and Prof Vervaeck in Brussels.

In several places there was a growing tendency towards making the expert facilities and knowledge of the university clinic available to the less indigent members of the community. This was partly due to obvious pressure, based on economic and social grounds, from the side of the public, who were contributing to the maintenance of these centres, and could not see why their enjoyment of the advantages so provided should be in inverse proportion to the amount they contributed towards their upkeep. In Scandinavian countries, in particular, this line of development has gone far, and I was able, as a patient myself in the private medical wards of the great Rigshospital in Copenhagen,[1] to see how much the patient gains by being treated in a public hospital fully-equipped for teaching and research. I was told however, by responsible administrators in the Government ministries, as well as in the psychiatric hospitals, that for the hospitals themselves the economic side of the matter is far from negligible since the fees received from private patients (though the charges are remarkably low in Scandinavia) are an important item in the budget. This matter was particularly stressed, from a different angle, at the neuro-surgical unit in Warsaw. Since the only fully-trained brain surgeon in Poland works there on a full-time basis, all, whether rich or poor, must become patients there if they want the best attention available in their country: but it is a public hospital which has a low fixed upper level of fees and will not charge well-to-do people in proportion to their income. The available money for the upkeep of the unit is very little, and the surgeon in question has to do as best he can with quite inadequate medical and nursing help. He deplores this, and, since he cannot get from the public authorities more money for staffing the unit on modern lines, he considers that it would be better to have a private department with corresponding fees, or else to allow him private practice, so that the money he thus earned from wealthy patients might be diverted to the staffing, etc., of the public unit, and to the financing of his research, which is at present hampered by lack of funds. In other places I was told that a private block in the public psychiatric clinic or hospital had had the advantage that the nurses and doctors, working, as they do, sometimes there and sometimes in the rest of the hospital, were found to be still more likely than ordinarily to have a friendly and individual attitude towards the needs of their patients, avoiding the impersonal or custodial attitude. I had no chance to judge what evidence there was for this belief. It certainly seemed to me that the situation of a psychiatric clinic as one of the separate departments in a complex of hospital buildings (with public and private wards), which made up the whole university teaching centre in medicine, was admirable for the training of nurses: Amsterdam and Copenhagen were conspicuous examples of this. Independent neuropsychiatric clinics seemed also in certain centres to provide equally good training, e.g. in Belgium. But the training of nurses depends so much on local conditions but it would seem idle to make too much of hospital layout and type of patient in this regard.

The level of psychiatric work in many of the places I visited could almost have been measured by the way they were pursuing and assessing the newer treatments, i.e. insulin and cardiazol for schizophrenia. In some, work was being well done, and its range extended on sound lines, but in many, little clinical acumen or ability in

---

[1] While in Uppsala in September 1937, Lewis fractured his radius and also contracted pleurisy. As a consequence, he stayed in hospital for two and a half months before returning to England in December.

Introduction to Report

planning and evaluating such a therapeutic experiment was being displayed, and the research possibilities were being neglected.

There is no single line of research in psychiatry which at the time of my visit appeared to be leading to a dramatic advance in the subject; there was an attack along a wide front, as the details of my various visits will have shown. The most impressive advance, taking the various European countries as a whole, seemed to be in the effort to improve institutional care, along the lines that are the recognised in England and other countries with a similarly highly developed social and medical system, as well as to provide adequate treatment and supervision for those whose mental disorder is not such as to demand in-patient care. So various, however, were the conditions and methods I observed that any general statement is in danger of giving a false impression.

Aubrey Lewis's Report on his Visits to Psychiatric Centres in Europe in 1937

HOLLAND[1]

Amsterdam

I visited Van der Horst's clinic. He struck me as much more alert than Bouman, and is, I gather, more popular with the students. The researches of which he told me were concerned with electrical reactions in cats that were being treated with insulin, and the neurological findings in their hypothalamus; also the effect on neurotics of air of different ionic concentration, humidity etc. I gathered that in both of these researches the work had not yet really begun. I think he is also proposing to observe the electroencephalogram in monkeys poisoned with mescaline. I got the impression in many places that a great deal of research is arrived at by the process of saying to oneself, "A investigates B or uses method B; X investigates Y or uses method Y: I will investigate B and Y together or use B and Y."

His chief psychologist, Van Essen, who succeeded Grunbaum, is an enthusiastic young man, whose training had been at first in comparative psychology under Van Boutdendyck [sic] and thereafter in Vienna under Karl Bühler for 3 years, where he wrote his thesis on "The psychology of decerebrate birds." He seems to have a free hand in his psychological researches on time relations of motor performance, and is to assist Van der Horst in proposed investigations of the Berger Rhythm[2] and in other electro-physiological work, though he seemed to me to have little intimate knowledge of the technique and principles.

Van Essen though without medical training also runs a pedagogic child guidance practice, to which children are referred by doctors. He is also working on reaction time in three tempos, following on some of Van der Horst's earlier studies on cyclothymia and schizophrenia and American tapping tests. He and Van Hasselt in the histological department are, as far as I could gather, the only two assistants who have remained

---

[1] Psychiatry in Holland experienced the reforms occurring in other countries over the course of the nineteenth century somewhat later. In the second half of that century, there were fewer asylums in Holland than elsewhere, and rather than constructing new buildings, older urban buildings were renovated. Administrative bodies held much more power over asylums than doctors, and there were limited reforms in treatment and management. In 1884 a law restricted the maximum number of patients within each institution, leading to the construction of new buildings. Throughout the nineteenth century and into the first half of the twentieth, there was a strong religious component to the social efforts to improve care of the mentally ill.

[2] Hans Berger (1873–1941) was a German psychiatrist who made original observations on the changes in electrical potential which could be recorded through the intact skull and which led to the development of electroencephalography (EEG), which records the electrical activity of the brain.

working in the clinic for years; the others have gone off into private practice. Similarly psychologists give up their work in order to go in for school teaching which is rather better paid. The rest of the laboratory staff at the clinic are relatively inexpert I should think, though Feitscher has had adequate training in psychometrics in Vienna. Feitscher discussed with me the psychological testing of children, which he does using Charlotte Bühler's methods. His original training was as a philologist; he is still interested in speech disorder in organic brain disease, though as far as I could gather he had not done much about it as yet; he was poorly informed about foreign literature on the subject.

Van der Horst told me he spent 4 to 5 hours a week in routine teaching, apart from his ward rounds. He has 150 beds, with five assistants on the clinical side and five in the laboratory.

I was told that the "Free" university is relatively poor in numbers and financially in danger of losing its privileges, unless certain requirements can be met. Of course, the Chair of Psychiatry and Directorship of the Clinic were not held by the same man until recently. I got the impression, not limited to this clinic nor indeed to Holland, that more research would be done if almost the whole staff were not engaged also in private practice, and so much time were not taken up in conducting university examinations. It seemed to be even truer of Bouman's Clinic in which the Professor spends relatively little of his time because of journeys abroad etc. Van der Horst's assistant, Wientjes, an alert fellow, interested in the somatic aspects, took me round the wards of the clinic. There is a fairly active child OP [out-patient] department, and as at Bouman's Clinic they take children into the wards. They have not time to do psychotherapy any more than at Bouman's Clinic.

At the Wilhemina[3] Clinic I saw first Bouman's chief assistant, Van der Waals, who runs the psychological laboratory. He has also psychoanalytical interests, chiefly in his private practice. In the psychological laboratory he is able to get most of his apparatus constructed by an excellent mechanic-carpenter he has, and apparently he can also get adequate funds for instruments, for example, a Michotte tachistoscope.[4] He is working on the apparent movement of successively exposed objects and does it well, I think, though without applying any strict mathematical way of determining the relationship between the period of each exposure and the intervals between them, or as to the rate of movement and effect on the apparent duration of the experience. His research would lend itself very well to an enquiry on time appreciation, from the point of view of external factors which influence it.

Van der Waals also has some interesting work in optokinetic nystagmus, especially its influence on after-images. There seems to be a complete gap between his psychological researches, which are of the academic sort, and his clinical work with patients; though he spoke rather vaguely about some perceptual studies on cerebral lesions. I had an impression that it was only to organic cerebral disease that he thought experimental psychological study applicable; probably he is influenced by Bouman's point of view. Van der Waals's psychoanalytical views seemed moderate.

---

[3] The Wilhemina Gasthuis in Amsterdam was built in 1929; with its modern laboratories and a neurosurgery section, it was a milestone for Dutch neurology.

[4] Albert Michotte (1881–1965) of Louvain University devised, in the late 1940s, an elaborate mechanical apparatus that allowed him to manipulate the animation of two objects on a projection screen, thus enabling experiments on the attribution of causality.

Bouman professes to be well-disposed towards psychoanalysis and told me that most of his staff had been analysed. I had the impression, however, that this had had very little effect on the general conduct of the clinic's work, and that psychotherapy of any sort in the OPD [out-patient department] is hardly practicable because the doctors cannot give the time to it. The same is true of the Valeriusklinick. Professor Bouman struck me as more interested in the cells of the cortex than in anything else, apart from travelling. He seemed convinced, in accordance with his earlier work, that cerebral cell changes in schizophrenia were constant and important. He has a dilettante interest in comparative anthropology, working in loose association with Kappers.

As in the other Dutch and the Belgian clinics, the buildings, equipment, space, libraries and so forth seemed excellent. Bouman's clinic is particularly well arranged in the provision for excited women, who are kept in large rooms, ingeniously arranged so as to appear open and very light. His continuous baths, however, have, like nearly all the European ones, either boards or canvas covers (with a hole for the patient's neck), which are really a form of constraint.

The provision for excited men was not so good. The cases Bouman showed me as interesting ones were nearly all of organic cerebral disease, and he told me he was working on the histopathology of Pick's[5] and Alzheimer's[6] diseases. He struck me as pleasant, and clinically very experienced, but old-fashioned and not stimulating.

The clinic which functions as a reception unit for the city is so arranged in the general hospital system that cases of cerebral concussion are all sent to him; his assistant Katt wrote a fairly comprehensive thesis about it last year. Evidently the compulsory writing of theses for a doctorate has this advantage, that it brings a fair number of people around the Professor, who do work which he suggests to them, or which he himself would like to do but has not the time for. Later these people drift away from the clinic, but at least it results in there being an interest in research and some activity.

The way in which cases are admitted to the various hospitals is part of an admirable system of health administration in Amsterdam. I heard about it from several sources but mainly from Arie Querido who is in charge of the psychiatric section. The arrangements are unified, covering at any rate 98% of the people of Amsterdam. The city is independent, and owns the Wilhemina Gasthuis and University, and employs under its

---

[5] Arnold Pick (1851–1924) described pre-senile dementia with focal cerebral atrophy in 1892. An assistant to Theodor Meynert and also to Karl Westphal, Pick later worked at the Wehnen County Asylum, and then became doctor at the Prague County Asylum in 1877. In 1878 he was made lecturer in psychiatry and neurology at Prague University. In 1886 he was professor of psychiatry and head of the psychiatric clinic at the German University in Prague. His work on the cortical localisation of speech disturbances won him international acclaim.

[6] Alois Alzheimer (1864–1915) worked at Frankfurt's asylum, collaborating closely with Franz Nissl, on the pathology of the nervous system. Alzheimer became director of the asylum in 1895, and from there conducted the research forming the basis of his description of pre-senile dementia now bearing his name, first describing in 1906 his observations on an unusual disease of the cerebral cortex. Emil Kraepelin suggested that the condition be named after him. In 1902 he went to Heidelberg, and then Munich where in 1908 he was a professor at the Psychiatric Institute and director of the clinic's anatomical laboratory. In 1912 he went to the Psychiatric and Neurological Institute in Breslau. Between 1906 and 1918 he edited, with Franz Nissl, *Histologische und histopathologische Arbeiten über die Grosshirnrinde*, 7 vols, Jena, G Fischer, 1904–1921.

Report

Chief Medical Officer a large staff of doctors, nurse-social workers and secretaries who supervise the distribution and aftercare or out-patient care of all illness. The system arose out of the situation that hospital beds were getting choked up with chronic or unsuitable material. So now, whenever anyone is sick the panel doctors calls in the city doctor (the system also covers schools, defectives etc.) who goes and sees the patient and decides whether he needs hospital treatment, and if so, to which hospital and which department he ought to go. Consequently a man like Snapper can get all the bone diseases, for instance, that he wants for research or teaching – he can get indeed all that there are in Amsterdam; in fact any recognised teacher or investigator has only to say the word and his material is obtained for him. On the psychiatric side the public health doctors decide what patients shall go to what psychiatric departments, if at all, and can keep in touch with them in the mental hospitals (which are, however, not under the city's control, though the city pays 300 guilders a year for each patient and can get the patients discharged from hospital much sooner than was formerly the case because it undertakes to supervise them).

The way in which the psychiatric section keeps some control over the movement of the mental hospital population is by its power of deciding which patients it will send to any particular mental hospital. If the superintendent is active and cooperates with the public health psychiatrists then more cases are sent to him. If not, he is embarrassed by not having many patients and therefore not receiving the sustentation pay for each, which would help the finances of the hospital.

The social workers visit the patients and interview them in their own homes after discharge from hospital, as they recognise it is useless to wait until the patients come to them. It is very much more efficiently done than in the corresponding arrangements in Moscow and Leningrad. Querido has, as his social workers, experienced nurses, (it would probably be an advantage for them to have more specialised training on the psychiatric side, but they do their work very well as it is). I was told that they get a good type of nurse in the mental hospitals because there is much unemployment among teachers and the pay is good. I was able to go out with Querido and his nurse and social worker to a particular call that came in when I was there, and to see how smoothly the system worked. This public health and aftercare service is excellently organised not only on the administrative side, but also as regards records, though they do not seem yet to have availed themselves of all the statistical opportunities which they system provides.

The legislative and administrative details are complicated, though it is clear that the system has saved the city much expense and has facilitated the early discharge of schizophrenics, for example. The city organisation, as a whole, almost seems to have been worked into the scheme and influenced by it, e.g. policemen report to Querido's department any instance of a man behaving oddly; sometimes he has even to check over-enthusiasm, as when a policeman would be inclined to take into custody some person who is behaving oddly, whereas the patient in question is a harmless paranoid or defective who is being quite adequately cared for extramurally. Querido's background is in physiology (which he did with Cannon in 1924 on a Rockefeller fellowship) and then public health work and moderate psychoanalytical interests. He is justly proud of his department, and enthusiastic. Some effort has been made to bring the child guidance movement in Amsterdam into the ambit of this public health activity, but there are difficulties in the way.

The psychoanalysts are less strict in their orthodoxy than the London ones, and seem still to be outside the official circles; thus, for panel purposes one cannot get recognised as a specialist in neuro-psychiatry unless one has done three years in a psychiatric clinic, and few of the analysts have done this. As elsewhere, it was clear that conditions of private practice and work were one of the chief factors in determining the direction of people's interests towards analysis. The more they are dependent on private practice and work is one of the chief factors in determining the direction of people's interests towards analysis. The more they are dependent on private practice for their clinical material or their research material, the more are they inclined towards analytical inquiry and treatment.

Carp in Leiden struck me as a good instance of this. He has latterly had to give up 10 of his 20 beds to a neurologist and has no control over the nature of the cases admitted to his beds, consequently he has to use the out-patients of his private practice for his clinical material, and so his likings and interests have turned from organic diseases of the brain, which occupied him formerly, towards psychopathology and more or less analytical enquiries only.

Child guidance seems to have got further from psychiatry in Amsterdam rather than closer to it. Dr Tiebout seemed to be torn between the desire to be more analytical in her approach to the children, and the manifest economic obstacles to that. The clinic anyhow seemed to be limited by its small income. I gathered however that the analytical trend had led to the raising of the question whether the training of social workers should take the form of personal analysis in Vienna instead of a regular Psychiatric Social Worker's Training course, as at the London School of Economics, but this proposal had not got any further than getting ventilated.

Mrs Querido, who is also a doctor, works in the child guidance clinic, so that there is a loose connection of a personal kind between it and the public health organisation of the city; possibly the connection will become closer.

At Revesz's psychological laboratory I found there was also considerable interest in children. A woman who is his chief assistant has been working on problems of co-operation, i.e. seeing how much better a child performs a task if another child is set on to it with him: they have examined children over the age of seven. It seemed a well-controlled experimental approach to the question. Revesz himself seemed very stimulating and eager, especially about his research on haptic perception; his work covers a wide field and is applicable, I should think, to some problems of organic brain disease. Like so many other people working in fields that have not so far in their experience touched closely on psychiatry, he expressed a keen desire to get on to psychiatric material. I should think he would certainly, given the free run of a psychiatric clinic, attach some of the questions in a fresh and productive way. He said half-jokingly that he would jump at the chance to spend 6 months in a clinic like the Maudsley. I suspect though that he may be a difficult man to work with, because of his variable temperament and impulsive frankness.

Similarly when I saw Snapper and discussed with him the work he was doing, he agreed with me when I remarked on how relevant some of his investigations were to psychiatric problems, and he told me that although he himself had not the time nor the opportunity to tackle these, one of his men had been appointed internist at the university clinic, and it was now the rule in each mental hospital to have one trained internist to deal with general mental problems; I gathered though that this full time appointment involved routine work much more than research.

From some of the people in Snapper's clinic whom I met, I gathered that there is a closer association between Brouwer's and Snapper's clinics than between Snapper's and Bouman's; Bouman is generally rather isolated from the rest of the Wilhelmina Gasthuis.

I went over to Brouwer's clinic, but he was ill, so I saw de Jong. He seemed preoccupied and sensitive about his position. He was very kind and showed me the effects of bulbocapnine. Most of the objections that have been urged against his work seem to have some validity, but certainly he is carrying on steadily and systematically with the observations on motor phenomena in cats and mice, chiefly, produced by various drugs. He seemed painstaking and tenacious but depressed, dull, and to my surprise unfamiliar with some investigations that had been published and touched closely on his work. Some of the more or less obvious investigations (for example, sympathectomy and the effects of curare or insulin) he had not yet undertaken; but he told me he was proposing to go to the Heymans in Ghent to prepare himself for studying electrical phenomena. His work seemed to be interesting as a pharmacodynamic study of motility, rather than as one shedding light on schizophrenic catatonia. His collaborators did not impress me much in the little I saw of them. De Jong is of course fairly well aware of the weak points of his work and theory but seems to shut his eyes to them. I went to Kappers' Institute, but he was away in America. I did not learn about researches bearing even remotely on comparative psychology etc., perhaps because I was shown round by a dry, highly specialized zoologist, Addens, interested mainly in the nucleus of the spinal accessory nerve.

Leiden

In Leiden I was not able to see Carp or Gorter as they were both away, or Van Hemmelen, however, I saw Wiersma. The arrangement there is fortunate for a child guidance clinic in that the chief assistant of pediatrics and Professor Carp's assistant both work in it; the social work is done by a medial woman. The clinic seemed comparatively small (they have an average of 2–3 new cases a week). They are probably not having all the material, though of course the cases with a somatic basis are weeded out at the beginning. Wiersma seemed keen on doing as much as possible of the psychological examination of the cases himself, but seemed hampered in research work by the smallness of his material; in his investigations on some psychometric tests he was contentedly taking the problem children as capable of giving him his general norms, and I thought his statistical methods were hardly refined enough for his small samples. He lives rather under the shadow of his father. He seemed likeable and sensible in his child psychiatry. I also saw Gorter's chief assistant, and discussed with the physicist there – Van Ormondt – the investigations they are doing on mono-molecular layers. The methods do not yet seem applicable to clinical work, though they might soon become of use in estimating albumen-globulin proportions and quantity of electrolytes in CSF [cerebrospinal fluid] etc. I don't know whether there is any important difference between what Gorter is doing with it and what Langmuir in America and the men in London and Cambridge are doing.

Rademaker I also saw. He told me of his interesting work on the striate area in the dog, and the effects of extirpation on the movements of the legs of the animal; also of his work on nystagmus etc. He seems much occupied with clinical neurology at present.

In Holland, as elsewhere, I found the oddest gaps in people's knowledge of work that was close to their own, going on in other countries. This was true even of people who knew the literature of their subject apparently well otherwise; often they would admit they had only just heard of so and so, but did not know the value of his work or the details of it. It seemed as though there was a need for two things (a) all-inclusive abstracts such as the Zentralblatt used to supply in neurology and psychiatry, and (b) reviews by competent people of work in all sorts of scientific departments, so that people in individual fields should not be unaware of work touching on their own in other fields. The existing abstracts and reviewing journals obviously do not meet the need, for various reasons.

I also found in Holland, as elsewhere, that clinical psychiatrists were doing little in the way of research that would commend itself to any of the research workers accustomed to modern physiology, etc. They seemed neither to take up other people's methods precisely and intelligently, nor to originate any of their own; of course, there were exceptions to this.

Utrecht

In Utrecht I saw Ziedses des Plantes who explained to me his ingenious X-ray methods. Like Feitelberg and von Muralt, he seemed to illustrate very well the advantages of having had a special training, (for example, in physics or engineering) beforehand.

I also went to Rümke's clinic – he has just obtained the chair. Silvies Smitt showed me around the wards; I gather he has great hopes of getting the neurology chair which is now to be separated from the psychiatric one. He seemed a balanced fellow with strong, candidly expressed views. He runs the child guidance clinic; it is not in a very satisfactory state financially, I gather, and they may not be able to continue to pay a social worker. A private donor may again supply the money. The question of the neurological chair seems a ticklish one with a political background. In Utrecht they have a large number of students in the medical school who take up a good deal of the teacher's time; Rümke was examining students when I was there.

I also went round to Professor Noyons. He showed me his wealth of apparatus and his laboratories, and told me of the various researches he was doing in basal metabolism, skin reactions in varying temperatures, sound, smell, disturbances of consciousness during rotation etc. If only one could enjoy his extraordinary richness of appropriate and ingeniously devised apparatus, some of the metabolic problems of psychiatry could be tackled with much greater precision than at the present time. He apparently has no contact with the psychiatric clinic himself.

Report

BELGIUM[7]

Brussels

In Brussels I saw Bremer. His work has an obvious application to psychiatry; although Bremer is in private practice and sees some psychiatric material, I gather he has not the opportunity particularly to carry over his physiological researches into the clinical fields. He surprised me rather by saying that he had obtained some promising results in the treatment of depression by photodyn – which is now generally discredited. I thought his work on the brain very stimulating.

I also saw Rodolphe Ley. He was extremely kind and helpful, in arranging visits for me, etc. He suffers from lack of material to work on, owing to unsatisfactory arrangements, and has to rely on brains sent him by others, like Van Bogaert. There are problems also about getting scientific papers published in a reasonable time. His histological work seemed sound rather than enterprising, though of course this could be accounted for by the somewhat difficult conditions under which he works.

From him I went to Laruelle's neurological institute. He showed me his "repèrage" method of neurological diagnosis (bubbles of air introduced by lumbar puncture), and the attempt he is making to benefit anxiety-neurotics by periods of continuous oxygen administration. I was not much impressed by the assistant, Andrée, who was carrying this out, but I was not there long enough to form an opinion. The best thing at Laruelle's clinic is his technique for cutting serial longitudinal sections of the cord instead of the usual cross sections. I gather that the whole of this work depends on his technical assistant, Mdlle Reumont, who is obviously very skilful and intelligent. It is a pity that as I heard elsewhere, there were obstacles in the way of her finishing her medical course. Laruelle seemed a man with plenty of ideas of a fruitful kind, but he does not publish much, apart from little things, and dislikes the hack-work of research. I could not find out whether it was a lack of funds or other reasons that had so far prevented him for applying his technique to the study of ascending and descending degeneration in animals; nor why he had so few collaborators. Although his institute is not official but lives on private funds, it seems to have an important influence on neuro-psychiatry in Brussels.

I visited the Dispensaire d'Hygiène Mentale, conducted formerly by Auguste Ley and now by Vermeylen, who sees only the children; all the adults being seen by Alexander who visits about four or five times a week in an honorary capacity. It seemed surprising that there was no regular paid official provision for the carrying out

---

[7] In the early twentieth century in Belgium there were fifty-four closed psychiatric establishments, belonging variously to the State, public administrations, individuals or religious organisations. From 1873 asylum directors had to be nominated by the Ministry of Justice; and in 1931 a jury was formed to check the qualifications and expertise of candidates; until then the head doctor could simply be the one living nearest to the asylum. From 1874 the law also required frequent inspections of establishments and the recording of any use of constraints. A system of open services for patients presenting no danger developed at the beginning of the twentieth century against the wishes of the judicial authorities; as a result of the controversy over this issue it developed illegally. In 1920 the law regarding inspections was extended to institutions for abnormal children. While demented children had to be held in asylums, they were, however, subject to laws on child protection. After the First World War, the mental hygiene movement led to the opening of numerous dispensaries for adults and children amidst an increasing concern with prevention of mental illness.

of some of the work which is entrusted to the centre, for example the supervision and treatment of cases referred from the prisons under the "Loi de la Défense Sociale".[8] The treatment at the Dispensaire is mainly social, I gather, and is carried out by a competent sister in charge and her trainees and voluntary helpers: the number of cases is such, that I should think Alexander must be overwhelmed with them. The children's department is organised separately so far as the five or six doctors go, and here too the treatment is mainly social. It is the only child guidance clinic in Brussels, except a Catholic centre which is practically limited to the diagnosis of mental deficiency amongst Catholic school children. Here, as in most of the other institutions which I came across in Belgium, the question of rivalry or partisan appointment in respect of sectarian and political influence cropped up. The work at the Croix Rouge Centre seemed to me to be well done, within their limits.

Professor Vermeylen's psychiatric clinic is, of course, excellently constructed, and combines a purely voluntary university clinic – like the Maudsley or the Henri Rousselle – with another independent building for "colloqués", i.e. a sort of observation ward. He has a disadvantage in that he is not able to keep his patients longer than two months. He is energetic and positive, though not profound or impressive from the research point of view. In the development of mental hygiene in Brussels, however, he seems an important influence. The research he told me of at his own clinic included some studies in reaction time in GPI [general paralysis of the insane] before and after treatment (which he thought might have a prognostic value); and an enquiry which he was just beginning into the effects of a compound allied to dinitrophenol upon the absorption of vitamins; also some work on the haemato-encephalic barrier – it did not sound very valuable. He is rather more interested in social developments and administration than in pure psychiatry; he has, however, the advantage of having done some work in applied psychology. His work on mental deficiency seems to have been somewhat original but based on inadequate experience.

I saw Louis Vervaeck at the Prison de Forêt. It is a pity that the enormous amount of work which he has done in the way of collecting anthropological and other data should never have led to any conclusions; he has a mass of material, but I couldn't discover that he was going to apply any statistical analysis to it, or otherwise study it. It looked like an unrivalled collection of data for research in criminology.

I was struck in various places I visited in Belgium by their keenness on social work, and yet their relatively inadequate training for psychiatric social workers; they were

---

[8] This law (of 9 April 1930) instituted a new juridical system for "abnormal delinquents", not only for those whose responsibility was completely annihilated, but also for those with diminished responsibility, on the condition that this diminution was permanent. The law provided for the placing of the accused under observation in a psychiatric annexe of a penitentiary centre for one month – this could be renewed monthly for a period of up to six months. Psychiatric experts would determine whether the accused suffered from dementia or a serious state of mental disequilibrium or debility rendering him or her incapable of controlling his or her actions; if so, the accused would be interned in a special establishment, initially for five years, raised to ten years if the crime required punishment by forced labour, or fifteen if it was punishable by death. (Decisions were susceptible to appeal.) Each case was re-examined every six months in the light of medical observations. Upon release, a magistrate and psychiatric doctors would determine whether freedom of the accused was on a trial basis or definitive. If there was no cure, the internment could be prolonged. In 1964 various amendments were made to the law, making internment, whatever the gravity of the act, by default of indeterminate length. This was felt necessary due to the inability to predict the duration of a treatment.

for the most part unaware of such training as that given at the School of Economics in London to which the Scandinavians and Dutch come. It would probably be a good thing if one at least of their people could come and see what the training is.

Louvain

In Louvain I visited d'Hollander's out-patient clinic where he sees the patients rather cursorily and such of the ex-prisoners as are referred to him under the "Loi de la Défense Sociale". It seemed to me, however, that this law cannot be working satisfactorily because one of the patients, whom d'Hollander saw that morning while I was there, had killed his mistress and was now married to a woman among whose immediate relatives four had committed suicide; moreover d'Hollander had not heard of this before though it was not the first time the man had attended the clinic. D'Hollander is old and will probably have to retire fairly soon. Though he is energetic he looks as though he will presently be physically incapable of going on. His chief interest in is histopathology, especially of sympathetic ganglia and fibres. He is attached to some theories abandoned elsewhere, e.g. the tuberculous nature of schizophrenia. He has clearly had a great influence in Louvain and has obtained extraordinarily good buildings for his laboratories and wards. I gathered that he had his own way nearly always, and plenty of money at his disposal for his work; and that his nominee – a tall young man whom I met at the out-patient clinic – would almost certainly succeed him.

I saw van Gehuchten in his out-patient clinic, where he suffers from having practically no one to help him. His, I think, is the only neurological chair in Belgium; it is because of his father's prestige that it still exists. He is working on the effect of lesions of the locus niger in animals. He is only just beginning his experimental work. It is a pity he has no better facilities. He is also interested in acute infective encephalitis.

Liège

I went to Liège to see Divry but unfortunately did not manage to meet him. I saw his out-patient clinic which is not well equipped; his research work is, as far as I can discover from his publications etc., concerned with histopathology and he is more of a neurologist than a psychiatrist. Fredering I could not see.

Antwerp

In Antwerp Van Bogaert showed me the Institute Bunge. Van Bogaert finds it an advantage to be independent of the University because of the rivalries which he thus avoids; he gets his pathological material from many sources. Van Bogaert has with him Scherer who is working on the different cellular structure of gliomas in serial sections, and on comparative pathology, as well as routine work. He has a plenitude of material, and excellent facilities. The atmosphere of the institute seemed very agreeable. The comparative studies are being done also in an interesting way in the chemical department where they are working out the normal serum and blood chemistry of monkeys, preparatory to studying the pathological changes. They seemed particularly fortunate in their relationship with the zoo in Antwerp; whenever one of the animals is ill, Van Bogaert examines it clinically and when it dies he gets the central nervous system;

part of it he passes on to Scherer and the other part to de Wulf, the superintendent of the Corbeeloo at Louvain, who is studying microglia by Hortega methods (which he learned in Madrid). I did not meet him. I also met the other people in the Institut Bunge, including an American CRB Fellow interested in neuro-surgery. A proportion of their time is taken up with routine work on the patients, but it is mostly research they do.

Van Bogaert seemed keen on enlarging the research activities of the institute: for example, I gathered that he felt that the physiological work was not being as well done as it might be owing to the incomplete training of his brother who looks after it. Van Bogaert distributes his interests so widely that, as he himself recognises, he does not go tenaciously and profoundly into any topic, but he struck me as an admirable man for directing a clinic because of his wide contacts and interests, his productivity in collaboration with others, his keenness and freshness of ideas, and his amiability.

In Antwerp I also saw the tropical diseases hospital and teaching school which seemed unduly magnificent for its main purpose. I gathered that in spite of the splendid appointments little research is done, though they do a lot of clinical pathological tests.

Van Bogaert also told me of the various more or less isolated problems which had been interesting him. There is no doubt as to his freshness and receptiveness. He had met with a number of infections and toxaemias of the central nervous system in monkeys and other animals; and endarteritis obliterans in the artery of the kangaroo's tail, confirmed by plethysmographic studies which he had been able to do; various forms of epilepsy, including one amaurotic one in animals. He is also very interested in fat metabolism, giving the patient butter and cholesterol, and then every half hour or so for the next 12 hours estimating the cholesterine, lipoid, non-saponifiable fat and phosphatides of the blood: he had had a case with cholesterol deposit in the cerebellum, xanthelasma, cholesterol in tendons and yet no change in the blood cholesterol. His interest in this latter problem was linked up with Epstein's work in Vienna.

Ghent

I also saw Professor Hyssen of Ghent whose chief interest is in reactions to pain (blood pressure, electrical changes etc.). He has practically no clinical facilities – no beds, etc., and he was very frank about the general conditions. Like some of the other professors in Belgium he has a policlinic only, and has to get his material for teaching from a mental hospital nearby, which in the instance of Ghent is very badly appointed.

I saw de Busscher in Ghent and he showed me the material which he had been able to collect as the result of his extremely energetic, almost excessively industrious activity. He has been able, partly through his experience and training, and partly because of his father who is head of the Department of Gynaecology in the "Byloque", to get a precarious attachment in that hospital, but without beds, out-patients or control of treatment: he was called in as a consultant. He is in consequence naturally discontented, and contrasted the conditions of work which he met with in America during his period as CRB Fellow, with the opportunities allowed him now. It seems very likely that his frankness is criticising and his hypomanic temperament would have stood in his way as much as the political bias in university circles. He has not refrained from telling the doctors publicly and plainly how gross the deficiencies are, for example, in the provision of neuro-surgical treatment for cerebral tumours. Although he has the position of *chargé-de-cours* in the teaching faculty in Brussels, where he is an exponent of very mild psychoanalysis to the Flemish-speaking students, he is unpopular with the strongly national Flemish who control the faculty in Ghent. It is proposed, I gather, by these people, to build a big hospital in rivalry to the "Byloque", (which is certainly badly provided with such things as X-ray, and where the pathological department has settled somewhat into a rut, so that the findings sent back from these departments cannot be trusted). De Busscher is the only neurologist in Ghent, and so in his private practice gets a lot of material as well as the "Bonne Maison", where he sees cases. Fortunately, de Busscher is on good terms with the professor of surgery, de Beule, who would be glad to co-operate with him in starting a brain tumour centre in Ghent: he has already more than 50 cases that have come his way. De Busscher has so much energy that if such a unit could be started it would certainly be productive on the neurological and pathological side, I should think. De Busscher is also on very good terms with Thomas, the pathologist, and would probably get on very well with anyone who was fairly young, and even half as energetic as himself.

Thomas took me to his department of forensic medicine and showed me his interesting and very painstaking work on the normal structure of the thyroid and the changes which occur in it in general toxaemia etc., as well as his work on artificial cancer in mice and rats. He took me round to Professor Gormaghtigh, who told me about his work on suprarenals and on kidney lesions and changes in blood pressure induced by excess of vitamin D. I also saw Heymans who described his experiments on sympathectomized cats and the factors influencing the circulatory distribution: we discussed the application of some of these points to psychiatry, particularly the difference between the sympathectomized cat with and without adrenalin; the outstanding manifestations of emotion in the former instance cannot be central; it raises interesting questions regarding peripheral influence in affect, and links up with some of Bremer's work on his cats with isolated encephalon.

Gheel[9]

At Gheel there were the obvious features, such as Kilgour describes, and which Pollock goes into from a wider point of view in his recent little book. The chief points of interest, otherwise, that occurred to me were (1) the attitude of the people of Gheel. Every psychiatrist stresses the importance of environment for mentally ill people, and the desirability that they should be surrounded by normal people and influences, of child guidance; what then is the reverse aspect? i.e. in this case, what is the influence upon the children and people of Gheel of having these lunatics and

---

[9] The origins of Gheel lie in a legend concerning Dimphne, the daughter of a king of Ireland, who in the seventh century clandestinely fled the country with her confessor, the priest Gerebernus, wishing to escape from her father who wanted incestuous relations. The fugitives were found by the king and his police in Gheel, on the path of a pilgrimage to Rome, and both killed. The legend tells of miraculous healings of mentally ill patients by the tomb of the girl; Gheel became a place of pilgrimage and inhabitants used to welcome and house the ill. Dimphne and the priest were canonized, and a church built in the eighth century had a "patients' room" where pilgrims prayed, and where Dimphne's relics lie. The welcoming of the mentally ill continued despite the construction in 1862 of an infirmary and then a psychiatric hospital, and after the colony became the property of the State.

defectives all round them, living always in their houses; and what is the effect of taking lunacy as a matter of course? Of not having the customary attitude of aversion to it, but living in a rather topsy-turvy state of acceptance of it as more or less normal? Actually by all accounts it makes very little difference at Gheel; in other words, growing up in a partly insane environment has there very little effect on normal children or adults, so that presumably a relatively well-endowed person is not a penny the worse for being frequently in contact with mentally unhealthy or unstable people. However, this question, so frequently raised in genetic studies, needs more investigation and seems to offer some interest as a research possibility. There is, for example, also the question as to what form hysteria takes among the normal peasant population of Gheel. Do they imitate psychosis and defect rather than physical forms of illness? Gheel supplies, as it were, the obverse of the psychiatrists' insistence on the desirability of a normal and healthy environment for the development of normal mental health.

Then there is the important point that according to Dr Raemaekers they have no sexual delinquency among the patients, no assaults on children etc., and no homicidal attacks. Seeing that there are so many defectives, this also seems a point for further investigation as to the social influence at work in bringing about such an excellent result. The children they have are all defectives, not delinquents. Among the adult women patients, however, I gather there is a case of pregnancy about once every 18 months, and they have had two homicides in the last 100 years.

Then there is the question as to whether a fair amount of what might be called ill treatment must be reckoned with. Some mild ill treatment there certainly is; the control is not close or constant and the doctors deliberately do not investigate trifling complaints of unkindness etc. It may be that that is an essential part of such a working scheme, and that, inevitably, living in a family in such circumstances will lead to some ill usage which should not be bothered about. It is true that in the Dutch colony there is stricter supervision and probably also in the French one but it is quite likely that one must strike a balance between licence and strict control. It may well be that for many of the patients it is less "normal" if they are not occasionally treated as they would be in any ordinary home of their class when they were troublesome. This seems reactionary, though there seems reason to believe that the application of mental hospital supervision to family care might defeat its own ends. On the whole there is probably scarcely any victimisation of the patients by the family guardians, but sometimes some of the patients do an excessive amount of work because their delusions urge them to; however, in a particular case which I came across when I went round with Dr Raemaekers I think the family were trying to dissuade the patient. The doctors, of whom there are eight to 3,600 patients, are not closely enough in touch with their patients to know them all well.

There is also the question of whether defectives do better if they are in homes with people of a rather low intelligence themselves, so that they "fit in", as it were, or whether that tends to result in quarrelling and stupid ill-treatment. I raised the point with Dr Raemaekers but he had not considered it particularly. The question really is whether understanding and care by intelligent people is better than a milieu to which the patient easily adapts and from which he is, in essentials, not far removed.

Report

The selection of cases for Gheel does not seem to be satisfactorily carried out. They have to take all the overflow of the mental hospitals. Judging from the numbers of patients they have in the colony, four more such places would provide for all the insane of Belgium; and the colony is of course much less expensive than the mental hospital. But I gathered that vested interests, especially the religious bodies, which control the mental hospitals, would be opposed to such a scheme, even if it were practicable.

It seems, however, certain from present trends that in the US and many European countries, especially Switzerland, there will be more and more family care, if possible on the colony system. Gheel is therefore very valuable: it is the best experiment, and offers many opportunities for research which do not seem to have availed of at all. (The Swiss procedure, as developed in Zurich under Bleuler and Hans Maier, is much more scattered and less satisfactory economically, as well as in some other respects). It is, for example, quite impossible to say what proportion of the patients at Gheel are defective, and what proportion have mental disorders. Nor could it be discovered how the patients do under the treatment; what proportion recover, what types of illness do best, how the duration of illness compares with that in mental hospitals, and so forth. The records barely exist and certainly are not detailed enough to give a basis for diagnosis. It is therefore impossible at present to form any useful opinion as to the value of the Gheel Colony method therapeutically (as against its economic advantages), much less compare it with prognosis or decide on the applicability of such methods elsewhere, say in the rural parts of England. Everyone who writes about Gheel puts a lot of stress on the religious background etc., whereas it is doubtful how far these historic and traditional factors now weigh with the population. It has been possible, for instance, to extend the colony into regions which were outside the geographical range of these traditional influence; girls from the villages and hamlets which are now included in the colony used, formerly, if they married a Gheel peasant, to find the care of a patient disagreeable until they got accustomed to it, but afterwards they fitted into the system quite well.

There are a lot of points upon which it is impossible to obtain precise information; there is for example the question of duration of stay and factors which may prolong it; for example, I saw one girl who stayed there largely because there was no one who would take the responsibility of looking after her when she went out, as her parents were separated and she had been in trouble through having an illegitimate child before. In this case they are really detaining a mentally healthy girl who is a potential social problem.

From the point of view of financial and administrative aspects of social psychiatry, as well as for psychiatric theory (influence of environment), Gheel seems to offer excellent material for research which could be carried out by a psychiatrist and social worker; they could extend their investigations to the other colonies and family-care schemes in Europe. At present the people at Gheel make no research use of their material; they do not, for instance, compare the incidence of tuberculosis in their schizophrenia patients with that of the normal population of Gheel, yet here is a perfect case for studying it, without having the abnormal living conditions of the mental hospitals to confuse the issue. They could also study the duration of life of their patients as compared with the average population living under almost identical conditions: there were a lot of old women patients about, and chronic patients stay there until they die. I think Dr Raemaekers would facilitate any investigations, but it is unlikely he could make them himself, partly because of his administrative duties which would, at any rate under present conditions, prevent him from giving enough time to it, and partly because his interests do not lie in that direction; but he has a benevolent attitude towards it, has done research work in pharmacology himself with Sollmann in [the] USA and seems hopeful of getting laboratory work going. It is a pity that one of the Dutch, psychiatric social workers, cannot be roped into a research of this kind; she would have the advantage of knowing the language.

There were several general impressions I got about conditions in Belgium. It was not that they were particularly different from those in other countries, but they were emphasized by the people I talked to. The fact that most doctors have to do private practice has, besides various clinical advantages, many disadvantages. Plenty of people would like to devote themselves much more to scientific work but cannot afford to; and on the other hand there is a great deal of the individualist attitude among doctors, i.e. they would rather earn the varying income of a competitive profession than have the fixed salary of a full-time professor or research worker. Vacancies are usually filled by appointing one of the people already in the particular city, so that there is on the whole not much interchange between the various universities and medical faculties. The clerical domination of some of the universities and of the mental hospitals is generally thought to tend towards conservatism and to result in inadequate medical staffing, along with unduly imposing buildings and equipment. It is perhaps partly due to this that Freudian doctrines are scarcely considered in Belgium, though Vermeylen is mildly favourable towards such a point of view; strict Freudian views of the kind met with in London are reprobated by the few people who know about them. Apart from Vermeylen, the general trend is strongly neurological, and even he is less speculative than some of them suppose him to be, I should say. Their mental hygiene movement concentrates on social results, and seems to have accomplished a good deal; of course the social conscience in such matters is fairly strong in Belgium. Sterilisation of the unfit is not an issue among them, and their rule is to have a procedure for therapeutic abortion almost as strict as the English requirements for certification of the insane. The secular nurses in psychiatric clinics are pretty well trained. I was told they do three years general training and one year special psychiatric training. I did not find out how the nurses among the religious orders are trained; d'Hollander said they were excellent.

Vermeylen seems to be the only professor who is particularly interested in psychiatry; the others are mainly neurologists or anatomists. The influence of French neurology and psychiatry is, of course, strong; consequently, and partly also because there is in many instances a dearth of material, people use the "casuistical" method of publication, ie of single cases. Moreover, there are few pathologists in Belgium. Van Bogaert says he cannot find anyone capable of co-operating in a virus enquiry.

Report

FRANCE[10]

Paris

In Paris I went to see L'hermitte in the Hôpital Henri Brousse, but he was away and I went round with de Massary, who is one of the senior people there. He seemed to me a poor clinician, examining his cases in a slipshod way and sometimes not knowing the essential factors about a patient. His treatment seemed of the blunderbuss kind, in the children's OP department. His clinical material, however, was very interesting. I later saw L'hermitte, who is still very active, and better informed about foreign literature than many of the other people I met in Paris. He seems to stimulate his people in various directions (e.g. I have just received, since I came back, a thesis by a Persian doctor whom L'hermitte had put on to a clinical and psychopathological investigation into disturbances of the body-image). His chief interest is, of course, in histopathology. At the Fondation Déjerine I saw many sections illustrating his studies of the changes in the dentate nucleus in myoclonus epilepsy; also the cell changes in the cords of rabbits in which he had injected anti-tetanic serum. He was interested in the latter problem because of some cases of paralysis in human beings which had followed injections of anti-tetanic serum. He seemed a little bold in the way he argued from rabbits to men, rabbits being, I think, particularly untrustworthy for such a comparison. He has with him a very good technician, Frln Kirchner, who had much experience of microglia and macroglia work with Bielschowsky before 1933.

I was interested to meet Paul Schiff, who belongs to the "évolution psychiatrique" group, and is particularly interested in applications of psychiatry to delinquency. He has had a good background in neurology and psychiatry and is also a psychoanalyst, but his present work is in the prisons chiefly. He has an official position examining and reporting upon the new prisoners. His appointment followed legislative action in which he had a large share behind the scenes. It will probably develop further, I understand. I read some of the reports he furnished to the courts, and it seemed to me that Schiff was doing the job very well so far as one man could cope with the amount of material. He is a rather melancholy, quiet man, but enthusiastic about his work. I learned from him that in Paris there is the same problem as in London – so many societies that one can spend every night going to meetings of those which have some connection with one's work.

In Lapicque's laboratory I saw Monnier, who showed me his work in recording simultaneous action-current at two points on a nerve and so calculating the rate of

---

[10] The primacy of French psychiatry in the first two-thirds of the nineteenth century had gradually been occluded by German psychiatry in the 1880s and 1890s. In the twentieth century, French psychiatry did, however, enrich the understanding of delusional states and contribute towards their classification, partly through the work of Gaétan de Cléraumbault and Joseph Capgras. And, as can be seen here, there were some highly influential psychiatrists in France, especially in Paris, at the time of Lewis's trip. Building on a heritage of studies in neurology, hysteria, and neurosis, French psychiatry was significantly organicist in bent – assimilating the recent physical therapies, which gained much ground in the 1930s, researching epilepsy and GPI, and searching for infectious causes of mental illness – but was also incorporating psychoanalysis, which in the 1920s made inroads in the form of organizations such as the Mouvement Psychanalytique Français and the Revue Française de Psychanalyse. The mental hygiene movement had taken off in 1920s, and in the 1930s there was a move towards modernization of services and a focus on prevention.

conduction, and he told me also of the lessened excitability and rate of conduction in motor nerves which he had found as the central effect of the injection of pyrethrine. I heard him give a lecture (to an engineering society, I believe) in which he showed an excellent capacity for expounding the matter clearly.

I saw Guillain at the Salpêtrière and attended his clinical demonstration. It was neatly and dramatically done, but on a superficial level; the examination was very brief and the commentary limited to one or two points of practical importance. I also met Mollaret, Roussy and Oberling – very briefly, and Ivan Bertrand with whom I spoke several hours. Bertrand is of course not entirely contented, and like most people in Paris does not see where the young men are coming from who are going to continue in research, the claims of private practice being imperative. Although he has the necessary apparatus etc., he seems at the moment to lack collaborators. His own investigations on the rate of regeneration of peripheral nerve when the spinal cord of a rabbit is used as a temporary substitute seemed an interesting piece of research applied to reparative surgery; he had done it in conjunction with Gosset. His other studies in conjunction with Guillain etc., were fairly straightforward pathological and anatomical ones. He is anxious to get Fessard to work with him and also to get some work going on comparative pathology of the nervous system.

The group that surrounds Eugène Minkowski seems to have scarcely any contact with the neurologists and holders of official chairs in Paris; not that there is enmity, but only lack of contact. Laignel-Lavastine is on friendly terms with this group, but is somewhat contemptuously regarded by the more neurological group. Minkowski's group "L'évolution psychiatrique" consists mainly of people interested in psychopathology, but there are also people like Guiraud in it, and a number of Claude's assistants as well as people at the Hôpital Henri Rousselle. Most of the more progressive people now seem to be associated with this group, for example, Heuyer, who has started a child guidance clinic (Minkowski also visits a children's home for behaviour problems, which is being run on sensible lines). Henri Ey who has done interesting work on hallucinations, Rubenovitch etc. Of course some of the members are psychoanalysts, but the French Freudians are not orthodox according to Vienna, and are certainly much less extreme than in London. They have their own society for discussing points of analytical technique. In Minkowski's society they take a broad psychiatric view. Minkowski himself seems still to be the most potent influence in maintaining this desirable emphasis on the broader medical aspects of psychopathology, and his strong philosophic bent gives depth to the general studies carried on by the group. In respect of psychopathology this small French group seems to me on the whole to be superior to many of the English and American workers who are either wholly psychoanalytical or inclined to be naively superficial and objective.

Guiraud, who wrote the textbook with Dide,[11] is chiefly insistent on his extraordinary findings in fresh foci in disseminated sclerosis. Certainly the things which he regards as parasites are visible in his stained preparations, and his Achucarro method seems safe enough, though it is surprising that so few people whom I have questioned

---

[11] M Dide and P Guiraud (eds), *La Psychiatrie du médecin practicien*, Paris, Masson 1922; 2nd ed. 1929.

about it even knew of the conclusions he had reached; certainly they (the conclusions) seemed hard to believe. He had with him, the day I was there, a young man, Delmond, who has written an interesting thesis on schizophrenia, and seemed quite alert and keen. I was surprised to find that although he works next door to Guiraud he had never seen Guiraud's preparations before. There doesn't seem to be as much communication as there might be between the various people and departments in Paris; of course the gulf between the "médecins des hôpitaux" and the "médecins des asiles" is wide. Guiraud I also saw in his OPD, where he is in his element because of his lively and plastic temperament. He struck me as a good clinical psychiatrist, and he must be a most amusing teacher. Although he knows the literature of psychiatry well, he seemed a bit behindhand in some respects; for example, he would tell commonplace things abut the result of malaria treatment in GPI as though they were fairly new.

The Hôpital Henri Rousselle seems to have fallen away from its original achievements and potentialities. Génil-Perrin is apparently a good clinician, but not particularly interested in research and progress and change of any kind. Of course he has only just taken over, but it is hard to picture him developing the place much; Mme Lebas, the secretary of the hospital, who has been there for a long time, seems to be chiefly responsible for the organization of it. They have a fairly busy OPD but from what Montassut told me there is not an adequate supply of doctors interested in working there, because they have to spend most of their time earning their living in private practice, and it is hardly worth their while. Moreover, there is no teaching there because it is all concentrated in the official hands of the Faculté. I gather they had no full time staff, but only part time people like Montassut, Schiff and Minkowski (though the latter hardly go there now), and house physicians. The doctors are former "médecins des hôpitaux" and psychiatrists without asylum experience; in other words the "médecins des asiles" have very little opportunity of getting into touch with the more psychological side of therapy etc.

In the laboratories at Henri Rousselle there did not seem to be much going on. The chemistry which was being done by Tscherniakovsky seemed old fashioned; they were doing out-of-date things like tryptophane, the Boltz reaction, but I understood that Tscherniakovsky had been away with Charcot on one of his polar expeditions and so perhaps had not been able to get things going. The younger Delaville – I did not see the elder one – was doing work on interferometry which seemed also out of date. They did not seem well up in the literature. In the psychological laboratories Lahy seemed more interested in psychotechnics and educational problems than in anything that had reference to the patients or psychiatry generally. Simonet, the director of the physiological laboratory, was away on the two occasions when I called. It seemed odd that the laboratories of the hospital should be quite independent from those of Claude which were only a few yards away.

I made repeated attempts to see Rubénovitch but he seemed in a dreadful hurry and passed me on to Lagache, who is the successor of Baruk and Rubénovitch as chef de clinique for Claude. Lagache is a Freudian, but fairly well equipped also on the somatic side. He will probably, however, drift into private practice, of which he already does a little. He seemed intelligent, and, like Delmond, keen on doing scientific work if he can get the chance. At present he is studying the psychopathology of jealousy, but the investigation did not seem likely to lead to anything particular. I could not find that much advantage was taken, at present, of the fact that Georges Dumas's laboratory is situated on the floor above the clinic, to bring about any application of psychology to psychiatric problems.

Fessard I found more original and very interesting. He has poor facilities at Piéron's laboratory – his wife has had to come in to wash up his vessels for him at times – his application of the Berger rhythm to problems of attention (studying the latent period) offered several possibilities. Unfortunately he is so shy and has in a mild way a feeling of inferiority and resentment towards doctors so that he rather distrusts them and fears that they will treat him as a technician, as though he had only some special skill. This made him dubious about falling in with Bertrand's invitation to collaborate; he knew of some of the common, rather unimportant, objections to Bertrand. He was actually eager, however, to work on clinical problems. He regrets the shortness of his stay with Matthews, and he would jump at the chance to get a further period in England, during which he might also find an opportunity of seeing clinical material and getting a working knowledge of clinical problems. The difficulty is, of course, getting spared from his teaching work.

Strasbourg

In Strasbourg I first saw Stahl who is continuing the work that he was doing in the USA. He is obviously very thorough and conscientious, and unhappy because he is unable to give all his time to research. His assistant and he are studying carefully the metabolic aspects, phosphatase, sodium, etc. of adrenal extirpation. The younger and more energetic people in Strasbourg seem to cooperate very well with each other. I met Keyser, Ginglinger and a number of the young people working with Leriche. Leriche's more or less experimental surgery struck me as bold rather than well-based. The originality of his ideas is very attractive but sometimes seems to depend on lack of familiarity with the relevant facts. Whether his therapeutic claims for sympathetic operations are justified, I had no means of judging. Surprisingly, he has not carried his operations into the psychiatric field, e.g. he has not treated anxiety cases surgically. I gathered, though, that Pferrsdorf is distinctly conservative. It must be stimulating to work with Leriche, but difficult if one is sceptically inclined. Keyser's studies on heat regulation were of interest and could, I should think, be carried over into the human field and applied to catatonic stupor etc., with some advantage, but he told me that the work is so exacting of time and patience that he would not like to have to repeat what he has already done (with pigeons etc.). His many other ideas were not particularly relevant to the problems of neurology and psychiatry. Ginglinger I also saw, but unfortunately Ancel, Bouin and Wolff were away on holiday, as it was Easter. Pferrsdorf seems to be mainly occupied, as he as been for years, with aphasia, and does not particularly welcome any fresh developments, though he is of course a good clinical psychiatrist.

Report

Lyons

In Lyons, at Easter, I had difficulties – as also in Marseilles and Geneva – in seeing the people I wanted to, because of the holidays. Dechaume, the Agrégé to Favre, took me round the medical faculty, and the neurological department at the Hôpital Edouard Herriot. Dechaume works a good deal with Hermann. From what Dechaume told me, the collaboration between the people in the different medical departments is fairly close; of his own papers, most seem to have been written in collaboration. He told me that they had no trouble there in getting satisfactory young people to do research, partly because it is the road to a career in Dijon, Grenoble, etc. He showed me the laboratories of Policard and Hermann, but unfortunately I could not see either of these as they were away.

Marseilles

In Marseilles I did not see Cornil because he was ill. Mosinger told me that Cornil has to spend some months every year in bed, and his heart is getting worse. Mosinger is very energetic and his enthusiasm seems to equal his output. It is hard to understand how he could have found time to write his big textbook on legal medicine, and his monograph in collaboration with Roussy, and at the same time have done his teaching and have got his various researches under way. He carries his interest in the hypothalamus as a secretory organ to considerable lengths, but the specimens he showed me suggested interesting lines of work. I had the impression, though, that he is inclined to pin more faith, and inferences as to function, on histopathological observations than one should. He is, however, quite aware of the more or less conjectural nature of some of the links in his chain of reasoning. He was full of ideas, especially regarding psychiatry; besides his interest in the prolan content in women with dementia praecox. He told me about his studies of vitamin A content in the livers of individual guinea pigs, in whom no difference of species or of diet could account for the difference of chronaxie which according to him corresponded to the lack or presence of vitamin A in these animals. If confirmed, it sounds a promising line of investigation, but as the administration of vitamin A in their diet raised the chronaxie, it seems surprising that diet can have had no part in determining the initial differences. Another and more interesting study that he was making in conjunction with Chevalier was a spectrophotometric investigation by means of which he would be able to analyse both quantitatively and qualitatively substances of relatively simple molecular structure, for example vitamins A and C and folliculin. In so far as it is a potential method of studying simple proteins in various tissues, it has some similarity to Gorter's study of monomolecular layers, though probably more practical at present.

Although Mosinger has not had training in psychiatry, he seems alive to its interest and importance and especially to the medico-legal implications. He struck me as overconfident, but certain to get a lot of interesting work done.

Neither in Lyons or Marseilles, as far as I could discover, does psychiatry really exist as such in the University. The professor, e.g. Lepine, is a neurologist and for his psychiatric teaching uses the material of the local asylum.

Aubrey Lewis

SWITZERLAND[12]

Geneva

In Geneva I saw Claparède who looks older than his years now, tired and unhappy because of the political disturbances; his family troubles too have been great and seem to have told on him. His teaching duties are heavy at the Institut Jean-Jacques Rousseau, and his assistants are so much taken up with routine that they cannot give him much help. He was one of the few psychologists I met who had had a medical training and recognised its value for research. His chief interest, as for many years, is in sleep and in speech; the latter has led him to a general interest in the question of cerebral localisation and he is in close touch with the most recent literature. I gathered that Bovet has also found it difficult to devote himself solely to his academic work because of his concern about the trend of political developments.

I also saw Piaget who discussed the opportunities of research in child psychiatry; he was not very ready to talk, however, but preferred to refer one to his books. He has a few people round him like Rey and Meile. He is at work on the development of mathematical ability in children which he finds is present surprisingly early.

Bois-Bougy

At Bois-Bougy I saw Löewenstein: he has resumed his work on papillary reactions and the study of movements in hysterics etc. In regard to the former he gives the impression that he will carry it to all possible lengths; he quoted cases where he had been able by its means to diagnose syphilis of the central nervous system long before there were any neurological signs, and when the Wassermann in the blood and CSF were still negative. In view of the data he gave and other things I have heard, some of his studies of this kind seem to require confirmation. There can be no doubt, however, as to the excellence of his ingenious and accurate method within its limited scope. His studies of motility by the well-known apparatus he used in Bonn, and by moving pictures, were of less interest. He is very enthusiastic about his two methods and draws unjustifiably wide conclusions from them, I thought; his skill seems to lie more on the technical side than on the interpretative. Of course, he is very much limited as to clinical material now. It is a pity because his papillary method needs to be applied to

---

[12] Psychiatry developed later in Switzerland than in other countries, and was initially linked to German psychiatry (three of the first four directors of the Burghölzli were German). Two individuals in particular helped place it on an independent footing: Auguste-Henri Forel (1848–1931) – who had fought for the pre-eminence of the head doctor as opposed to the financial administration in asylums – and Eugen Bleuler (1857–1939) – under whom a wave of therapeutic optimism emanated from the Burghölzli. Asylum directors were *ipso facto* professors of psychiatry in the corresponding university. The five most significant university clinics were Bel-Air, Cery, Burghölzli, Waldau and Friedmatt. From the days of Bleuler's direction of the Burghölzli, psychiatry began to be located in a wider territory than just the asylum. A move towards placement in families developed a little; while in Cery, in Waldau, a colony of patients was established. From the 1930s onwards, psychiatric policlinics – corresponding to the *dispensaires d'hygiène mentale* in France – developed significantly. Instead of making a rigorous distinction between closed and open services, and voluntary and obligatory placement, Swiss psychiatry tried to give establishments the air of a *service libre*. Acknowledging the significance of both hereditary and environmental factors, Swiss psychiatry was also fairly receptive to psychoanalysis; the Swiss Society of Psychoanalysis was founded in 1919. Binswanger's existential and phenomenological views were also influential.

neurological material (disseminated sclerosis etc.). Löewenstein is also rather limited in his outlook, it seems to me; he had not followed some of the lines of investigation by his method which seemed obvious, and he knows only the German literature. At the Bel-Air Sanatorium he has charge of a house where psychopathic children are looked after.

Geneva

I saw Friedheim in Ashkenazy's laboratory. He had had a preliminary training in psychiatry with Bleuler (and Kraepelin I think) before he took up bio-chemistry and pharmacology. He has collaborated with Meyer (the son of Hans Horst Meyer), but finds little support from Ashkenazy who apparently dislikes any complicated apparatus or new fangled methods. His idea that dyes act as catalysts for cellular respiration and might therefore be used therapeutically in malaria and trypanosomiasis opened up an attractive line of investigation. It struck me that it would be a good thing if he were to extend his studies to GPI. We talked of work done on these lines also which might be applied to continuous narcosis. I could not judge whether the latter line of work would be productive or not: he had not yet been able to make the preliminary experiments.

I tried to see Walthard and de Morsier but they were both away on holiday. I also did not see Ladame, but I was told in Geneva that since he had the chair he has been more or less swamped by administrative work, and had not undertaken any research.

Lausanne

In Lausanne I saw Steck (the successor of Preissig) who was rather annoyed with himself for not having carried further his experiments with insulin as a form of treatment for schizophrenia, which he proposed years ago. He still thinks that insulin is efficacious in smaller and less drastic doses than Sakel advocates (though when Steck advocated this method years ago, it was a death which resulted from it that put him off continuing with it). He is critical and like most people has come to the conclusion that insulin can bring social benefit, e.g. by making the patient quieter or by bringing about general improvement in the state of some chronic or hopeless cases, and that sometimes it is prompter in cutting short an attack than other methods. However, he had had one case of status epilepticus due to it, and a number in which the treatment had done no good. Cardiazol he dislikes. Like most people, he has seen a number of relapses after temporarily successful insulin treatment.

Yverdon

I saw Georgi at Yverdon. He has built up this private mental hospital (which was very badly run and had a bad reputation before) very successfully; but it is necessary if he is to get on at all that he should get a Swiss qualification, and the preparation for his examinations is now hanging over his head. He works very hard. It is a pity that Grünthal did not welcome the proposal that Georgi and he should work together in one place. Georgi has managed with his modest equipment and his one technical assistant to do a remarkable amount of chemical serological research on the patients who he had treated with insulin and cardiazol. I saw his method and clinical material and discussed with him more or less controversial points. He has obtained a remission in 70% of his cases, some of them after four and even six months' treatment by the method. He also has observed social improvement in long-standing cases – making them quieter. He is combining cardiazol with insulin. He believes that epileptic convulsions occurring during the treatment are an advantage whereas Müller does his best to avoid them by giving luminal. He is making a study of the blood electrolytes, the permeability of the "barrier" to bromide, etc., in his case.

Wherever the insulin treatment was being carried out it was clear that one had to separate the three aspects of the matter (1) immediate outcome of the present attack, (2) outcome of a case in the long run, (3) theoretical and research possibilities offered. Hardly any of the people who carried out the treatment in the places I visited were aware of the American work on sodium amytal, nitrous oxide and other substances which temporarily produce a dramatic change in catatonic stupor. When I told them of it they seemed almost abashed, because so much emphasis has been put on the dramatic immediate effects of insulin as indicating that it is something quite different from what has previously been tried in the treatment of schizophrenia. Naturally in discussing the treatment most of the people who were using it a good deal said nothing about its making any patients worse; I gathered, however, that this sometimes occurs.

Landeron

I went off to Landeron to see Bersot; his hospital seemed rather haphazard in its organization but he himself keen in a slightly dilettante way; he has worked on the development of children, and published a paper on the excretion of vitamin C; he is interested too in insulin treatment and cardiazol, which he has employed. However, his main merit seemed to lie in his advocacy of mental hygiene, and his statistical efforts. For the former he writes many pamphlets, worthy and well-intentioned but curiously old-fashioned in tone. For the latter, i.e. statistical work, he struck me as having the necessary industry but lacking in any critical attitude towards the figures he was offered. He seemed to regard the diagnostic and other data compiled from the official Swiss sheets as quite reliable, though I learned from others that the doctors hate filling out these compulsory sheets, which are rather detailed, so they do it carelessly; and in any case even if they took trouble with it, there would be the question of varying standards of diagnosis. I could not find that Bersot bothered himself about sources of error. He did not know how to work out percentages and movements of mental hospital population in a statistical way; he does not know the literature of this subject as well as is desirable if he is going to continue with his task of collecting the mental hospital statistics for all Europe. Still, the task is so formidable that, unless one were blind through enthusiasm or lack of criticism to the certain deficiencies in any figures obtained, one could hardly make a beginning in such as task. When I enquired in other countries less advanced psychiatrically than Switzerland, it was clear that their figures were of varying degrees of unreliability and that very few were in a state in which they could be analysed with profit. In Italy, for example, the only person who seemed to have any data collected was Modena; I tried hard to see him but did not succeed, and in any case people told me that he had not yet got trustworthy data.

Similarly, or more so, the Russian statistics were very much to seek [*sic*]. Bersot is, at any rate, doing his best to collect such data as he can obtain; it is necessary as the first step – there will be plenty of people to point out how unsusceptible of useful analysis such figures are. Perhaps the time is hardly ripe for attempting to get general European figures when the standards of public provision for mental disorder and deficiency and the standards of diagnosis etc., vary so much, not to speak of the difficulties of ascertainment.

Berne

In Berne I saw Klaesi who showed me the many improvements he had made in his mental hospital. He is so self-centred and talkative that I found it difficult to discuss any matter with him. He talked a great deal but mostly about administrative matters – the private rooms he had built and so forth. He is ill-disposed to the use of insulin though he is using cardiazol, which, along with continuous narcosis and psychotherapy, seems to him to provide everything in the way of treatment which insulin could. On occupational therapy he has strong views, believing it to be greatly over-rated. He has altered the organisation of his hospital so that there are now three divisions. In the clinic, which is the admission section and main university teaching department, he has made the rooms rather comfortless and removed all reminders of home on the theory that the patient should not have anything to make him so satisfied with being in hospital that he would be willing to stay indefinitely; similarly he will not let them work in the garden as it would be too agreeable. Of course for the chronic patients these Spartan regulations are not imposed. Though he claimed extraordinarily good results in avoiding noise in the wards of his hospital, I could not discover that herein it was different from any other modern psychiatric hospital either in its methods or the success attained. He is so positive, that one was forced to doubt some of his conclusions; for example, when I asked if he had the impression that the special colours on the walls of the rooms in which manic and depressive patients are treated had proved effective, he said, "We have no impression about it, we have certain proof that it does"; the evidence was not forthcoming. He is a very skilled clinician, especially in dealing with schizophrenics. It is difficult to form an opinion about his work because so much seems to depend on the phase in which one comes across his variable and forceful personality.

One of his assistants (Brieben, I think) showed me the new children's clinic, actually an old inn which they are converting for the purpose. They will use it as a reformatory and observation centre for up to thirty difficult children, to judge their conduct, psychiatric condition, etc.; they will not keep the children longer than six months. The children, I gathered, will be sent there willy-nilly, but defectives will not be sent; parents will not have any say as to whether or not their children are to go to a place situated, as this is, in the grounds of the mental hospital.

I met some other assistants of Klaesi and the superintendent of a cantonal mental hospital who was visiting him: the latter told me that he used family care for his patients, roughly up to 50% of them going into families, mainly the families of the female nurses of the hospital. The nurses have, as throughout Switzerland, a pretty thorough training and there is a fair supply; Klaesi has come to the conclusion, incidentally, that ugly nurses are less beneficial for the patients, especially the depressed ones, and regulates his staff accordingly (it was difficult, with all his statements, to make out if they were considered opinions).

I was told that there are about 100 medical students; there seem to be more universities in Switzerland than the population of $4\frac{1}{2}$ million people require, and it seems doubtful whether they can go on getting enough suitable men to teach and do research in their departments, now that they are reluctant to take anyone from outside as they used to.

Schizophrenia seems to be the aspect of mental disorder that very much colours Klaesi's outlook; his interest has, of course, always been on that side of psychiatry.

Grünthal and his technical assistant were busy. He showed me his comparative studies on the thalamus, and told me how he found the ontogenetic sequence in his mice-embryos reflected in the phylo-genetic series he has accumulated. He is proposing to study the function of the thalamus by the use of the electro-cautery. He is also continuing his Würzburg studies in brain volume and brain swelling. He has an interesting programme of further studies to deal with the anatomical basis for what is specifically human instead of seeking in the usual way for what is common to human beings and other animals. I went with him to his Policlinic too. He seems very satisfied with his present situation and opportunities (he has the chronic organic cases under his care in the hospital, which suits him because of his longstanding interest in such cases).

In Berne I also saw von Muralt, who was excited about the discoveries he was just then making about the chemical changes in the nerve fibre. He was right in the middle of it, working very hard, and hoped to be able to report to the Royal Society in June that he had found that a cholin ester is produced for very short spaces of time in the nerve fibre itself during stimulation, instead of only at the synapse of where there is an interruption of lipoid continuity. He had not so far been able to test the influence of eserine, etc., because of the difficulty of getting through the lipoid barrier in the nerve sheath. His work seemed to raise a lot of possibilities as regards time relations in nervous transmission and their chemico-physical basis. He is still busy reorganising his department, and has been successful in getting an arrangement working by which one of the more promising people in the department of internal medicine comes to him for a year; he has a man from there studying blood volume by a new method which von Muralt had devised. Although he is thus collaborating with the Department of Internal Medicine and is proposing to apply some of his methods to studying the blood volume of anaemias, emotional excitements, etc., he is not sanguine about the possibility of getting collaborators from the clinical side as he finds them so often vague in thought and unprecise in technique. He makes ingenious use of optical methods for studying the respiration in a frog's heart preparation, basal metabolism, etc. There is also a man studying the influence of pyruvic acid, etc., on haemolysis. Von Muralt also told me he was going to study the changes in metabolism of cretins at high altitudes at the station on the Jungfraujoch, carrying the cretins up and down by the funicular railway, while the estimation was made by his interferometric method.

Report

Münsingen

I went to Münsingen and saw Müller and the people who are working with him on insulin and cardiazol treatment. He had 20-odd patients at the time under the treatment, which was directly under the care of a German woman doctor, called May – an émigré working there voluntarily, I gathered, who would soon have to leave. They were treating several patients in one room and did not seem to worry about one patient seeing another in the throes of the treatment. Müller, however, feels strongly that one must individualise as regards dosage, etc., after one has acquired some experience with Sakel's original method. It was significant that he was not treating with insulin the large number of schizophrenics that one found in the hospital when going round. It wasn't that he thought it would harm them, but he didn't believe it would do any good either, except to a few of the noisy ones who might be quieter after it. He did not believe that there were ever any physical ill-effects, but this is probably due to his doing only the more obvious laboratory investigations; Georgi has found cylindrical casts and albumen after the insulin treatment. He does not take quite the same precautions as Georgi does in regard to cardiazol, but on the other hand thinks it would be a little dangerous to combine the two treatments. He mentioned also that he had known a patient whose recurrent depression had been cut short by insulin, but who complained afterwards that the recovery was not so satisfactory as when it occurred without such treatment on previous occasions; he also finds that he gets better results with catatonic and paranoid forms of schizophrenia than with those in which psychogenic and reactive features are obvious. I found, however, that many of the cases which had done well with insulin in this hands, particularly the paranoid ones, were such as would be diagnosed as mainly benign depressive ones at the Maudsley, and, I think, at the Phipps or Boston Psychopathic. I could not find that he or anyone else had made an investigation into the effect of insulin on the duration of recurrent benign attacks, i.e. mainly manic-depressive forms. Müller had once tried the treatment on an old obsessional case which was almost schizophrenic but it did no good. This question of diagnosis and type of case benefited seems to me one of the central points of the whole matter, and then there is the question of what they mean by good results: often in Müller paranoid cases it was a recovery without insight, which is, after all, a dubious kind of recovery.

Müller is very honest about his cases though, of course, inclined towards enthusiasm, but I think that he is disposed to put undue emphasis on the single case, which proves little or nothing. He is very ready to concede the provisional nature of any conclusions reached. If the contention of most of the insulin therapists as to its efficacy in early cases comes to be accepted, then people may come to have much the same attitude towards schizophrenia as towards cancer, namely that it needs to be diagnosed early and treated drastically, and even then the results are rather unsatisfactory. Obviously, at present, no one can tell whether the apparent good effects last. One interesting thing about this wave of interest in the physical mode of attack on schizophrenia, by insulin or cardiazol, is that psychotherapeutically-minded people, like Müller, Kronfeld and young Forel, take up the method enthusiastically. It is interesting that Müller, who identified himself a few years ago with psychotherapy in schizophrenia, does not do any psychotherapy on his insulin cases after the treatment.

Müller seems to have organised a sort of little training course in insulin treatment, and gives some certificate to those who have worked with him for three months or more. He is certainly very careful in some directions; for example, he takes electro-cardiograms on every case; this, no doubt, follows on the work which he did in conjunction with Hadorn on the subject. Using such precautions he thinks the dangers of the insulin treatment have been exaggerated, but from what I have seen elsewhere, I doubt this; at any rate for the average psychiatric clinic or hospital. There are, of course, a lot of other points with regard to insulin which strike one, not only at Münsingen by also in Vienna, and in many other psychiatric clinics I visited, but they resolve themselves, apart from technique, into questions of standard of accuracy in diagnosis and reliability of statements about recovery. Nearly everyone who has used it agreed that some cases will benefit by it which they would not have expected to be benefited by anything; that it is not a panacea; that it is no good for chronic cases; that no one can say how long the good effects will last, and that animal experiments suggests the possibility of cerebral damage (which would, however, be a small price to pay if in fact it arrested for good a progressive schizophrenia). The research possibilities which it opens are very many and seem to be pursued fairly widely at one or other clinic – Georgi on the bio-chemical and permeability side, Angyal on the motility side (in Budapest), etc. It looks to me as though in the long run the chief merits of the treatment would lie (a) in the research opportunities for studying bodily reactions in schizophrenia, and (b) in the fillip it has given to the therapy of schizophrenia on the physical side.

At Münsingen I met also Rittmeister and some of the other assistants. Rittmeister was formerly a pupil of Minkowski in Zürich and is now carrying out an investigation on finger tip patterns in schizophrenics (which Katzenstein suggested to him).

It seems that a fair number of German schizophrenics come for treatment into Switzerland to evade sterilisation. I was told that although the diagnosis in the case of German patients referred to Münsingen may, in Germany, have been given as something that does not call for sterilisation under German law, nevertheless, when the patient returns to Germany, sterilisation will probably be carried out whether the patient has recovered or not, the diagnosis of schizophrenia being either inferred from the fact that he has been at Münsingen or from the history given by his employers, etc., in Germany.

Zürich

In Zürich I spent some time with Hans Maier and was much impressed by his quiet and competent way of examining patients, and by the extraordinary amount of work he gets done both personally and in the clinic as a whole. It was the first European clinic I came across where records were kept fully, more or less in the manner customary in the United States and England; the contributions from the social agencies to the history were remarkably full. The chief thing that impressed me about Burghölzli[13]

---

[13] The Burghölzli – the Psychiatric University Hospital in Zürich – was founded in 1875, with Bernard von Gudden as its first director. Other directors included Julius Eduard Hitzig, Auguste Forel, Eugen Bleuler, Hans Wolfgang Maier and Manfred Bleuler. Karl Abraham, Franz Alexander, Ernest Jones, Carl Jung, and A A Brill were among those who spent portions of their careers at the Burghölzli.

was the way the clinic was organised on social lines, research taking a second place. Alcoholism is, of course, still one of the most important psychiatric problems for them, but court cases, where women referred for a recommendation as to whether an abortion is appropriate or not, and other such issues, take up a great deal of their time as well. As far as alcoholism is concerned, it is interesting that they will not take cases on for a cure in a Heim for anything less than a year.

The organization of the policlinic, which I also visited, was explained to me by Glaus, the senior Oberarzt at Burghölzli, he sees special cases but the test of the work is done by three assistants; they do not reckon to treat the cases psychotherapeutically, but there are a few people who come regularly for "control" – mostly drunkards, I gathered. If a case needs psychotherapy they refer it to some trained therapist in private practice, of whom there are so many in Zürich that their charges are relatively small and the insurance may pay for it. The bulk of the cases at the policlinic were would-be abortions referred by private doctors, by gynaecologists in private practice, or by the gynaecological department of the university hospital for an opinion; a few of the cases come spontaneously. It is expected that in the projected legal code for Switzerland there will be a paragraph on the practice of abortion, which at present varies from canton to canton. In Zürich the psychiatrists are more generous in their interpretation of what justifies therapeutic abortion than in England, for example, though in principle the difference is not great. I was surprised that they were not overwhelmed with applications, but this apparently is avoided because the patients do not regard the psychiatric clinic as either the first or last point in the arrangement, but only as an accessory intermediate step between their private doctor or the gynaecological clinic at the beginning, and the gynaecological clinic at the end. There are a lot of other details in regard to the carrying out of the procedure and concurrent sterilisation which were interesting as bearing on the developments in other countries. It is interesting also that as a routine contraceptive they now recommend the Knaus-Ogino safe period. I gathered that nearly all the time of the doctors is taken up with examining these cases in the afternoon, and writing reports on them in the morning, so that the Policlinic and the doctors in it see little of the actual psychiatric material such as one would see at the Maudsley Outpatient Department, for example, and the policlinic does not feed the hospital itself. The whole situation seems bound up with the "psychiatrization" of Zürich by Forel, Bleuler, Jung, etc. so that there is a plethora of trained psychiatrists and psychotherapists; partly also it is due to an increased demand for social services from the doctors of the clinic which leaves them little time for OP work of the general kind. The bulk of the doctors exercise in a large measure the functions of the German Amtsarzt.[14] Another aspect of the "psychiatrization" is that doctors cannot practise as psychotherapists unless they have an adequate training in psychiatry; consequently, apart from pastors and lay therapists, there does not arise the situation that exists, for example, in London, viz, psychotherapists without any psychiatric background. The situation is somewhat like that in Holland, though of course more highly developed.

Owing to the thoroughness with which the social responsibilities of the psychiatrist are undertaken by the clinic and the methodical way in which patients are examined from many points of view, and records made, there is little time left over for

---

[14] Public health officer.

independent research. They have been studying continuous narcosis, as formerly; also Huntington's chorea,[15] Rorschach's test,[16] and the effects of castration. The laboratory research is chiefly looked after by Wespi, who did not have anything particularly interesting to show or tell about; the laboratories seemed little used except for routine investigations for which they are well equipped, and which seem to be done thoroughly on all the patients. Hans Maier told me of an unusual investigation he was doing on the irradiation of the liver in schizophrenia; they are also working on alcohol.

Besides the clinic itself, I saw the separate house for children, similar to the one I had seen at Klaesi's hospital in Waldau; Lutz, who also runs a children's policlinic in the town, is studying juvenile schizophrenia. In the most acute wards of the hospital I was surprised, as in other Swiss clinics, to see that mechanical restraint is still used not infrequently.

Binswanger, the other Oberarzt (a half brother of Binswanger of Creuzlingen) who is leaving shortly, I believe, explained the family care arrangements which are in his charge. He goes out and inspects at least once a year every farm where they have a patient, which is a difficult task because the farms are scattered over a wide area. As in Gheel and elsewhere it is mainly a peasant population that takes the patients. The cases are selected, and include a large number of defectives; there are of course also schizophrenics, in accordance with Bleuler's views on the advisability of early discharge from the mental hospital. The troubles they have, arising out of family aftercare, are accusations of exploited labour and a very infrequent case of suicide or arson; brutality or ill-treatment hardly occurs at all. The system works moderately well and is growing, but its applicability to other countries, and particularly to England, seems doubtful, perhaps because of the lack of a corresponding peasant population here. They do not as a rule put their alcoholic cases out in family care. Binswanger explained the various provisions, including an intermediate home to which they send difficult cases. They lack adequately trained social helpers in the Inspektorat, which is an important defect. Their social workers have been trained in a general way, not specifically for psychiatry.

At Minkowski's brain institute and neurology clinic I saw Minkowski and Katzenstein. Katzenstein is much under the influence of Monakow's doctrines as one would expect, but singularly fertile in out-of-the-way ideas for investigations, for example, crystallo-graphic studies in the CSF. He seems much more active minded than Minkowski. They are working on the minute cerebral changes after head injury; their specimens, showing rapid infiltration of the cortex by proliferating strands from the

---

[15] A rare disease of the central nervous system characterised by progressive dementia with grimacing, gesticulation, ataxic movements, finger twitching, speech disorders and other involuntary movements. It was named after George Sumner Huntington (1850–1916).

[16] Hermann Rorschach (1884–1922) studied psychiatry at the Burghölzli university clinic under Forel, Bleuler and Jung; he graduated in medicine in 1909 and took a position in the psychiatric hospital in Münsterlingen. He became interested in Jung's word association tests, as well as in psychoanalysis and reflexive hallucinations. In 1913 he went to the Waldau psychiatric clinic near Bern; and in 1915 was made associate director of the Herisau asylum in eastern Switzerland, where he stayed until his premature death. In 1918 he had resumed his previous experiments with inkblots as a means of accessing associations, and published his work in 1921, in *Psychodiagnostik*. After Rorschach's sudden death, Hans Huber published the book anew and the work received increasing attention. An institute was founded in Rorschach's name in New York in 1939.

pia, the collapse of blood vessels, presumably through shock to their innervation, and cellular changes in this perivascular territory, were very interesting. Katzenstein has also been looking at the furrow across the palm usually found in mongoloid idiots, and is inclined to think that whenever this is present in a normal person one will find in other members of his family epicanthus and other mongoloid features, and that if a mongoloid idiot has not got the furrow other members of his family will have it. It is a new and surprising observation.

He is also studying camptodactyly and related digital anomalies which he says he has never found except in families with an accumulation of mental degenerative features; I don't believe this can be right. In collaboration with Rittmeister at Münsingen he has been testing Poll's opinion that there are average finger tip formulae for each sex; Rittmeister thinks that the majority of schizophrenics have formulae of the feminine type; this also sounds improbable. Katzenstein has been studying the heredity of some rare neurological conditions, but like Hans Maier doesn't seem to know some of the literature on these matters, e.g. Julia Bell, Sjögren. He doesn't seem to be going on with his earlier studies on the effect of extirpating parts of embryos. He is also interested in the spontaneous drawings of patients, of which he has an interesting collection. (It is surprising in how few psychiatric clinics I found any interest in the spontaneous products – artistic or otherwise – of the patients.) Minkowski is rather taken up now with clinical neurology, so that he has very little time, he told me, for detailed researches, like his famous earlier ones on the movements of the foetus. He has, however, recently done his investigations of the olive in epilepsy, and is working with Katzenstein on brain injury. He is also examining methodically Monakow's brain.

In W R Hess's Institute, I found Jung from Freiburg, who was just finishing his studies there; it seemed a good thing that someone should apply strict histological study to Hess's work. Hess will not use any anatomical distinction or criterion for his notions of "vegetative" and "animal", so that the lack of precision in these terms, which is not noticeable so much if only functions, hierarchies and purposes are under consideration, becomes evident if one tries to get Hess to correlate his ideas with what can actually be observed in the central nervous system. He would like to apply his point of view to psychiatry, but in its present stage it looks as though it would merely add another to the various psycho-biologies already existing. I put some psychiatric problems in connection with sleep to him but he could not offer suggestions as to how to tackle them, though he could offer interpretations in terms of his functional views. His explanations of psychiatric problems were all plus and minus explanations, which is the usual functional way of looking at psychiatry, but conceivably a bad way. Hess's method is, of course, far from being exhausted; he is carrying on interesting further investigations himself, and it is being applied elsewhere in Zürich by Krayenbuhl, and in other countries. Hess seems to ignore unduly the endocrine influences. I also saw in Zürich von Wyss who keeps up with the literature but doesn't seem to do much original work.

With Oberholzer I had an interesting talk about the position of the psychoanalysts in Switzerland. Although Oberholzer is a Freudian, he and his group are not members of the International Psychoanalytic Society. This is partly an outcome of the fact that nearly all these Swiss psychoanalysts have necessarily to have a psychiatric training which seems to have interfered with their full acceptance of the Freudian doctrine. Of its development in England, as influenced by Melanie Klein, he, like all the analysts I met abroad, was distrustful, if not derisive. Oberholzer and the group with him use all psychotherapeutic methods – hypnosis etc. – and he expressed what seemed to me sensible views about the suitability of psychoanalysis for psychiatry, and its possibilities. On the organization of an out-patient service he had views essentially the same as those held, for example, at the Maudsley. Oberholzer is also very interested in the Rorschach test; he knew Rorschach well. He considers that this interest has prevented him from getting one-sided and being only psychoanalytical in his outlook instead of having a broad psychiatric viewpoint; in short, he acknowledges the perils of a private practice in psychotherapy. Rather surprisingly he did not know the work of Vernon, Beck or other English and American writers on the Rorschach method. Indeed apart from the physiologists there were few people I met in any country who were as well acquainted with English and American work as they were with German. Knowledge of French literature was very variable, and on the whole poor except of course in France and Belgium.

Krayenbühl, the neuro-surgeon, (his brother does the pathological work for Hans Maier, and runs a private hospital), is keen on studying the psychological effects of frontal lesions, but as he himself knows, he does not grasp the psychiatric intricacies of the matter, e.g. release of preformed tendencies, etc. More interesting is his proposed investigation (using Hess's method on the exposed brain) into the depth at which one must stimulate to get a motor or other response, especially in the frontal region. He is keen on using Hess's method still further, but has to go cautiously.

It is surprising how little cooperation there is among the various very good people working on or around the CNS in Zürich. It is also surprising, in eastern Switzerland particularly, to find how little influence Bleuler's psychopathological approach to psychiatry has had. It is true that notes are kept more fully here than in other European clinics and approximate to English and American standards of detail, and that the teaching is thorough and sound, but apart from the analysts, psychopathology is not studied. Jung has very little influence on or contact with the medical circles now; I gathered that he would like to, but only on conditions which are unacceptable.

Basle

In Basle I visited Verzar's Institute. The work there on the relationship between adrenal cortical activity, vitamin B_2 and B_6 and reabsorption seemed applicable to some of the nutritional problems of psychiatry, also to fatigue. Their attempts to apply their findings to clinical problems seemed somewhat unorganised. Laszt, Verzar's assistant, did not strike me as particularly intelligent, though he is apparently industrious and expert in animal operations; perhaps he is so preoccupied with individual investigations that he cannot see their general purport. Verzar's work on fat and carbohydrate metabolism has led to a linkage with general medicine – coeliac disease, Gaucher's Niemann-Pick[17] disease, though not so far with the psychiatric clinic. I also learned

---

[17] This was named after Albert Niemann, a German paediatrician (1880–1921) and Ludwig Pick (1868–1944) a German pathologist. It is a disturbance of sphingolipid metabolism characterized by enlargement of liver and spleen, anaemia, cherry red spot of the macula with progressive blindness, lymphadenopathy, and progressive mental and physical deterioration.

of their work on compensatory increase in the lung when aeration is inadequate, as in asthma, and also on the metabolism of parts of the body, e.g. different perfused muscles, and their diminution in size with various poisons.

In the psychiatric clinic, unfortunately Staehelin was away, but young Manfred Bleuler took me round. There, too, there was a quite extraordinary ignorance of any but German literature, in spite of young Bleuler's having spent a year in the United States. They have done a fair amount of genetic work (Brugger's etc.) influenced by Rüdin (probably because of his formerly having had a chair there). They seem to hanker after compulsory sterilisation; the ostensible basis for it seems to be the prevalence of deficiency, but young Bleuler admitted that there were no statistics on which to base their views, and that it was rather a matter of principle. The clinic seemed well run and quite active, but a little behind the times, e.g. they are studying the use of Sodoku, and are thinking of introducing tryparsamide in the treatment of GPI. Anatomical and chemical researches are not bothered about much, though Staehelin's interests are chiefly on the pathological side.

Also in Basle I saw Demole at the Hoffman La Roche works,[18] and Professor Rotholin at Sandoz.[19] Demole seems to have got quite away from his former neurological and psychiatric clinical interests, and to have concentrated on vitamin problems.

ITALY[20]

Pavia

In Pavia I saw Margaria. He has only been there a few months, and has very little assistance and most of the routine work to do, e.g. 4 lectures a day on 3 days a week. His laboratory, which was built by his predecessor, Gayda, is on an unduly generous scale considering that Margaria has only two assistants. The pay is so small that it is clearly impossible for most people to undertake such work, for example, Margaria, as professor, gets the equivalent of £3.10–£4.00 per week and his assistants get half or three quarters of that until they themselves obtain a chair, say at the age of 45. Some of Margaria's work he can get his students to do. He is energetic and is starting a

---

[18] In 1896 Fritz Hoffman-La-Roche founded F Hoffman-La Roche as the successor company to Hoffman, Traub and Co. It became one of the largest and most successful pharmaceutical companies in Europe.

[19] Sandoz Ltd (now Novartis Ltd), in Basle, was set up as the Chemical Company Kern and Sandoz in 1886, by Dr Alfred Kern (1850–1893) and Edouard Sandoz (1853–1928).

[20] Several influential figures in the second half of the nineteenth century – Camillo Golgi, Augusto Tamburini, Eugenio Tanzi and Cesare Lombroso – put Italian psychiatry on the map. By the second decade of the twentieth century, psychiatric work was shared between a minority of public asylums, neuropsychiatric divisions of general hospitals and private asylums. Teaching, in university clinics, was dependent on the Ministry of National Education. Psychiatry, however, took a downhill turn after the work of the founding fathers; teaching tended to privilege neurology and the asylums went into decline, partly due to indifference amongst the administration as well as doctors, who preferred private work, and of course to the cultural isolation of fascist Italy. Although Italy did not instigate purges and repression to the same extent as the Soviet Union and Germany, and there was not a similar move to create a purely Italian/fascist science, certain textbooks by Jewish authors were proscribed (mostly after 1938), and in the fascist period racial laws accounted for significant losses of professors, particularly in the sciences, medicine and law. Of the 1,200-odd professors with chairs, 98 had to leave because they were Jewish – almost one in twelve (a higher number than that leaving due to voluntary emigration or forced resignation for political causes). (Edward R Tannenbaum, *Fascism in Italy: society and culture 1922–1945*, London, Allen Lane, 1973, p. 338.)

lot of studies, influenced by Meyerhoff, A V Hill, Bancroft and others – (metabolism of the red cells, pyruvic acid influence, and particularly lactic acid studies in work and fatigue). I had the impression that his lactic acid work is somewhat concerned with the present interest in sport physiology, of which Donaggio is the most extreme instance. (Like most of the other reputable people, he is contemptuous of much of Donaggio's work which has, however, received a great deal of official support.) In his study of carbohydrate metabolism he was applying the method used by Verzar (moniodoacetic acid).

I also saw Riquier, the professor of psychiatry in Pavia. He also has only been there a few months, having come from Padua to follow Rossi. Rossi had put all the emphasis on neurology, and was evidently a dominating figure in neuro-psychiatry in Italy. He had organised the clinic on research lines, but it does not look as though under Riquier this will be continued to any extent. Riquier is a much smaller person, and knows little of conditions outside Italy, He is very proud of the open wards which he had in Padua, and proposes to introduce them in Pavia. The Pavia Clinic, which is derived partly from private benefaction (a rare thing in Italy), is fairly well constructed. The women nurses are nuns here; the men have little training. They have a ward for encephalitics, as have most of the other university clinics that I saw; it is the outcome of the advocacy by their Queen of a Bulgarian quack remedy which she had heard of in her native Montenegro and which has turned out to contain belladonna. They are treating patients with insulin and proposing to take measurements of metabolism, blood pressure, etc., but without much realisation, apparently, of the snags in doing so; when Margaria, who was with me, pointed these out they seemed surprised. Riquier is anxious to develop neuro-surgery, and would like one of his men trained in it. He favours sending him to Olivecrona or Clois Vincent. He is anxious to link up surgery of the central nervous system with pathology and neurology and would probably provide good facilities when his man had been trained. The clinic is the admission hospital for the town, but can draw material from the local mental hospital or send cases there; there are about 60 psychiatric beds. As regards the teaching of the students, I learned in Pavia that De Vecchi, the former Secretary of Public Instruction, had ordered the Professors to teach clinical neurology and psychiatry in 25 set lectures, to be given to the students in two batches, i.e. twice over. This had made an unnecessary amount of work for the professors, and indeed Lugaro told me that when he received orders to teach by set lectures instead of by clinical demonstrations as he had always done, he ignored it because it was so impracticable. Margaria was spoken of elsewhere in Italy always with respect as a sort of white hope of Italian physiology, and it became clear from conversations that there are few promising men coming on; an academic career does not attract the more brilliant younger men because of its lack of rewards, and such of them as go in for it tend to be diverted into more or less practical applications, e.g. sport physiology, aviation physiology, psychotechnics. The older men of established reputation, like Giuseppe Levi and Lugaro, are tolerated but not encouraged; they get no financial support from the authorities, whereas the younger people or men like Pende often do.

Report

Milan

In Milan I found little to see. I visited Gemelli's laboratory in the Catholic University, but it is notorious that he does hardly any actual work himself there, is almost entirely occupied in his semi-political activities as Rector of that University, and in planning a similar university in Rome, where I believe he is President of the new Pontifical Academy. Gemelli still publishes interesting psychological studies but it is generally said that all he contributes to them is either the original idea or the review of the literature; he reads enormously. The actual work is done by Padre Galli and Dr Pastore. He has also had with him people working on electro-physiology, e.g. Rohracher and on animal psychology, but phonetics is his chief subject. He writes excellent orientating reviews also e.g. in *Scientia*. The laboratory is extravagantly equipped with instruments, but it looked as though there was no one there particularly trained to use them intelligently.

In Milan I also called on Prof. Medea who is mainly a neurologist, but is President of the Italian Mental Hygiene Society. They have a good school for abnormal children in Milan, but they have so much leeway to make up in these matters, that what is particularly good there, would not be so in more advanced countries. Medea is not the full professor; the man who holds the official chair, Besta, has no beds, and is not interested in psychiatry particularly, I was told that neuro-surgery under Clivio had been the main interest of the clinic latterly.

Turin

In Turin I saw Levi and his assistant Jablonsky (from Albert Fischer's laboratory in Berlin) and Fräulein Mayer. Levi has to work under some unsatisfactory conditions, but is carrying on his cytological studies very thoroughly. He has neuro-fibril cultures that have been alive for 14 months, and which show the anastomosing of the network that forms, so that the strict theory of neurones can scarcely be sustained. The possible clinical application of what he is doing seemed to lie in his study of the resistance of neuro-fibrils in artificial conditions: and one of his assistants is studying the ageing process in peripheral nerves, which might have a bearing on senile psychosis. Levi is also investigating the rate of growth of the new (or rather the regenerating) fibrils. Levi reads enormously, and is *au courant* of almost everything physiological and neurological.

I also saw Herlitzka. He said that he had been diverted into the physiology of aviation and submarines after the war, and could not get away from this field, though he would prefer to be doing electro-physiology. Whether because of his annoyance over sanctions (about which he feels strongly), or for other reasons, he said nothing about the research he does. He talked, however, about other people – Donaggio, Pighini and Pende (all of whom are well-in politically, but are regarded as scientifically negligible).

Lugaro, whom I also saw, is no longer so active, but is still one of the few really well-informed psychiatrists in the country. Everyone speaks of him respectfully, and from his writings it seems likely that if he had published in some more widely diffused language than Italian he would have had a considerable European reputation. He had anticipated Kappers in regard to neurobiotaxis, and Bleuler in regard to dissociation phenomena in schizophrenia. The width of his interests and his detailed work make one feel that he is an outstanding figure, but conditions have become unfavourable to him, and he is no longer productive, though still, I should think, capable of it in better circumstances.

In Turin I asked particularly about any people doing psychiatric criminology and genetics; the connection with Lombroso occurred to me, but neither here nor elsewhere in Italy is there any satisfactory research in this field, so far as I could discover. There is a woman, Gian Ferrera, carrying out twin-studies rather incompletely along the usual lines, but I could not discover any of the current work on forensic psychiatry or constitution which, for example, Kinberg so praises. I asked after di Tullio, who has written a textbook, but they said he was not connected with psychiatry in any way. Pende, of course is keen on constitution studies, but without any bearing on psychiatric or neurological problems.

It is of interest that Lugaro is almost alone in holding the view that the chairs of neurology and psychiatry in Italy should be separate, instead of as at present combined. Certainly as Lugaro pointed out, the effect has hitherto been a neglect of psychiatry. Insulin at the moment is resulting in a slight revival of psychiatric interest, but not a very intelligent one; for example, Cerletti treats schizophrenics in this way, but his methods and opinions struck me as ignorant. The poor state of affairs in psychiatry seems to be partly due to the fact that all the clinical professors do private practice and are dependent on it chiefly for their income. This, with all the teaching they have to do, leaves little time for such detailed work as psychiatric research actually demands. Then, of course, there is the political aspect. Moreover, all the professors are dependent for their clinical material on a smallish admission hospital, largely devoted to neurological beds; their contact with the mental hospital is a permissive one, since they have neither administrative control nor any privileged position, apart from the right to borrow cases for teaching.

Genoa

In Genoa I was able to see a large mental hospital. I was taken round by Rieti, one of the doctors who had been trained in French psychiatry a little and also in psychoanalysis: (there are very few psychoanalysts in Italy and they exert no influence). The superintendent of this hospital, Alberti, has the title of professor because he has passed the appropriate examinations, but he has really no university position. He had a political pull, at any rate, to the extent of getting a great deal of money from the authorities of the Province for his hospital (his brother is a Senator). He obtained roughly £200,000, I was told, to build his new admission hospital, and managed to spend all they gave him and more, but the upkeep has proved so expensive that the authorities have regretted their generosity. The money has actually been spent extravagantly on a hospital for 400 patients containing every conceivable apparatus, many of the most expensive ones never having been used, nor likely to be, it seemed, (great X-ray apparatus, electro-cardiograph, diathermy, short waves and other electrical apparatuses for this form of treatment, which is so popular in Italy). The patients, however, in the wards are, many of them, senile and advanced chronic patients for whom the splendid surroundings are quite inappropriate and pointless. There is neither segregation, occupation, nor proper nursing as far as I could see. There were private wards but the patients in them seemed, from the way they were dressed etc., to belong to the poorer classes. Moreover, in the wards the sanitary and other arrangements were at a surprisingly primitive level from the point of view of privacy, etc., but Rieti and others clearly regarded it as the last word in modern mental hospital provision.

In the laboratories they have a physiologist and histologist, Massazza, in charge who has various doctors doing histological and pathological studies under his direction, but I did not hear of anything of importance. The "libero docente" degree which entitles one to be professor and so is valuable in private practice, has hitherto been fairly easy to obtain if one had published a number of papers and could pass the necessary examination; hence everybody feels that it is important to publish research papers, but the standard attained is low, (while I was in Italy the regulations for obtaining the "libero docente" were tightened up by an administrative decree). From this probably springs the bulkiness of their periodical literature. At this Manicomio, for example, which I visited in Genoa, they publish independently the researches carried on by their own doctors, and a lot of other clinics and hospitals do likewise; there is no editorial sifting of all this stuff, except what is submitted to the two or three journals which have standing. Certainly a great deal of work published has been badly done, without personal competence or competent direction by others; it is sometimes the experimental animals that have to suffer most, in futile and amateurish experiments.

As far as the clinical work in this mental hospital was concerned, I was surprised in looking a their books to see what an exceptionally high proportion of GPI they have there, perhaps it is due to the fact that Wassermann is done as a routine and so is X-ray of the chest of every new patient, but I could not find any that they had made any particular use, so, far, of the data so obtained. Rieti does a psychological examination, which really amounts to a full mental status plus a Rorschach and perhaps a Rossolimo.[21] He is enthusiastic, but suffers from lack of training which he proposes to remedy by going to New York; he ought, however, to improve himself in straight clinical psychiatry before he goes in for research in clinical psychology, as he proposes.

In contrast to the absurdly grand admission hospital, was the other part, the old, much larger section of the Manicomio. The conditions under which the patients were looked after there were definitely out-of-date. It seemed to me that if they had spent their money on proper nursing, occupational therapy, rearrangement of the available buildings (built in 1860) so as to permit of proper grading of patients, etc., and on purchasing their apparatus and building their laboratories at a scale on which they were likely to be used, it would have been more to the point than building this admission block of which they are so proud. In keeping with their general outlook is the fact that here, as in many other Italian clinics, they have a keen nose for anything new. They

---

[21] Grigorii Ivanovich Rossolimo (1860–1928) became a lecturer in Alexis Yakovlievich Koshewnikov's neurological clinic in Moscow in 1889. He then became head of the department of neurological disease at the internal disease clinic run by Ostroumov. In 1911 he founded an institute for child psychology and neurology, and in 1917 a department for child psychoneurology at the State University in Moscow when he became professor of neuropathology there. He is most famous for the experimental psychological methods he devised. His name is associated with several of these methods and instruments; these include a brain topograph, a diadochokymograph, an orthokynometer, an orthostatometer, and a dermografometer.

had, for example, discussed the propriety of introducing Moniz's method of treatment by destroying tissue in the frontal lobes,[22] at the Psychiatric Congress in Naples the week before I was there. They try insulin and all these other advanced methods, while in fact their general care and use of well-established methods of treatment are lagging behind those of other countries. It is not mainly a question of money, seeing how much they lavish on building and equipment, though actually they apologise for their deficiencies on the ground of poverty. Mental hygiene has a real field in countries like Italy where the level of treatment of mental disorder, judged by modern standards, both in hospitals and by means of policlinics, is bad.

Medea, who is President of the Mental Hygiene Association in Italy, told me he had been preaching better provision, on the ground that it will diminish through early diagnosis and prophylactic treatment the number of people in mental hospitals; this seemed to me a much less sound basis than would be an insistence on the fact that extramural care would be possible for many cases, duration of illness would be, in some cases, shortened, and a much better and more decent standard of adaptation and care obtained for the chronic cases. I was told everywhere in Italy that this new admission block in Genoa is regarded as a model which the others hope to imitate. Many people gave me to understand that the majority of mental hospitals were over-filled and very backward.

In Italy, as in Russia, one had the impression that a good deal was sacrificed to outward show – fine buildings etc., and that the political pressure on scientific people to work on problems that had an immediate relevance to daily affairs had, in fact, resulted here and there in some unsatisfactory work on problems not suitable for attack by the rather precise methods familiar to the experts in question. In Italy I gathered that some of the physiologists regarded their applied studies of this sort as a sop, so to speak, whereby they obtained funds for their more customary researches; one man told me he had got the money for an animal house on the pretext that he was going to use the animals for research in the physiology of aeronautics.

Also in Genoa I saw de Lisi, who has the university chair. The clinic is here, as elsewhere, predominantly neurological in its material. The laboratories are extensive, but de Lisi deplores the fact that he cannot use his surgical theatre because he has no surgeon; he hopes that a former pupil of his in Cagliari, who has studied in Paris and in Baltimore, will fill the gap. As in some of the other clinics in North Italy, their neurology is influenced by Paris more than by Germany; as for English neurology and psychiatry their knowledge of it often seems to be summed up in Kinnier Wilson's disease[23] and Hughlings Jackson's name, more or less.

De Lisi is an accomplished man, probably a stimulating teacher, very vivacious and alert; he can read English very well but won't talk it. He seemed one of the few men in

---

[22] Egas Moniz (1874–1955) is often spoken of as the discoverer of cerebral angiography and prefrontal leucotomy. He became professor at Coimbra in 1902, transferring in 1911 to the new chair in neurology at Lisbon where he remained until his death. He also worked for a time as a physician in the Hospital of Santa Maria, Lisbon. He served as a deputy in the Portuguese parliament until 1917 when he became Portuguese ambassador to Spain. Later in 1917, he was appointed Minister for Foreign Affairs. Moniz was awarded the Nobel Prize in 1949, although John Fulton is often considered prefrontal leucotomy's true father.

[23] Samuel Alexander Kinnier Wilson (1878–1937), a British neurologist, described, in 1912, "progressive lenticular degeneration", a familial nervous disease associated with cirrhosis of the liver. It is also known as hepatolenticular degeneration.

Italy who was doing anything interesting in psychiatry; he has been working on motor constitution, in association with Pintus who was formerly with him in Cagliari. He is proud of his bound volumes of case records, representing improvements he made in record keeping when he came to Genoa: they seemed so average when one looked at them, though, that one could infer that previously the records had been deplorable, and indeed it seems that in all the clinics and mental hospitals the records are bad on the whole. He followed Cerletti in Genoa about a year ago. De Lisi has encouraged Rieti in his psychopathological enquiries and they are now writing an article together. I also learned in Genoa a little more about the Milan Clinic; Besta, the professor, had a clinic for soldiers who had had head injuries in the war (like Isserlin's one in Munich) and had as his assistant, Clivio, who now works independently as a neuro-surgeon, and is said to have good results.

I also in Genoa met a German lawyer, now practising in Italy, and asked him about forensic psychiatry in which he is interested, but it seemed to be a quite stagnant subject.

Rome

In Rome I visited Cerletti's clinic. After the death of Sante de Sanctis the combined chair was again broken up; Cerletti became professor of neurology and psychiatry, and Ponzo, a former pupil of Kiesow and associate of Gemelli, became professor of psychology. Cerletti has an adequate enough clinic from the structural point of view, but seemed very ashamed of it, and is apparently shortly going to have a much grander building. He is mainly a neurologist, but is concentrating somewhat on insulin treatment at the moment. He seems incapable of recognizing the clinical condition of his patients; for example, he showed me one young man as a "cure" following insulin treatment, who in fact revealed himself quite obviously as a dissembling paranoid schizophrenic and indeed, when I talked to him for a little time, he disclosed that he was still having hallucinations and delusions; Cerletti had accepted at face value his statement that he was now quite well and quite rid of his morbid disease. Similarly Cerletti said that he did not think that a woman in the ward was schizophrenic because she didn't satisfy Kraepelin's test obeying the command to stick out her tongue so that a pin could be stuck in it. However, Cerletti has working in his clinic a German refugee, Kalinowski, who has had a good psychiatric training, so that probably corrects the deficiency. They are also using cardiazol and observing the effects of this substance and insulin upon the behaviour and the cerebral structure of the dog. One dog to which they had been giving cardiazol and producing fits regularly, behaved as though it were now demented in consequence. The pathologist at the clinic showed me brains in which structural changes had occurred following insulin administration. The histopathology seems to be well done in Cerletti's clinic. He is said to be a good neurologist and to have had a good training in neuroanatomy. He talked of some interesting work he had done earlier on the effects of intoxication with morphine in cats etc., but he doesn't seem to have been pursuing anything of that sort of late years.

I went to Ponzo's laboratory but he was away and I was shown round by his associate Professor Banissoni, who is actually an Austrian from Trieste. It is clear that the greater part of their time is taken up in lecturing and teaching; all sorts of people have to be given semi-popular lectures. The research they do seems to be concerned mainly with psychotechnics, and did not strike me as very advanced, though Banissoni himself is very knowledgeable. Ponzo works in collaboration at times with Gemelli and the other people in Milan.

I also visited Pende's institute. I did not see him, but was taken round by one of the younger men, who showed me all the apparatus which is used for testing the school children and workmen who come there for examination of their constitution. A great deal of what I was shown struck me as eye-wash. In one laboratory I was shown a lot of apparatus for testing special senses: I asked my guide what purpose this served, and he said that it was essential for making typological examinations, but when I asked him how the tests were done, he hesitated and admitted he did not know. On several of the instruments in question, when we took them out, the rubber was quite perished so that they had obviously not been used for some time. My guide then admitted that they had discarded this particular set of investigations.

In the large laboratory where reactions are measured there was a great display of special apparatus for measuring various professional aptitudes, etc., but again it seemed designed for show rather than for any scientifically justified end. My informant said that there had been no exact statistical examination of any of the data collected, but showed me lots of charts, including some which correlated Pende's constitutional types with the particular occupations to which they were suited. It may be, of course, that my informant was ignorant, and so misled me as to the work done, but he assured me that he was actually in charge of the largest and most used of these laboratories for vocational testing, and what I heard in other places about Pende's work confirmed the impression I received here. He has, of course, wards in the same building but I could not discover that he did any special research on the patients in them. Altogether I had the impression that the work on constitution for vocational selection is badly done and is mostly for outward show. Bastianelli made a very different impression. He is extra-ordinarily well-read in the literature of neurology and physiology, but his main interest is, of course, in malaria. He usually has a small number of beds occupied by patients with GPI whom he uses for his experiments with malaria. He mentioned several interesting observations which do not seem to have percolated into the literature of GPI therapy – largely, I suppose, because they have been published in malaria journals. He has, of course, no official university status, and judges fairly severely the value of a great deal that is done by the professors in Rome. His own institute seems to range further than malaria studies alone; for example, one of his men is doing interesting wok on electrocardiographic responses. His brother, I gathered, is doing a good deal of cerebral surgery in Rome.

I tried to see Modena, who, I was told by Kalinowski and others, was the man entrusted with the statistics of mental disorder throughout Italy. Although they are so proud of their statistical work generally in Italy, so far as psychiatry is concerned it seemed to be negligible. Modena, however, works at Ancona and is only occasionally in Rome, and I did not manage to see him. I have heard since from Kalinowski that Modena is conscious of how much there is to do and wants to start on it.

Report

Naples

In Naples I visited the biological station, and Dohrn told me of the various researches going on. At the moment, however, the only thing that has any bearing at all on the central nervous system was a study on tissue respiration; they were using the customary Warburg method. Fragnito's psychiatric clinic in Naples did not seem of any consequence.

Florence

In Florence I went to Zalla's clinic and was shown round by his "Aiuto", Roberti, a disciple of Lugaro, who is hoping to get a chair of his own within the next few months in the South of Italy. The university clinic is situated almost in the same grounds as the mental hospital and there seems to be a closer liaison between the two than in any of the other places I visited in Italy. Roberti, who is a lively, active-minded person, is pursuing some researches into hallucinations and the influence of "vegetative" drugs like physostigmine upon them. He talks quite intelligently about the matter until one questions him closely on any issue, and then – as in the rest of his conversation – one discovers that he is profuse and superficial, though undoubtedly with a widely-ranging mind. As so often in Italy, when I asked if they had such and such a department or did such and such research, I was given an affirmative answer which more detailed questioning showed to be unfounded; for example, Roberti talked about "insane art" and when I asked about any collection, said, "Oh yes, there is a good one", but when I asked to see it, it turned out to consist of one bad specimen done by a mental defective. His tongue runs away with him; when I asked him if he had seen any cases of peduncular hallucinations he said he had seen lots; which struck me as improbable. Roberti said that the nursing was done by peasants who had little or no training, though they were, in his opinion, none the worse for this; elsewhere I had been told that the nurses had training; presumably there are local differences. I was taken across to the mental hospital and met the superintendent, Simonelli, whose training had not been in psychiatry but in biochemistry. He seemed, however, no longer to have much interest in the latter subject nor any particular competence in the former, though perhaps he is a good administrator. (He had had to make a choice between turning into a mental hospital superintendent or remaining an "Aiuto" – he decided for the administrative job.) He was dull and loquacious; when I asked him about any biochemical researches on patients he was very vague and branched off into a discussion of Donaggio's work. There is no organised occupational therapy and the patients are left apparently a good deal to themselves.

Padua

In Padua I saw Terni. He is very active and has been particularly occupied with the preganglionic fibres of the sympathetic and their relationship to the intermediolateral tract of the cord and the white rami communicantes. He doesn't seem now to be so occupied with his anatomical work, e.g. the abducens accessory nucleus, though he writes critical general reviews, for example, of the relation of the vegetative nervous system to the endocrines and of the theory of surgery of the sympathetic. In his cytological work he is using ultra-violet rays mostly for damaging the cells, and his laboratory seems to be well equipped.

He has also modified Policard's method of micro-incineration; instead of incinerating he gradually increases the temperature to 400° using a specially constructed microscope; as the temperature rises the colour changes, the fats etc., alter, so that he can detect proteins and fats, where Policard is concerned only with minerals. He is looking round for expert chemists for this work, he told me. One of his associates has been doing very patient work counting the number of fibres in cross section of nerves; he finds that the number of fibres is diminished in old age. Terni is obviously one of the most energetic people at the medical faculty and keen on furthering psychiatry and psychology as much as he can. He is collaborating with the physicist in Padua, Rossi, to see if there is anything in the influence of cosmic rays on cells, I gathered.

Terni arranged for me to meet Berlucchi, who was recently appointed Professor of Neurology and Psychiatry. Berlucchi has obviously been diligent, especially in neurological research, but seemed to have no independent ideas at all. He is, however, diffident and has no command of foreign languages so one can hardly compare him with a confident, voluble person like Roberti. Terni has a good opinion of Berlucchi and thinks he will do good work. His inaugural address reviewing morbid psychomotor phenomena had been stimulating. He does his best to obtain familiarity with foreign literature, but has some surprising gaps. He is more interested, he said, in psychiatry than in neurology, but in the past seems to have worked on the latter mostly, and he has now only about 10 psychiatric beds – (Riquier's former clinic, quite divorced form the mental hospital and not a pure admission unit). He had spent a short time with Gerstmann in Vienna. I gathered that they had hoped to get de Lisi in Padua and that Berlucchi is a second best. He doesn't seem to have any ideas for research in psychiatry at the moment. I also met Truffi, the Dean of the Faulty who, is, of course, mainly a syphilologist.

Terni also arranged for me to see Musatti who is at first a little unprepossessing, but is actually enthusiastic and intelligent and doesn't, like so many others in Italy, give a quick reply which he cannot support if questioned further. Musatti is a pupil of Benussi's and follows in his footsteps. In the "concours" for the chair in Rome he was one of the three candidates finally selected, but Ponzo got it because Gemelli and de Sanctis supported him; the third candidate is now in Ferrara and is a painstaking, dull man. Musatti is, from his training, interested in Gestalt and in perception of movement. He mentioned the work he had done on the efficacy of even minimal convergence or divergence on perception of depth and apparent movement; it linked up with the Frankfurt work on the divergence of hands as influenced by colour and some of Rademaker's work and Cerletti's studies on the movements of the eye muscles in cats in whom sight had been extinguished from the beginning. His investigations are not at any point in touch with clinical material, though he is a psychoanalyst and treats patients. Although he has never had a personal analysis he is accepted by the Italian Psychoanalytic Society, and is one of the judges who decide who shall be admitted to it: it is surprising how in each country the analysts cut their coat according to their cloth. Musatti has no established position, he teaches philosophy and history at the Lyceo to earn his living, and has a little apparatus in his rooms.

He told me that neither Benussi's chair nor Kiesow's had been filled: Gemelli is now mainly a politician: Galli is a man without ideas: Ponzo is busy with his applied work and teaching, as is also Bannisoni who also runs a general medical practice – so psychology is not much cultivated in Italy at present. The philosophers are opposed to it because of the prevalence of Croce's ideas and the trend towards idealism and against anything materialist or positivist.[24] Educational psychology has similarly been displaced by semi-mystical and empirical methods of approach. So little contact has there been between the psychiatrists and the psychologists in Padua that, as Terni told me, Riquier did not even know of the existence of Musatti. So far there has not been contact between Berlucchi and Musatti, though probably Terni will be able to effect it. If Musatti were given the chance he would probably do good psychological work, I should think. It is surprising how neglected subjects like animal psychology are (though Gemelli has just written a review on it in *Scientia*). Psychopathology, genetics and social anthropology also seem to be neglected in Italy. It is also noteworthy that the difficulties they have in travelling have led to their being ignorant of much that goes on elsewhere; even Terni did not seem to know some of the things that are going on (though Giuseppe Levi from his reading was very well informed); Musatti had never heard of any mescalin studies.

In various places it was suggested to me that Reggio Emilia might be worth a visit, but actually it seemed hardly necessary to go there. It is still one of the biggest of the mental hospitals and one of the few where research is tackled on a large scale; the influence of Tanzi and Morselli is responsible for this (just as in Florence Tamburini or Mingazzini is responsible): but Pighini, who is the chief person there, is not regarded as in the least reliable by any of the people I met. Buscaino in South Italy is better spoken of, but more for his wide reading and remarkable memory than for the value of his researches, (which are mainly chemical, of course): this confirms the opinion one forms from reading his publications.

HUNGARY[25]

Szeged

In Szeged I saw Miskolczy. His psychiatric clinic, separate from his neurological one, is an old dilapidated building, but he has done his best with it, and in some respects

---

[24] Benedetto Croce (1866–1952) was an influential historian, philosopher, and senator. Although he never held a university position, he published widely (on Hegel, Marx, Goethe, history, poetry, and art), elaborating an idealism influenced by Hegel. He was Minister of Public Instruction from 1920 to 1921, and during the Fascist era was one of its major opponents. After the war, he was a minister in the new democratic government, and from 1943 to 1947 was president of the reconstituted Liberal Party; he retired from politics in 1947 and established the Institute for Historical Studies in Naples.

[25] Psychiatry took off in Hungary in the second half of the nineteenth century. The National Asylum was created in 1868 in Budapest and, towards the end of the century, treatment improved and legal changes were effected. Between 1900 and 1916 the number of people treated in asylums or hospital services tripled, with treatment ranging from baths and diets to bromides and opiates, with psychotherapy available in private institutions. After the First World War progress slowed, however, despite the inauguration of some new psychiatric services attached to public hospitals, mostly in provincial towns. Gyula Nyiro and Fabinyi, in the 1930s, enabled the extension of psychiatric care to neurotics, as well as the first ambulatory care centre. Insulin and electroshock were increasingly used for the major psychiatric illnesses; and in psychotherapy, hypnosis, psychoanalysis and individual psychology were dominant. Sándor Ferenczi (1873–1933) had

even (for example in the use of isolation) it seemed better than more pretentious clinics. Miskolczy struck me as sensitive, and justifiably proud of what he had accomplished there. He is determined to push on with his research, though handicapped financially. The neurological clinic is, of course, in much better condition than the psychiatric one, and there he has reasonable facilities for histological research and routine biochemical investigations. He has collected special cases systematically and so has an unusual number of brains of Pick's disease, etc., for the studies on the heredo-degenerative conditions which he has published in the monograph with Schaffer. He is Dean of the Faculty this year, which rather hampers his work; moreover, one of his men is away in America and another in one of the other medical departments in Szeged. He has, however, with him at present an assistant called Benedek who seems keen.

Miskolczy is about to make detailed studies of the brain in GOI [*sic*, presumably GPI], going further afield than previous investigators, who concentrated on the cortex; he has some interesting ideas in connection with this, bearing on the cause of remissions. He is also getting the cooperation of chemists in studying neurofibrils; one of his men, who is spending two years working with Szent-Gyorgyi, will soon be returning to him to cooperate in this. Also, when his colleague, who is now with Percival Bailey, returns, the neurosurgery will get under way. He impressed me as thorough and critical, and with original ideas on the structural basis of psychoses; his research has the advantage of collaboration with Szent-Gyorgyi, Raczyska, Jantschow, (the spirochaete man), and others at Szeged. Apart from his own qualities, he seemed to illustrate the advantages of working in a small university city where all the university professors know each other and may, if they are on good terms, collaborate with great profit, in contrast to a big city, where people in different fields seldom meet. Among the side lines with which Miskolczy is occupied are: the effects of various substances, such as adrenalin and other hormones and physostigmine, on the cells of the central nervous system; some work in comparative pathology in regard to a familial recessive disease of the central nervous system of fowls, probably cerebellar; the relation of the shape of neurons to their functions, e.g. Purkinje and pyramidal cells; the effect of Szent-Gyorgyi's new vitamin P on patients who bruise easily ("insane" ear, ecchymoses, etc.). As regards his views on schizophrenia, he is very well aware of the possible objections, but he refuses to follow the speculative lines which some of his critics prefer. Certainly what he reports can be taken as reliable.

He took me round to Szent-Gyorgyi's laboratory, where I heard of something of the recent work on the treatment of diabetic ketosis with succinic acid, the vitamin P, and his more fundamental work on the chemical processes which are the essential sources of energy (the work similar to Keilin's). He professes to dislike the clinical application of his work; yet it seems to occur fairly promptly, anyhow.

Raczyska [Racesyska], in the Medical Clinic, told me of his interesting work on the use of histamine (by gradually working up the dose) to prevent surgical shock, and his blood pressure work.

---

been the main figure behind the National Psychoanalytic Association in 1913, becoming professor of psychoanalysis at Budapest University in 1919 and effectively the head of a Budapest psychoanalytic movement which saw Hermann and Michael Balint amongst its members. The Second World War put an end to these developments, with Balint, Sandor Rado, Rapoport and Franz Alexander pursuing their careers elsewhere.

Report

Budapest

In Budapest I visited Bela Johan's Institute. He explained to me how public hygiene has been developed under his direction. He is not at the moment particularly interested in mental hygiene, but is pulling up the standard of the work in mental hospitals by exercising his power of selecting the doctors for them. There can be no doubt, judging from recent appointments, that good people like Meduna are now getting a chance, but Johan's power in this respect cannot really be complete because at the mental hospital, although the superintendent has not been there long, the place is badly run, and I was told that he is a lazy, incompetent person, who obtained his appointment only because of some family influence. I get the impression that Johan considers that the mental hospitals must be pulled up before social services and policlinics for mental disorder should be taken in hand; the state of the mental hospitals suggested that this is the desirable point of view. There is a great contrast between the excellence of the public health organisation and the model institute of hygiene on the one hand, and the mental hospitals on the other. I suppose when Johan decides to concentrate on the mental health field that, too, will become a very good service. He is so thorough and has been obviously so successful in organizing the rest of medicine.

I saw Meduna several times. He is ambitious, hard working and conscientious. He has a good book knowledge of psychiatry and some practical experience, of course, but as he has never been out of Hungary to study, his knowledge of practical arrangements and day-to-day clinical work is disproportionate to his abilities. He works in close association with Nyiro whom I also met; Nyiro is responsible for a well-run Sanatorium in the grounds of the hospital where patients are treated on a voluntary basis. Meduna is enterprising, as of course cardiazol shows, and has done good, if humdrum, pathological work under Schaffer. His material prospects at the moment are not particularly good. He is aware that cardiazol is not the beginning and end of schizophrenia, and would like to organise a wider scheme of research into the whole problem; it seems unlikely that he could alone direct efficient research, but he would certainly supply on the clinical side good cooperation and probably ideas too. As regards the cardiazol, he makes no extravagant claims for it, but clearly in his heart of heart has high hopes. There can be no doubt that some patients in whom the prognosis has seemed poor do well with cardiazol. He has the common weakness of calling every anergic patient catatonic, so that some retarded depressions are likely to be diagnosed schizophrenic. One of the points constantly urged against cardiazol treatment, especially in Switzerland, is that it is not only disagreeable to watch but unpleasant to experience, and certainly in the Swiss clinics many of the patients struggled against having another injection. At Meduna's clinic, however, where a number of patients were being injected, there was nothing of this; much must depend on the attitude of the doctors who give the treatment.

I also visited Benedek at the University Clinic. Many people seemed to be of the opinion that Miskolczy had had just as strong claims on the chair as Benedek, when Schaffer retired. Benedek struck me as very energetic and versatile, but not at all original-minded. He seems to pick up every new thing, and to do some work on it. He is said to give a great deal of his time to his private practice and to be a martinet in his clinic; his assistants seemed almost servile in his presence, and all complained of being overworked and looked it. Anyhow, it has the result that a lot of work is done in his clinic. His chief assistant, Angyal, is mainly interested in the motor phenomena during insulin shock, which he has analysed skilfully. He has worked with Gerstmann. Juba, the histopathologist, is working on the structure of gliomata and on some neurological problems, e.g. lyssa. He and another assistant came with Benedek from Debreczen; the latter assistant works in the cerebral tumour ward, making a great deal of use of stereoscopic radiography. They are not doing anything very remarkable but what they do is probably reliable. Most of the assistants look ill.

I tried while in Budapest to see also Szondy, who works on endocrines, but he was out of town. Meduna showed me round two of the mental hospitals in Budapest; the patients in one were lying in rows along the stone corridors, elbow, to elbow, and altogether in a primitive state.

AUSTRIA[26]

Vienna

In Vienna I visited Pötzl's Clinic. Hoff took me round. The organisation of the place seemed bad; in the OPD it was not so much the number of patients as the haphazard way in which they were seen that led to confusion. Hoff would no sooner start to examine one patient than he was called away to the wards to see someone else, and he was not able to give proper time and attention to the examination of any patient, as far as I could see. The level of routine work seemed bad, although individual patients are no doubt examined very carefully if someone is interested in them. Stengl, for example, is interested in the association of obsessional symptoms with diseases of the brain stem, Pötzl with the more neurological disorders, Pichler is doing some anatomical work, etc. and so on. Hoff who is the chief figure in the clinic, as far as I could make out, works very hard but gives some of his time to a semi-private clinic which he has near the hospital was well as to private practice. Wagner-Jauregg and others told me that it is really he who prompts Pötzl and runs the place. Of course insulin is their chief topic, but they don't do it as well as the Swiss do it now, and are far too interested in the publicity aspect to be able to view it dispassionately. They are

---

[26] Before the Second World War, Austrian psychiatry was concerned largely with the foundation of psychiatric institutions and the improvement of conditions for patients. Research was primarily practised in university clinics, while psychotherapeutic schools were being developed in private societies. The law on admission and length of stay was reformed in 1916, making public establishments, university clinics and private institutions subject to the same regulations. This reform led to the requirement that the situation of an individual being kept in an institution against his or her will had to be examined within a month by a judge-led commission, advised by an independent psychiatric expert. In the universities, neurology and psychiatry were taught together from the beginning at Graz and Innsbruck, and in Vienna from 1911, until relatively recently. This led to a priority being given to organic research, which led to three strands: new treatment methods (Julius Wagner-Jauregg and Manfred Sakel); legal and clinico-descriptive psychiatry (Richard von Krafft-Ebing, Josef Berze, Erwin Stransky), which itself led to contributions in the nosology and psychopathology of schizophrenia and the manic-depressive psychoses; and cerebral psychiatry (Paul Schilder and Otto Pötzl). Psychoanalysis was of course a hugely significant product of Austria, which was also incorporated into the more organic psychiatry by several figures, including Pötzl. Psychoanalysis and individual psychology became distinct fields after the separation of Alfred Adler from Sigmund Freud in 1911.

also interested in trying out other therapeutic methods; for example, Hoff is trying out of the treatment of melancholia with a combination of thyroid extract irradiation of the thyroid and physostigmine, and some other substances. I do not recall the exact details but it sounded unlikely to be of value. He was also anxious to introduce Benzedrine. He seems to be dabbling in several fields, because he told me he was also working on a virus investigation in poliomyelitis and encephalitis. Kauders, I believe, is working on it in a more serious way in Graz. Pötzl has so committed himself that it is difficult to get an opinion about some aspect of the insulin treatment from other professors who have come in contact with it, e.g. Marburg, and Chiari; the latter has examined the brains of patients who died under the treatment, but was disinclined to speak of what he had found in these brains because Pötzl might not like it; Marburg has been afraid to do animal experiments with insulin for the same reason. I heard some conflicting statements; for example, Hoff said that in Vienna the schizophrenia group is much more stringently delimited and prognostically much more unfavourable than in other centres, diagnosis being restricted in the tradition of Meynert and Wagner-Jauregg; Wagner-Jauregg, on the other hand, told me that they are very loose now in their diagnosis of schizophrenia, and have quite departed from his own strict notions of dementia praecox. Hoff made the point to me that insulin treatment could still be advantageous even if the results were not lasting, because one might have thus given the schizophrenic four or five years of normality, but apart from the fact that there has been nothing to tell how many years of normality the apparently recovered cases have, his argument is weakened by the premise from which he starts, namely, that schizophrenics don't do any good at all except spontaneously. Of the possibilities of treatment on general lines, e.g. according to Adolf Meyer (whose merit he questions) he has no notion. Hoff admitted that Sakel, who started the treatment, has no knowledge of psychiatry and indeed no capacity for learning it. According to Hess, Sakel is enthusiastic about his work and cares nothing about fame and money, etc. It appears, however, that some of the early publicity which Sakel managed to obtain for himself caused a great deal of resentment among the more responsible people in Vienna, who felt that Sakel, and Pötzl's clinic incidentally, were almost starting "a racket".

I gathered from Hoff, Wagner-Jauregg and others that the quality of the doctors at the clinics is steadily and rather rapidly deteriorating now because many appointments are not decided by the medical faculty, but by the political authorities who override the latter's recommendations.

There have also been a number of dismissals on purely political and racial grounds. The responsible people who talk about it seem concerned at the way in which the level of scientific work is sinking.

Marburg told me of his investigations on experimental epilepsy in animals and showed me the reprints of studies done in the previous two years. Chiefly, however, he wanted to talk about the lack of resources, which he considered would hamstring his work. I gathered that whereas Wagner-Jauregg used to refer the neurological material to him and the brains to von Economo, Pötzl does not do so, and that Marburg is not on such good terms with the psychiatric clinic now. I was told that he was a poor clinical neurologist, unsystematic and variable in examining cases, but of course a good pathologist. Certainly he has collected an immense material. He does not give the impression of having any stimulating ideas, but he knows the literature very well, of course.

I got in touch with the psychoanalytical group around Freud. Anna Freud, who seems active and sensible, has working with her, amongst others, an American psychiatrist (formerly with Macfie Campbell) and Mme Laforgue, the wife of the psychoanalyst in Paris. They are doing at the Montessori Kinderheim an interesting investigation into the diet which children under the age of two years spontaneously choose; the direct connection with psychoanalysis was not obvious, but I was told that the object of the study is not only the children's choice but the extent to which they get back their primitive pleasure in eating; the physical side of the children is attended to also in that they are examined physically and weighed every time they come.

In talking to the various analysts I met – Kris, Wälder, Julia Deming, Sterba, Hartmann (formerly in Pötzl's clinic), etc. I got the impression that in Vienna the analysts treat character disturbances very much more than actual neurotic illness, i.e. they seldom get cases of straightforward phobias, obsessions, etc., but a great many people with sexual and other personality difficulties, yet no definite symptoms. Consequently they are not much interested in therapy and practical problems of the OPD or the clinic, and cannot understand the medical point of view. The group is not as coherent as one had thought; Nunberg has been spending some time in America, there have been secessions, Federn has never been analysed himself, and they have switched over towards the non-medical side. The Viennese analysts, however, distrust the line of development which psychoanalysis has taken in England under the influence of Melanie Klein's work with children. The analysts in Vienna have had less and less to do with the university clinic, so that Stengel is practically the only one working there now.

I spent some time with Pick in the Pharmacological Institute, where I met also Rössler and some of the other assistants. Some of Rössler's work on pharmacodynamics of the circulation seems to have a bearing on schizophrenia and corrects the notions of Meduna and others as to the mode of action of cardiazol. The most interesting work that I saw in Pick's clinic was being done by Feitelberg, a Latvian, working there. He had set about measuring heat changes in the brain as a direct way of determining the functional activity of different parts of it. His previous training as an engineer has enabled him to devise a very ingenious way of measuring the temperature changes, comparing those of the cortex with the brain stem in rabbits and cats, and with the temperature of carotid blood. He was using the method to test stimulants and depressants, e.g. narcotics, and to determine their site of action; (in accordance with the Meyer-Gottlieb theory). He stimulates the tissue by a method similar to Hess's. After an interval of 10 minutes or so the temperature of the separate parts of the brain under narcotics becomes the same, but in the meanwhile there are significant differences. He has found also that the temperature of the occipital lobe rises when there are slight stimuli; it would be interesting to test the effects of mescalin. His method is very ingenious and seems capable of yielding valuable results in several directions. He had, however, to interrupt his work for $1\frac{1}{2}$ years to do his compulsory military training in Latvia last year and the year before.

Report

Pick also discussed the prospects for pharmacological research in psychiatry, mentioning for example that he thought that nowadays much of the initiative in synthesising the new preparations must be left to the big manufacturing chemists because of their much greater technical facilities and experience. (This is not quite in accordance with what Supnieswski does, but seems to apply, except in very special cases.)

Chiari I found to be quite uninterested in the central nervous system, except that he has an assistant working on the changes in the brain in periarteritis nodosa. Their pathology seems to consist entirely in examination of clinical material, without regard to experimental work.

I saw Durig in the Physiological Department. He turned me over to Lippay who was busy with chronaxie studies and fatigue phenomena and excitability in denervated muscle preparations. Rudolf Allers, the Adlerian, works there also on sensory physiology, but has now little interest in experimental work of that kind. There seemed to be little contact between the different departments in the Physiology Institute: Lippay, for example, did not know what the others were doing.

I met some people who talked mainly on general topics, e.g. Wagner-Jauregg who was very informative about the present state of psychiatry in Austria, Kris who worked on the psychology of art from the psychoanalytical point of view, and Wäler, the sociologist, who edits the *International Psychoanalytical Journal*. Berze I did not manage to see; some of the others spoke disparagingly of him. Gerstmann's work is of course careful and painstaking; a contrast to Hoff. Eppinger and Hans Horst Meyer I met very briefly. Epstein who works in the Kaiser Franz Josef Hospital on the chemistry of fats, etc., seems to have no connection at all with the neurologists and physiologists whom I met; most of whom had never heard of him, and Pick seemed to know very little about him.

I saw Karl Bühler, who explained to me his views about the uselessness of collecting further facts about psychology, instead of bringing those which are now available into a coherent scheme. He has sketched out the lines upon which he proposes to formulate a more or less complete psychological system, having due regard on the one hand, to physiological and biological requirements, and on the other hand, to the complicated psychological phenomena which fall outside natural science. It is obviously influenced by his studies on language and development. He is very critical about the psychoanalytical theory and about the Gestalt writers, and Kurt Lewin and Spearman. He is much more alive and stimulating than the people I met in the clinical departments. Although Bühler thinks that more than enough piling up of data is going on, Brunswik is going ahead with some experimental work in his laboratory, and Bühler himself keeps well in touch with recent work.

Prague

In Prague I went to Gamper's clinic. He is chiefly interested in the brain stem and the analysis of symptoms produced by diseases in that region. His methods are the conventional ones. Surprisingly, he said that he did not find it difficult to distinguish the organic from the psychogenic symptoms: I told him how often we found it impossible to be sure whether an apparently extra-pyramidal syndrome was hysterical or not, and he said that he thought that might depend on the fact that different clinics had very heterogeneous material. He, for example, had scarcely any neurosis among his out-patients and very little introspective productivity on the part of the schizophrenics such as he was familiar with elsewhere, of the Heidelberg material [sic].

The person of whom I saw most in Gamper's clinic was Klein. Gamper has an arrangement by which his chief assistants alternate each year between the psychiatric and the neurological clinic; the neurological clinic is regarded as the heavier in its demands (which indicates their predominant interest). Klein is at present on the psychiatric side. He told me that as far as laboratory work is concerned, they do not go in for histological studies, limiting themselves to a determination of the site of cerebral lesions. Klein is interested in aphasia and apraxia; he seemed quiet, reliable, and well-informed in his own field; has probably few new ideas, but critical.

Both Klein and Gamper were very apologetic about the structure of the psychiatric clinic, but it is not so old actually, and it seemed to me airy and large enough if only the nursing were to be improved. There were lots of Gitterbetten [children's cots], apparently used as a substitute for supervision and nursing; on the women's side things were a little better than on the men's side, but there seemed little attempt to give the patients occupation, or to treat them as individuals. The clinical material is really that of an observation ward or reception station, there seemed few chronic lunatics and some neurological cases. They are situated just above the mental hospital, which similarly suffers from lack of nursing and occupation for the patients, etc. Patients lie about and look depressed and degraded. The corresponding Czech psychiatrists, Haskoveç, who has the university chair, and Mysliçevek, who runs the mental hospital, are more in touch with French psychiatry; they publish single cases and pathological studies in the French journals. I was not able to meet either of them, and was dependent on hearsay and articles of theirs which I have seen.

In the neurological clinic there is Kral, who is the other chief assistant to Gamper. We discussed the reaction which he and Gamper have reported as characteristic of schizophrenia and some organic diseases of the central nervous system; he is quite definite about its regular occurrence, and told me that he had carried out a small number of control investigations on non-organic, non-schizophrenic diseases, the results confirming his views. The number of investigations done, however, did not seem to warrant his conclusions; the work has not been adequately tested elsewhere. Kral seemed more lively and more energetic than Klein. They are also anxious to try the reaction which Lehman-Facius reported at Frankfurt a few months ago, but cannot get details from him.

In Rihl's Institute of Pathology I saw Reiss, who showed me his technique for removing the pituitary in rats, and told me of his work on that and on adrenalectomised rats. He is no doubt a good endocrinologist, but when it comes to clinical application, he seems a bit ignorant and credulous (for example, as to the effects of provirol on impotence). Like a number of people in these countries he is troubled by political trends, finds himself out of sympathy with the Germans and for various reasons is eager to publish his work in some English-speaking journals.

I attended a meeting of the Ärzteverein in which Knaus, the gynaecologist, and von Jaksch took part. There was an incidental discussion about contraceptive methods and population problems: Knaus was, oddly, rather ill-informed about the latter. In

Budapest I was told by Meduna that deliberate abortion is quite a problem in some of the villages in Hungary. I did not have an opportunity of meeting anyone especially interested in eugenics. I was told that, apart from Benedek, (whose interest is fitful), and Somogyi, who is a school teacher, no one is much concerned about it at present in Hungary; and in Czechoslovakia I did not find out who were the authoritative people interested in the matter. The people I met seemed to regard eugenics as a simple issue between compulsory sterilisation in the German style and laissez faire.

At Tschermak's physiological institute I saw Schubert: Tschermak was away. Some of his work in optics and acoustics is certainly applicable to psychiatric and neurological problems, e.g. to depersonalisation and toxic states, but the methods are too complicated for the non-expert. Schubert has worked on aviation physiology, and on electrical phenomena in the stomach in normal subjects (using similar apparatus to that for electro-cardiography).

I gathered that one of the other men there is working on calcium metabolism in relation to muscular activity, but Schubert could not tell me the details. Although Tschermak's researches are so applicable to psychiatry, I could not find that there was any liaison between his department and Gamper's. As so often elsewhere, I was impressed here by the urgency and importance of their matter of collaboration or fertilisation within the university or city: people seemed to try out work of which they had only read in a foreign journal in preference to what was being done next door, or perhaps in ignorance of it.

POLAND[27]

In Cracow I went to the Psychiatric Clinic which was shown me by Prof. Pienkowski and his assistant Godlowski. I could not find that the professor was at present engaged in research; he was not pursuing his former studies on the hand symptoms of extrapyramidal disease, and he seemed depressed and tired. He mentioned various additions to the work of the clinic, e.g. a children's department, and spoke of the research which he and others were trying to initiate on the inheritance of mental disorder, but in discussion he did not give the impression of being at all familiar with the problems, much less with the methods of attacking them; he spoke only in general terms of the need for a firm basis, thoroughness, etc. The clinic was apparently intended mainly by Piltz, when he designed it, for neurological cases, and it seems neither adapted for the treatment of severe psychosis nor to contain all the varieties desirable for

[27] The first psychiatric hospitals on Polish territory emerged in the first half of the nineteenth century, and from mid-century psychiatry courses began to be part of the medical programme. After Poland's independence at the end of the First World War, the Polish Psychiatry Society was founded in 1920 – although meetings of neurologists, psychiatrists and psychologists had been taking place since 1909 – and was principally concerned with consolidating therapeutic approaches and with juridical questions. Biological tendencies dominated, although Borsztajn and Forstig published psychoanalytic works. The Society's 1933 meeting dealt largely with heredity and the prevention of mental illness, and ended with a formal protest against the eugenicist use of sterilization for psychiatric patients, which had just begun in Germany. Polish psychiatry was to suffer under Nazi occupation; all universities were closed, and virtually all psychiatric patients were killed in the Nazi euthanasia policy. Sixty per cent of psychiatrists did not survive the war. (See Jacques Postel and Claude Quétel (eds), *Nouvelle histoire de la psychiatrie*, Toulouse, Editions Privat, 1983.)

teaching, etc., in a university clinic. The nurses seemed poorly trained, and it was a little inappropriate that Prof. Pienkowski should put so much more emphasis on the structural arrangements of the clinic, of which he evidently thought highly, than on the standard of the nursing. There were many evidences, as I walked round, that this was well below what is now regarded as necessary. I was told that occupational treatment was employed, but during the round I saw no signs of patients working or of the customary facilities for it. Although lack of money was emphasised as responsible for some deficiencies, the more glaring ones, to the casual visitor, were such as could probably be remedied without much expense. Several of the laboratories which Piltz had set up were now unoccupied; the only research of which I was told was anatomical and experimental – chiefly by Godlowski, the Agrégé, who was doing careful work cutting the posterior commissure in cats and observing the effects on motility; his interests are on neurophysiological lines, and in conformity with a general trend in Poland (e.g. Rotfeld in Lvov and Orzechowski) they centre on the vestibular apparatus. In the museum of the clinic there were a lot of brains awaiting examination and I was told that they had all been collected there in the fifteen years since the clinic opened; the extraordinarily high death rate seemed to be partly due to their cerebral tumours not having been operated upon and to their having senile cases in the clinic. This is no doubt related to the neurological bias (there were only thirty odd psychiatric cases and these had to be together, e.g. a hysteric near deteriorated and noisy schizophrenics, etc.). There is a larger, more varied material at the reception ward in the general hospital, but their interests there are also mainly neurological. Prof. Pienkowski told me that he has four polyclinics, one of them for alcoholism alone, and that psychotherapy is employed, but as he said that there were 30 or so new cases at each session, it was clear that time and probably experience would be lacking for so much work of this sort. The physicians are occupied with their private practice in the afternoons. Their clinical outlook was not impressive, e.g. several cases of cryptogenic polyneuritis were shown to me, but the possibility of a vitamin deficiency was not mentioned, though a lot of less probable causes were; for a case of spontaneous hypoglycaemia they were going to irradiate the hypophysis; a rather popular therapeutic procedure in Poland at the time, without considering the possibility of pancreatic tumour. In spite of Cracow being such a small place, it did not appear that the people in the clinic had very close contact with the other research workers, e.g. physiologists, pharmacologists: Godlowski's scientific connections lay elsewhere. They were, however, in touch with recent literature, especially Godlowski, who seemed able and well trained, and the most active influence in the clinic.

In the Pharmacological Institute I saw Prof. Supniewski. He told me of his work on mescalin and allied compounds, and on synthesised substances related to acetylcholine. At the time I saw him he was much handicapped by not having any competent assistants; the lack of adequate pay or prospects in his department made it impossible to get people to take up the work. His incidental remarks on political and social matters showed that he was psychologically hampered in his productive worked by dissatisfaction with the general conditions prevailing in Poland and Europe. He seemed interested in pharmacological questions bearing on psychiatry, but to lack the nexus with psychiatrists; I was to try the effect of some of his cholinergic compound, which he offered me, when I got back to London. He was disposed to reticence about the uses of mescalin now, as he had not worked on it for the last few years.

Warsaw

In Warsaw I first saw Opalski, the neurologist, who was then working in Prof. Masurkiewics's psychiatric clinic, in order to qualify for any vacant chair in the combined subjects. He was responsible for the insulin unit, which seemed, as in so many European clinics, to be conducted more light-heartedly from the nursing point of view, etc., than the risks require but his chief interest and research lay in straightforward histo-pathology.

Prof. Masurkiewics showed me round the clinic; the buildings are very old. He showed me some unusual cases of aphasia, etc., and explained to me his theoretical views of the pathology of mental disorder, in which the vegetative nervous system plays a large part; he makes a curious fusion of the views and findings of Orbeli, Hess and Bourguignon. One of his assistants, a woman, Madame Skrzypinska, had gone to Paris to work with Bourguignon, and the research was still going on. Prof. Masurkiewics struck me as unusual, in that he had developed an original point of view in psychopathology, without losing touch with practical clinical problems and concrete (as apart from speculative psychological) research.

I also visited Prof. Orzechowski at his neurological clinic; he seemed to have a heavy burden of cases there, and I could not discover that he was actually pursuing any research.

Chorobski, the neuro-surgeon, was working in a unit arranged for him in the "traumatological" hospital, which is directed by a military surgeon, though Chorobski himself is officially attached to Prof. Orzechowski. He could not resign himself to the material and personal difficulties which he met with in Warsaw; he contrasted it with conditions he had known during the years he spent in the United States and in Western European countries. Temperamentally he seemed rather ill-equipped to cope with adverse conditions. He was very busy, but could not get good assistants who would stay; he was just about to lose his excellent American trained nurse and his chief medical assistant, both of whom were very reluctant to go but could not afford to remain. Practical difficulties such as lack of money for equipment, the right to diagnose and select cases, etc., preoccupied him rather. Nevertheless it seemed clear that he was building up a sound neuro-surgical unit and that there was no effective hostility to this in Warsaw. His reputation as a good brain surgeon is high in Poland, and he seems to be educating the rest of the profession in regard to the possibilities of surgery of the CNS. His chief interest on the research side was in the sensory fibres of the sympathetic, and in the relation of arterial tension to brain conditions and the psychological evidences of impairment. It seemed a pity for his proposed work in the latter that he had not had a good training in clinical psychiatry. For the development of his department it would possibly have been better if he had been allowed private practice; he would then probably have been able to get and put more money into the surgical unit. At present they do not even take private paying patients into the unit. So that well-to-do people are operated on there without paying fees which could help greatly towards developing the unit along desirable lines. Chorobski's keenness and industry seemed to promise that he would not have neglected his main work, even though he had had some facilities for private practice; he would very likely have been able to get on with research more satisfactorily.

I saw Konorski and Stefan Miller and Mdlle Lubinska at the Nencki Institute. They showed me their conditioned reflex laboratory and discussed the special use of the motor response in their experiments. It seemed, allowing for the objections made by the Leningrad workers to this method, that it could be extended to the study of some psychiatric problems in children, especially in regard to inhibition. The keenness of these three workers and their interest in some of the applied problems arising out of their research were impressive.

RUSSIA[28]

Moscow

In Moscow I had some difficulty in getting to see some of the people I was most anxious to visit. The first I saw was Dr Victor Minor, who did not appear to have any laboratory; I called on him at his home. He discussed with me his work on the distribution of the sweat glands, especially the importance of mechanical or physical factors, the relation of sebaceous to sweat over-activity and his interesting speculations in regard to the differences between sweating due to heat and that due to emotion. At present he seems to be one of the most active of the lecturers on medicine to the general public. I saw next Prof. Lina Stern, but on none of the three occasions when I saw her – twice at her laboratory and once at her home – did she seem inclined to speak in other than general terms of the current research work in her laboratories, evidently centred on the haemato-encephalic barrier as in her earlier Swiss days. She seemed always very tired and was working very hard. She, her friend, the daughter of the late Prof. Bach, discussed the question which I raised, of the efforts made to co-ordinate and direct scientific work towards specified ends in the USSR; Miss Bach repeated the theoretical and general arguments which I had read elsewhere, but Prof. Stern seemed to have little interest in or esteem for these arguments, and I gathered that in physiology, at any rate, she did not consider there was any real difference in the present Russian way of initiating and determining the trend of research and that followed in other countries, though there were manifestly considerable differences in detail.

---

[28] In nineteenth-century Russia, debates about psychiatric theory and practice were situated in a context of the wider opposition between Slavophiles and Occidentalists; there was, however, a keen interest in both French and German psychiatry. In 1861, after the abolition of serfdom, the newly created *zemstovs* – assemblies of doctors, engineers, and statisticians – established agricultural colonies for the mentally ill. The first psychiatry Chair was created in 1857 at the Medico-Military Academy in St Petersburg, held by I M Balinski. U M Bechterev held the post from 1893. Moscow's first psychiatry chair was given to A J Kojevnikov (who isolated continuous partial epilepsy). Grigorii Ivanovich Rossolimo and Vladimir Mikhailovich Kernig were two neuropsychiatrists who became well-known throughout Europe; figures such as S S Korsakov and V C Kandinski were also influential. Interest in psychoanalysis existed before the Revolution, but became more marked between 1917 and 1928; from 1928 onwards, however, a highly vigorous intellectual culture was repressed; only Pavlovianism was acceptable and indeed became State doctrine. All Western developments, psychoanalysis and existentialism especially, were condemned.

Report

I visited Prof. H Müller's Institute; he was away and his associate, Gershonson, showed me round. There seemed to be more original serious work going on here than in any other institute I visited in Moscow; several of the research workers explained the details of what they were doing: influence of X-ray dosage on mutations, splitting of the Y chromosome, estimation of the size of the genes in the metaphase chromosomes (by Raphael and another American), etc. Gershonson also told me of the ingenious research being done into the fixity of gene characters, by transplanting bits of growing germ gland on to a Drosophila's egg (other tissues from the larva were also being used); the bearing of this on "Penetranz" and other fundamental questions of heredity was discussed. They were also good enough to tell me of some of the research in applied genetics being done on sheep, rust-resistant wheat, etc. by the Institute. I asked also about Prof. Müller's views on artificial insemination in human beings; Gershonson implied in his answer that this was a private vagary of Prof. Müller's.

I next went to the Brain Institute, where they were occupied with four problems – variability of the different brain fields à la Brodman, "Entwicklungsmechanik" (observing the effect upon other regions when a piece of embryonal or growing brain is cut off), Berger rhythm, and very careful serial studies of the changes in Pick's disease. They were also busy dealing with "élite" brains, e.g. of Gorki, Pavlov. Undoubtedly their painstaking work in mapping the human cortex and in making beautifully accurate atlases is extremely useful; fortunately they seem to have experts who enjoy doing that as their permanent total occupation. Their work on the Berger rhythm seemed to be more fruitful of results than that of reliable people elsewhere, although technically they did not seem to be taking all the customary precautions to ensure accuracy; they were working on the changes produced by artificial tumours such as implanted myoma and on the effect of drugs such as chloroform and strychnine. Unfortunately the man who does all the work in this department was not available, and consequently I could not get any detailed information about his research.

At Prof. Levitt's Institute he told me of the work going on under his direction. Like so many of the scientists I visited, he spoke proudly of the large number of assistants he had, forty-six, I think – but they were scattered in different institutes, and I gathered from what he said that many of them can scarcely have any genetic knowledge, e.g. he has two men working on heredity of psychoses of whom one is a psychiatrist ignorant of genetics (the other is a pure geneticist): Levitt said that he knew of only one other man working on psychiatric genetics. He mentioned Ignatiev. He showed me the children's clinic, in which he keeps twins for six days' observation; some of the precautions taken to prevent infections seemed excessive. I had read and heard of his enormous collection of twins – 2000 pairs; but when I asked him about them I discovered they were mostly children under 10 and that he had occupied himself almost entirely with average children; he had few morbid twin collections of any size. The method of ascertainment of his twins would, it seemed to me, preclude their being used as a representative sample for psychological studies, since, besides those discovered by inquiry at houses by field workers, he accepts spontaneous applications (which might conceivably include an unduly high proportion of intelligent, enthusiastic or neurotic subjects). He told me that so far as psychiatric disorders were concerned he did not see that any other methods were applicable than the familiar ones, namely, family studies and twins. His collaborators were working on some two hundred schizophrenic pedigrees. An inquiry into a problem of educational psychology was being carried on by a woman in his department, who had earlier collaborated in this work with Luria (observing the extent and duration of improvement in performance and also in perception when a model is presented for copying in which the constituent parts are not separately visible). I was surprised to find, however, that they had not extended the investigation beyond the point which it had reached when it was reported on in their article two years before; possibly this was due to the withdrawal of Luria. Levitt also told me of his interesting studies of the incidence of achlorhydria in the immediate relatives of patients with gastric ulcer; the incidence of accentuated secondary aortic sound in the siblings of patients with hypertension; and other such work, looking for the early or premonitory signs of disease. It seemed to me, however, that at any rate in his use of the urinary concentration test on the relatives of patients with diabetes insipidus he was being unduly influenced by his notion of what anomaly would be a signal or a constitutional feature of an impending disorder; in the psychiatric field this difficulty would become of much greater importance than in the subjects he has so far worked on. His use of the twin method for histological correlations, e.g. correlating the height of the T wave in the electrocardiogram with the size of the heart seemed to me an interesting and new method, but more limited in its possibilities than he believed. He also spoke of the serological test he had been using and from which he had expected much. He seemed full of original ideas, e.g. he had taken pieces of skin from a patient with an atrophic skin disease and cultivated them in vitro to see if the atrophy persisted; if it had he would have supposed it to be a constitutional or inherent quality.

In view of the semi-political cloud under which Levitt was reputed to have been earlier in the year, it was interesting to notice with what energy and emphasis he interspersed his account of his researches with rather irrelevant or seemingly naïve remarks about the superiority of Marxian arguments over capitalist science, e.g. he brought the Marxian arguments against natural selection into a discussion of this work on dominance, and he said that it was only in Russia that the capitalist mistake of anecdotal or "literary" selection of twins had been avoided; he is obviously so familiar with the international literature of his subject that one would hardly think he could have meant this seriously.[29] It was also noteworthy perhaps that, after he had asked me to look over the English of an article he was sending to an English journal, the Voks guide, [he] made a point of asking me for the article and reading it forthwith, and of being present when Levitt eventually called at the hotel to get it back from me.

Next I saw Prof. Kroll, who told me of his histological studies with a functional background, i.e. secretory function of neuroglia, activity of sympathetic nervous system and adaptation of skin to temperature and other changes; his work on the thalamus was interesting. He showed me his laboratory and suggested various psychiatrists and other research people in Moscow whom I ought to see; for reasons that I could never fathom properly, nobody was able to arrange, however, for me to get in touch with

---

[29] These remarks suggest that Lewis was not aware of the extent of the anxiety that must have been felt by people in Levit's position and the extent of their possible persecution.

these people. Among them were Lubitchev (or some such name) at "Viem", Gurolevsky and his associate professor, and Mark Serejski and Gilarowsky the histopathologist.

I saw Speranskii at his Institute. We spoke of his views, developed in his book, about the influence of the nervous system on somatic disease, and the converse. His observations and experiments were very interesting but when I asked him about the application of this theory to some concrete issues in psychiatry he would not commit himself in any way and referred me back to the book. He said that a number of clinicians were now applying his method to the treatment of their cases, but here again it was impossible to get any definite details or illustrations of how this was done; he had not yet attached any psychiatric problems but was reluctantly yielding to the solicitations of the psychiatrists to do so; I could not discover what he had in mind to do, although I raised such questions as: did he mean to collect more facts in the light of his theory or to rearrange the present ones? How would it apply to such a matter as the treatment of GPI? The neuro-psychiatric complications of pernicious anaemia etc.

I made several attempts to get in touch with some psychologists, but neither in Moscow nor in Leningrad was I able to do so. I had a letter from Dr O'Brien for Hellerstein, but nobody seemed to know what had become of him;[30] Kroll thought that he was working in Lina Stern's institute, but she told me that she knew nothing about him. I got an impression, rather than a definite statement, that he had been caught up in psychotechnics of "pedology", and after that their initial flourishing these branches of psychology had not justified expectation and had been more or less liquidated. Since then I have seen the account (in Sir E D Simon's book on Moscow) of how educational psychology, mental testing, etc., had been indicated as anti-Marxian and Prof. Blonksy had publicly retracted his alleged errors. I cannot imagine why no one in Moscow told me of this plainly when on the subject, since it was no secret, the decree of July 1936 had been published and the matter ventilated in the Moscow Daily News. Luria, Kroll told me, had taken up medicine, and was busy with his examinations so that I was not able to see him.

I saw Propper, who also suggested various people I ought to see, but nothing much came of it; he took me round, however, to Ivanov-Smolensky's laboratory in the Institute, Ivanov-Smolensky was in Leningrad, but I was told of their work on the sympathetic response to conditioning in children; as with many other interesting things, the work was at that time projected – "in construction" – rather than actually under way there.

Propper told me of his own work on epilepsy and on pain. He was stimulating the cortex diffusely by electrodes put on the skull and then observing the biological changes (effect of perfused frog's heart, etc.), and producing toxic effects by injecting an emulsion of brain tissue into animals of the same sort, i.e. more or less repeating Forster's experiments; he had done similar work with pain stimulation in animals, though there seemed to be a possibility that the BP and other effects he observed might be due to an adrenalin-like substance.

---

[30] O'Brien, in his letter to Lewis (O'Brien to Lewis, 23 February 1937, p. 8), describes Professor S G Hellerstein as the Director of the Psychotechnical Laboratory of Institute of Experimental Medicine, saying that his field is applied psychology.

Kroll kindly took me along in his motorcar to the Institute Gannushkin where Serejski and Kronfeld work. The director unfortunately spoke only Russian and a few words of German, and did not (as I had hoped he would) just hand me over to Kronfeld (whom I had known in Berlin in 1928). They have treated a lot of schizophrenics with insulin, 250 in one year, under the direction of Kronfeld and another German exile, Sternberg. Schizophrenia is a diagnosis more generally applied in Moscow than in Western countries. Many cases we would call depressive, manic, or psycho-neurotic they label as schizophrenia, – especially schizophrenia mitis. Although this is a reception hospital, they said 80% of their admissions were schizophrenic (an extraordinarily high figure). I saw eight or nine recovered cases playing ball to music, under an instructor; apparently this recreational therapy is mainly for convalescent patients. In the occupational therapy department there were four rooms, mainly adapted for more or less skilled trades, e.g. making woodwork and toys, and for painting street rubbish-bins, and doing other socially useful work. I was told that a sixth or less of the patients work there. One or two of the men patients whom I saw there were, I was told, quite well now, but had elected to remain, and they continue their work in the shops while living outside; there seemed a good deal to recommend such a plan, but, on the other hand, I would have thought that therapeutically it would be more important to use these places and the work-rooms for patients who were still ill. In short, their occupational therapy is on the old plan – not so much to benefit the patients' health, as to benefit others by the work of a few, usually chronic or convalescent, patients. I was told that other patients work in the wards; I did not see this, as when I was there it was rest time. They also have an X-ray and electrical department of which they are very proud; young doctors from other places come there to learn the technique, but it was reminiscent of some Italian and other clinics I had seen where there was much equipment for giving static electricity and other forms of instrumental treatment either obsolete or of solely suggestive value. I also visited the histological laboratory where the pathologist (an elderly man who had evidently had a severe hemiplegia) showed glia stained by his own method. In the wards the nurses were people of little training. I was told that this would be remedied later on. The "disturbed" ward was very disturbed. Kronfeld had been given charge of a department and was extremely enthusiastic about Russian psychiatry and the treatment that he had received from Narkomzdrav.[31] I was not able, however, to speak to him at any time except in a group of people, which I regretted because his praise was so excessive in some instances where the facts were quite obvious to anyone who knew psychiatric conditions outside Russia, that I found it difficult to believe it to be his genuine opinion. I asked whether he was still pursuing the work in psychopathology and psychotherapy, for which he had been so distinguished, but he and the rest of the doctors seemed embarrassed by my question, and I learned that psychopathology is not much pursued in Russia and that for psychotherapy there is either little time or little inclination; psychoanalysis is frowned on.

When the patients are discharged they come under the neuro-psychiatric specialist for their district. I could not, however, get any information about the numbers and organisation of these cases in Moscow, being always referred for details to someone

---

[31] An abbreviation of Narodny Komissariat Zdravookhraneniya – People's Commissariat for the Protection of Health.

else whom I never discovered. I tried to get the figures about the rayon service also from Karanovitch, of the Narkomsdrav, but whether because of the language difficulty, or some other reason I could not get them. In Leningrad, however, I did get information to this point.

My last visit in Moscow was to Karanovitch who, I was given to understand, was their chief authority on the statistics of psychiatry. As he spoke only Russian it was unusually difficult to make clear to him what I wanted to know, and to the most simple questions as to the percentage frequency of this or that disease he would answer with a long statement. I gathered from him that there has been no marked change in the distribution of the various mental disorders, e.g. they have as many manic-depressive psychoses as formerly, but that they now hospitalise traumatic cases, which they did not do before, and this has apparently altered the hospital incidence of the other conditions. He said their statistics were still incomplete even for Moscow, that extra-mural psycho-neurotic cases were not yet included in them, and that differing criteria of diagnosis influenced them, as one would expect. He thought I would be able to get better information in Leningrad. From the figures available it seemed that they have still an enormous deficiency of beds (the present number being perhaps one-sixth of what are needed). They have little provision for mental deficiency per se; nor for senile and arteriosclerotic cases, hence the predominance of patients in the earlier decades of life. Moreover, cases seem to be discharged too soon, judging by the high figures for re-admissions. To draw conclusions, however, from their published statistics as to the frequency of particular disorders is to court error; one does not know whether, for instance, the high percentage of schizophrenics (nearly one-third of all admissions) may be a matter of diagnosis, or of factors determining selection for admission. The figures do, however, seem to show a great advance on the psychiatric provision available in earlier years.

Leningrad

In Leningrad I first saw Koupalov; he showed me the chambers used for the conditioned reflex studies and how he puts the food in fluid form directly into the dog's mouth, thus eliminating the secondary cause of salivation, e.g. chewing. He seemed almost entirely taken up with the physiological side of his problem, and therefore opposed to movement studies such as those of Konorsky because of their complexity and their variability. He seemed wedded to Pavlov's "cortical" theory of inhibition, etc., and unaware or unable to see how unsatisfactory this is found to be by psychiatrists, for instance; it seemed unlikely that the direction in which he was pursuing his researches would result in illumination of morbid psychological problems.

Next I went to Podkopaev, but he seemed indifferent or reluctant to see me, excused himself and handed me over to Gersuni who was studying action currents of the 8th nerve (Wever-Bray, etc.) and observing the effects of other stimuli on this, the relation of loudness to intensity and chronaxy, also the noise phenomena produced by an electrical current through saline in the external ear. He seemed competent and keen. He was interested in the question of the influence of drugs which I raised with him, but had not so far studied it.

At the Filatov Hospital Krasnogorsky showed me two experiments on conditioned reflexes which he was doing, one on a slightly neurotic girl, and another on a myxoedematous patient in whom the basal metabolic rate had fallen to -40, and who, while in this condition, did not develop conditioned reflexes. His experimental rooms were much less well equipped than others that I saw in Moscow and in Leningrad; his apparatus was old and worn, though adequate for his purposes. Krasnogorsky is obviously energetic, original-minded and enthusiastic about his work. He told me about the various forms of research in paediatrics, nearly all of them concerned with original problems, usually of therapy, e.g. his method of treating enuresis by a planned salt control, which however might only be effective with those in whom the enuresis was due to an irritable spinal micturition-centre. He also told me of his work on sleep and of his reasons for giving up the notion of inhibition, speaking of more and less excitability instead. Although the pure Pavlov followers in Leningrad evidently regard Krasnogorsky's work in the field of conditioned reflexes as too uncontrolled, dealing as he does with human beings, he seemed to be the only one really attempting the necessary work of applying the method to clinical problems. Others seemed hampered by Pavlov's theory about the cortical happenings.

Gurevitsch, of the mitogenetic rays, showed me his laboratory and his method. In talking about his research he was fairly plainly on the defensive; he brought in A V Hill's contemptuous remarks about his work, and also Bateman's critical article in *Biological Reviews*, of which he spoke bitterly; this was perhaps understandable considering how devastating Bateman's article had been. I also saw his assistant, a psychiatrist called Braines (of whom Ossipov spoke quite highly). Braines made startling claims, and seemed very confident. He had found that in mania there was a great increase in the mitogenetic activity of the blood, but in depression no such activity at all, and by treating depressive schizophrenics with the blood of manic patients he had, he thought, brought about recovery; irradiated blood had exerted a similar good effect; also by the injection of a manic patient's blood, he got to take their food satisfactorily. It all sounded very improbable. I gathered elsewhere that Gurevitsch was likely to lose suddenly and completely the strong support that he had for his researches, as soon as the government, i.e. the political heads of scientific work, concluded that it had no real value; that this withdrawal of support was imminent; there had been no published criticism of his work in Russia because it would have been indiscreet in the circumstances, but that this had not meant that it was generally accepted. People thought Gurevitsch was honest but misguided.

I saw Ossipov at the Military Academy and at the Brain Institute, where Bechterev was formerly. The clinic at the Military Academy was, surprisingly, not full. The accommodation, which was generous, was for a hundred patients. They have laboratories but, apart from some research on mescalin and hallucinations, they did not appear to be doing much research there just then. In the Brain Institute, besides the morphological work there was evidence of there having been formerly considerable interest in psychology, especially the comparative psychology of apes, but here, as in Moscow, psychology seemed to have become rather a taboo subject; no successor had been appointed to Wagner, the last professor. In the electro-physiological department, the influence of Orbeli's views was evident. Mdlle Novikova, who had been in the

Report

USA, was investigating the effect of cutting the sympathetic rami on the nerve muscle response of frogs (stimulation of peroneus) which had had a hemisection of the cord. I also saw Petrov's work on the influence of electro-magnetic fields on nerve muscle preparations. I was impressed by the investigations in the biochemical department where they were analysing the calcium, potassium, sodium and magnesium in the grey matter of brains from the embryo onwards, seriatim, and the oxygen exchanges of the grey matter of rats. In decorticated dogs, the physiologists were observing the conditioned reflexes using the standard Pavlov technique; they told me that the decortication had been complete but it was evident that the dog they brought in was using its occipital visual cortex still. Ossipov gave the impression of a well-trained psychiatrist of the old school; his outlook seemed to be substantially that of Kraepelin, under whom he had studied.

At Ivanov-Smolensky's clinic (formerly Pavlov's) I found that continuous narcosis was their chief interest. Ivanov-Smolensky uses Cloettal on patients with catatonic stupor and considers that his 50% remission rate represents a substantial therapeutic advance; he seemed to be unduly influenced by Kraepelin's 15% recovery rate. Walking through his wards, however, the cases that he showed did not appear to be severe catatonic stupors but looked more like what we would call melancholic semi-stupors. It was difficult to discuss psychiatric matters with him, partly because of the language difficulty and partly because he seemed to resent as criticism such questions as: what were the figures for a control series of his cases not treated by continuous narcosis; whether the good results obtained were regarded as supporting Pavlov's theory of over-excitability and need of rest in these catatonic cases, and if so whether the success of the treatment in manic-depressives did not indicate that the same theory would apply there; what criteria were used to determine whether the stuporose patients were narcotised continuously (he said he used response to pain and light reflex, which seem an unsatisfactory way). He was treating some cases with insulin in pursuance of his views as to the vegetative changes in the sleep treatment. He assumes that in schizophrenic patients there are toxic phenomena which must be attached. His other research, i.e. the examination of all new cases by a modified conditioned reflex method, seemed to have little to distinguish it from the familiar reaction time and learning experiments, but done in a Pavlov chamber; the results, however, were interesting. There was also the mechanical hypnotising apparatus.

From Ivanov-Smolensky and Ossipov I learnt that there are 10 rayons for Leningrad, with its population of approximately three million; each rayon has on its staff a neuro-psychiatrist with two doctors assisting him. There are about 200 neuro-psychiatric patients in the rayon, the doctors spend $4\frac{1}{2}$ hours a day on two days of the (6-day) week seeing patients who come to them, and three hours on two other days of the week going to see patients. In the $4\frac{1}{2}$ hours each doctor sees about 20 patients. All the questions of commitment to a mental hospital are decided by the doctors; there is no legal aspect to the procedure. From what Ivanov-Smolensky told me the number of cases in the mental hospitals in Leningrad is small in proportion to the population; like every other psychiatrist I asked, he said he did not think that there were fewer manic-depressives in Russia than elsewhere, and said that the statistics were not as yet complete enough to permit one to say.

Prof. Orbeli took me first to his electro-physiological department where interesting work was being done on Vedensky inhibition and on the autonomic fibres in mainly motor nerves, e.g. to gastrocnemius, rectus abdominis, artorius, (in relation to Orbeli's theory concerning the different stages of evolutionary differentiation). Orbeli spoke of his views and observations on the regulation of reflex activity by sympathetic influences. He was studying the influence of sympathectomy on metabolism and on the mesencephalon investigated by the Hess method. One of his assistants was observing the trophic changes in the eye of the rabbit following excitation of the Casserian ganglion on that side. At another visit I saw Orbeli operate, cutting the vagus in two dogs and suturing it to observe the gradual effect of the regeneration on gastric and intestinal secretion; the other vagus had been cut three years before. He showed me various animals that had been operated upon (one had the impression in Moscow and Leningrad that more animal experiments are done there than anywhere else in Europe): cats in whom the posterior columns had been out high up with consequent disturbances of motor behaviour – some of their symptoms were exactly like those of a man with visual agnosia; the assistant, Pancratoff, working on this was also studying catatonic patients in the psychiatric clinic and comparing their motor disorder with that of dogs in whom the cerebellum had been removed. Other animals with experimental lesions of the cerebellum and the thalamus were also brought in. Orbeli spoke of the influence he believes the cerebellum to have upon intestinal and other forms of sympathetic activity. Also there were animals in whom the effects of labyrinthectomy could be studied.

I also saw Prof. London operate. Although so much less deft in his technique than Orbeli, he does his remarkable three-stage operation with surprising rapidity. The originality and wide applicability of his method to the study of bio-chemical problems made one wonder why it is relatively little employed elsewhere. It was a relief to be in the company of London or of Orbeli, who are so direct and clear, after having contended with other people who seemed more bent on impressing the visitor than on discussing their research itself.

Lindberg showed me dogs at various stages after ablation of one hemisphere, and of the pre-frontal region on the other side; it was surprising to see how little they used their smell to locate food thrown to them in their hemianoptic field. Having apparently heard from someone else before I came to him, that I had spoken of the difficulty of getting in touch with various people because of their working in several different institutes, he told me I had been misinformed on this point, and that most people like himself do all their research in the one place. (I gathered from others, however, that it is still necessary for many doctors, probably not the research men, to take up a number of jobs to earn a fair living.)

Rosenthal was also working on the effects of removal of the hemispheres, with particular attention to the effects of the removal of small pieces of cortex upon complex activities; he tests not only the ordinary conditioned reflexes as Lindberg does, but also such motor conditioned responses – or trained habits – of the dog as giving alternately first one paw then the other. He was also, like Lindberg, interested in seeing how far tactile disorientation was preserved after decortication (conditioned response to stimulus on one spot and not on another). He had a number of plans: he wanted to modify Dusser de Bareme's method, and test the effects of electro-coagulation of the top two or three layers of the cortex instead of all six; also by the "trace" conditioned reflex to attach the problem of memory, also "negative" stimuli. The question of the part played by sub-cortical mechanisms is little regarded; for example, it seemed that stimulation of the labyrinth by hot and cold water might be used to throw light on this; he said it had not been done. He stated his conclusions about the area striata and other regions of the cortex in such a form that it seemed he was finding that a conditioned reflex should be established as long as the area of cortex which received and dealt with the appropriate perception was intact, e.g. if all the cortex except the area striata were removed, visual conditioned reflexes could still be obtained. I discussed with him the bearing of this on Lashley's work and he said that Pavlov had believed that there were many centres of nuclei where specific "elements" were concentrated but that simple "elements" for some purposes were distributed throughout the cortex.

I next saw Prof. Osowsky who conducts one of the university clinics in an outlying suburb, and is chiefly responsible for the collection of psychiatric statistical data for Leningrad. He told me that what published statistics there were might be found in a book by Dr Persakoff (or some such name) which he would send me, but like some other books and papers promised me by people in Russia, it has not reached me. He said he had not the impression that manic-depressive psychosis was any less frequent in Russia than elsewhere (he had studied in Halle and knew German psychiatry well), or than it had been formerly in Russia; and that he would be surprised if it were so. He himself saw few psycho-neurotics because they did not come his way; his clinic, like most of the others, selected its material from the general hospitals, the dispensaries, etc., and therefore he and his university colleagues were not in a position to form a personal impression of the frequency of the various forms of mental illness. It is usually after a preliminary period in the clinics (evidently reception hospitals) where the patients can stay as long as the doctors wish, that they go on to the mental hospital if necessary; consequently a majority of the manic-depressive cases may recover in the clinic and never be included in mental hospital statistics. He did not believe that any figures were available concerning the patients seen in the rayon; he had not even the figures for his own district, though his clinic is in the locale of the dispensary of the rayon psychiatrist there. I asked him about the content and form of the usual groups and it seemed that there was nothing particularly different from what is found in other European countries, e.g. the hysterics have psychological rather than coarse neurological-looking phenomena; obsessionals look like masked schizophrenics; anxiety states, however, he said were more often discreet anxiety attacks than chronic states. Fortunately, also, he was responsible for the treatment of alcoholics – a subject on which I had been able to find out nothing except vague generalities from others. The arrangements for alcoholics, and indeed for all the outpatient specialist treatment by psychiatrists in the rayon, are still restricted to the big towns, the team there consisting of a neurologist, a psychiatrist, a "narcologist", a psychotherapist and, rather pointlessly it seemed, a neuro-pathologist (probably a man who does laboratory tests, as for syphilis, etc.). Cases of acute alcoholism are sometimes admitted for 24 hours to the hospitals in Leningrad. Severe alcoholics are sent to an institution, containing 25 beds, where they seldom stay longer than two months. On discharge there is no control of their drinking, but if they commit anti-social acts, they are punished according to the act and not for the alcoholism. Alcoholism is not accepted as an excuse of plea of lessened responsibility for delinquency. The treatment in the institution, which is too small to deal with all the cases, consists of work therapy and perhaps subcutaneous injections of oxygen, or some other fashion of the time, e.g. hydrotherapy. He said that after discharge the patients do not, as a rule, relapse and that new drunkards do not develop among the younger people because "unlike people in the capitalist countries" they have plenty to occupy and interest them. He attributed the improvement to the general social improvement and the milieu, and partly also to the lectures which are given in the factories and to children in school about the dangers of alcohol; this is not done "by private societies as in capitalist countries", but by the state. He did not mention this prophylactic side until specifically questioned on the point and did not seem very enthusiastic about it; when I asked him if the emphasis in these lectures was put more on the social wickedness or the physical ill-effects of the habit, his reply gave the impression that it was left to the individual lecturers to decide what they should say. He said that there was no control of the sale of alcohol to drunkards, nor, I gathered, when the alcoholic has come before the courts for anti-social behaviour, is the penalty greater for a second offence. He described the outpatient surveillance or treatment of the cases by the narcologist vaguely as social care (a nurse is trained to do the social work) psychotherapy and oxygen injections. Anything more precise was not forthcoming. A patient had to attend the dispensary if told to do so; the rayon doctor could ask a policeman to bring him by force if he did not come, this was, however, seldom necessary. Some of the things Prof. Osowsky told me seemed to have been more rosily presented than other evidence suggests. The most recent statistics I obtained from them showed alcoholics to make up nearly a quarter of the total male admission to mental hospitals during the year. There were almost as many alcoholics as male schizophrenics; the total alcoholic admissions included a considerable number of re-admission (about half of them as far as I could make out). Evidently alcohol is a very much bigger mental hospital problem with them than in England or the USA, though their figures may be swollen by the compulsion put on alcoholics in Russia to undergo treatment. In Moscow I noticed several men drunk, some of them in their twenties and thirties; one drunken young man who was causing a scene in the crowded restaurant of the Park of Culture and Rest, seemed to excite sympathy and amusement among the other people there, and was treated with extra-ordinary forbearance by the policeman who was called in (I was told by the people I was with that the young man was protesting that he had to work very hard and was entitled to sleep or sing at the table if he wished, and that people sitting nearby were taking his side).

I asked Prof. Osowsky about what is done for feeble-mindedness, and wayward or delinquent children. He did not regard these problems however as a matter for psychiatrists or even for doctors of any kind to attend to. I gathered from other sources that juvenile delinquency had been increasing in the last five or six years, and is causing much concern. He mentioned occupational therapy and educational measures but by the former is meant in Russia what has been the custom in the less energetic mental hospitals with us, i.e. getting such patients as can do useful work, rather for the sake of the work than of their own health.

Report

Since the denunciation of "pedology" in 1936, the whole subject, and especially mental tests and psycho-technics, has been under a cloud, almost to the point of extinction; consequently I could not find that there was any special training for defectives on a large scale. As I did not, however, manage to get in touch with anybody who spoke with first-hand knowledge about the matter I was left uncertain. Although Osowsky had been specially picked out for me as the man who would know all about the statistics for Leningrad, he was unable to give data which one would ordinarily be able to get from official records, and altogether the statistical side of psychiatry seems unaccountably neglected. Even at Davidenkoff's clinic for neurological and neurotic cases (formerly Pavlov's clinic), when I asked what were the proportions of different types of illness at the clinic each year since its opening six years or so before, I got the only too common answer to any definite question, namely, "they were just getting it out", "it would be ready shortly"; and when I asked how many of the cases were neurological and how many neurotic, they could not even tell me that. I was eager to find this out because, according to Osowsky, a lot of the neurotics go to the internist, as in other countries, or to the neurologist, rather than to the psychiatrist.

At Davidenkoff's clinic I asked about the treatment of the neurotic; they emphasised that they did not use psycho-analysis but employed a little hypnosis and persuasion. I gathered that they do very little psychotherapy at all. Davidenkoff's chief assistant could not give any concrete illustrations, it seemed, of his reiterated statements that they studied and treated their patients by physiological methods and that through Pavlov, psychology had been superseded by physiology, etc., etc. When I pressed for details and method, they kept laughing and saying "Oh, something concrete he wants," and repeated their phrases about applying the knowledge gained from dogs to the study of human beings. In the long run what they do, as far as I could make out, is to give full doses of sodium bromide three times a day but with no control of the chloride intake (at first they said vaguely that they did and when we got into details said they had not done it yet, but they were just going to begin it). Similarly with the classification of patients into four types according to their temperaments, the only criteria apparently, apart from a rather subjective total estimate, were how the patient had responded when his life had been in danger and what were his responses to fatigue and work tests (Kraepelin – Schults, ergograph, dynamometer: chiefly the latter). They were doing some research on sleep, taking electrical records of eyelid movements in subjects who are falling asleep; the work was being done mainly on a "narcoleptic", whom I saw, but who seemed to me probably a hysteric. They were treating a "narcoleptic" by sleep conditioning and said they had "cured" him, though I found that he still had his cataleptic attacks. They work in a large hospital and can pick their cases to suit themselves. They were also doing some conditioned reflex work on motor reactions, on orthodox lines. I asked about Davidenkoff's genetic studies, of which I had known something before, and one of the assistants, who was responsible for that part of the work, told me she was studying the heredity of sleep in twins and ordinary siblings. Her results, however, will be a little unreliable, I think, because she gets the necessary data as to length, uninterruptedness, etc., of sleep from the children themselves whom she is studying and from their parents, rather than by direct observation. In the wards she showed me a number of myopathics and dystrophics and said that in various neuro-muscular conditions (including Myasthenia gravis) she had good results by giving "myelisat" which they use very widely for the non-cerebral neuro-muscular affections. There were a number of interesting cases, e.g. an epileptic, who had been conditioned to have a fit whenever light of a particular colour was turned (he had formerly had his fits on awaking from sleep, their onset being detected by the electrically recorded lid movements). On the other hand, in a woman with a remarkable tic beginning in her eyelids, they had not made any attempt to register these initial movements and analyse them on their apparatus. In the wards the doctors talked freely about the patients' neuroses in front of them, talking Russian to the interpreter quite loudly. The beds were a little crowded but the clinic well laid out for its purpose. As in other clinics, there seemed many more doctors about than would be expected in other countries, but since punitive taxation has practically killed private practice, these clinics may not be representative of Russian hospitals as a whole; probably the profusion of doctors has not quite the significance one at first attaches to it. It seemed clear at any rate that in the clinics the number of doctors is out of proportion at present to the amount of competent work done or even the number of hours spent at it (so many finding it necessary to work at several jobs). In the department dealing with vegetative anomalies, Dr Weinberg showed me a number of endocrine cases, some of them very rare, and a collection of patients with migraine. Apropos of the somewhat uncritical approach some of them showed to endocrine therapy, even Ossipov told me he had had great success in treating melancholia with an interior pituitary preparation given by the mouth.

Conditions in Russia, even for a visit so remote from political questions as this, were different enough from those in other countries to call for some general references to them. There was first of all the baffling difficulty in getting to see the people and places one wanted to. Though I repeatedly asked in Moscow and Leningrad to be allowed to visit a large mental hospital, this could never be managed. I had hoped to see Prof. Bronner early in order to get a general understanding of the organisation and line of development of psychiatric work, but this was impossible (I was variously told that he was ill, away at a congress, and on holiday); nor, though I asked if I could call on any of his assistants who could inform me on these matters, was I able to do so. Similarly, I was never able to see Prof. Astachoff, Prof. Uktomsky, or Prof. Davidenkoff; and, as the explanation varied, (e.g. one day Prof. Uktomsky would be too busy to see me, they said, another day his telephone had broken down, another day he had already been away for a week from Leningrad) one felt that it was easy to arrive at false conclusions from what one saw and heard. Moreover, it was impossible to spend the time as profitably as elsewhere, since far fewer visits were arranged in the time that I was accustomed to pay ordinarily, and some of those whom I saw seemed so bent on impressing the visitor and answering questions without consideration, or else defensively, as if criticism were implied that it was hard to form a clear picture of their work. A neutral inquiry was treated as though it were a statement containing objections out of which one was to be dissuaded. It was noteworthy that the senior people, like Kroll, Orbeli, London and Lina Stern, and some of the younger, abler physiologists and geneticists were free from this. They talked reasonably and did not keep trying to reply to some argument supposed to lie behind one's question. The psychiatrists, however, were prone to wander round the point, and to paint a diffusely rosy picture, on the details of which they would hedge. Some of them talked more like salesmen than scientists.

Although more or less familiar with main trend[s] in other countries, they seemed in psychiatry, and to a less extent in physiology, out of touch with the nuances of opinion elsewhere, e.g. the malarial treatment of GPI and continuous sleep treatment of psychoses were to [sic] as though they were recent and still highly disputable discoveries. Orbeli's attitude towards protopathic and epicritic sensation is an example of the same thing. No doubt it is due to the very limited contacts even the foremost men can have with their fellow workers outside Russia, and, though less significantly, to the difficulties in getting hold of foreign journals, (this is apparently not the case in physiology but is so in psychiatry). The younger clinicians, who have never been abroad, seemed to suffer most from this limitation and the ones I met at the Gannushkin clinic and in Leningrad seemed unpromising and ill-informed, judging from the very little I saw of them. Their notions of the outside world in its medical aspects are naïve on some points; advances in Russia, which by our standards would be belated and fumbling, they presented as daring triumphs of Soviet thought in medicine. However, I feel particularly diffident about my impressions: what with the language difficulty, the delays in seeing people and their reticence or vagueness in some cases when I did get to them, I could not feel confident that I was finding out what I wanted to know. Moreover, I had extremely few opportunities of seeing anyone without the interpreter's company, even though in most cases there was no interpreting needed: where I did see people alone they talked much more freely and enabled me to see how misleading, on some matters, the interview *à trois* had been. I was enjoined not to publish what I had been told or indeed what I had seen, because it might rebound – as had happened before. I did not gather that the best scientific workers in this branch of medicine are happy, or that what is done in Moscow and Leningrad is representative of the rest of USSR, or even of RFSSR: the discrepancy is extreme. Criticism of scientific work may be hampered because of its political repercussions as with Gurevitsch's work; or suddenly whipped up by a political change of wind.

Psychiatry, even at its best, seemed on a much lower level than physiology and genetics, and probably than brain morphology. But I could not get to see enough people to judge fairly, and when I did meet someone like Kronfeld, who could describe the position fully, he hid his knowledge and opinions behind exuberant praises.

I had supposed I might find in Soviet psychiatry great licence of speculation and experiment, original points of view, and enormous development of the social side of this subject. But in this I was disappointed: I always asked what they were doing that was new or different from what is done elsewhere, but found that the work was mostly along familiar lines: as far as social psychiatry was concerned, I heard of no new sides and no enthusiastic progress. "Pedology" and vocational psychology had been dropped, with public repudiation of mental testing, because they conflicted with political views, or had been misapplied. Speransky and Braines certainly had unfamiliar things to tell but the one was unspecific and the other dependent on a biological theory that is discredited. The actual yield from original theories, e.g. of Speransky, or from formerly stimulating ones, e.g. of Pavlov, seems meagre.

As regards the practical work in psychiatry I had the impression that the nursing is poor, though on the upgrade, and that of psychiatric social work, as understood in England or the USA, there is little: they seem to rely (understandably but, as things are, rather shakily) on large-scale, and not on individual, social measures. Of a psychiatric approach to delinquency I could not find evidence nor of any detailed sociological approach; I was told that the number of offences by children had increased in the last few years. There were many indications (e.g. in the Park of Culture and Rest) of the earnestness with which the people are instructed in medical, as in other more or less technical, matters. Except with regard to alcohol and syphilis, mental health appears to play little part in the popular education.

I had the impression that scientific congresses are long and unduly numerous and time-consuming. Teaching inevitably takes up a great proportion of the senior men's time too. The statements about the number of people engaged in research in this and that institute needed qualification; many of them seemed very much in *statu pupillari*, and the amount of serious work done depended on a few people, trained and competent. Like so much else in Russia, the significance of all this varies according to one's response to the assurance "it is in construction; come again in five years' time and you will see".

I expected that in psychiatry the Soviet insistence on research being directed towards practical and previously defined ends would be obvious and interesting. But it seemed doubtful whether such planning was really working, in the way one had read of, in the field of medical research, or whether there was much co-ordination of effort. The directors of departments had to submit budgets or indicate in advance what they were aiming at, but this was done, at any rate by some, perfunctorily and with a belief that in research you could not predict what you would have accomplished, or even what you would be working at, by the end of a year or two. I did not gather that the members of the party who meet regularly in each institution interfere with straightforward research. I was unable to meet people like Prof. Bronner who could have informed me of the lines of development planned in medicine. However, a casual visitor can see that the political and social background casts much light and much shadow on scientific work, and that broad statements about it cannot be taken at face value.

FINLAND[32]

In Helsingfors I saw Prof. Fabritius. His outlook on psychiatry was considerably coloured by his earlier, predominantly neurological interests. He mentioned some of

---

[32] Psychiatric hospitals, such as the Lapinlahti in Helsinki, that near Kuopio and the Kakisalmi and Pitkaniemi hospitals, began to be built in Finland between 1835 and 1900. From 1840 the management and care of the mentally ill became the State's responsibility. After the First World War there was much development in psychiatry; most provinces had their own asylum, or shared one with a neighbouring province, and psychiatric departments were established in general hospitals. German psychiatry had influenced Scandinavian psychiatry heavily until the Second World War, and many Scandinavians went abroad to study the subject. Freud's theories were not very influential until after the Second World War; until then Scandinavian psychiatry emphasized somatic and constitutional aspects. The concept of schizophreniform psychoses was much used (it had been elaborated by Langfeldt), and from the 1920s malaria therapy and the convulsive and shock therapies were increasingly used, a little later than in other European countries.

the principal difficulties that arise in regard to staffing, through the prevailing nationalist feeling and the Finnish-Swedish dispute. He mentioned that his most promising assistant, Gordin, who had lately written the excellent monograph on torsion-dystonia, was being blocked in his advancement for reasons of this sort.

In Helsingfors there is the familiar problem of short-time workers, i.e. the doctors of the clinic are unable to keep adequate records, do scientific work, etc., because so much of their time is split up between a number of jobs in order to earn a living. His first assistant, for example, has a private practice, prison work, court work and some other jobs, so that he is able to spend only a few hours a day in the Clinic. The professor is himself apparently much occupied in writing expert reports and in teaching undergraduates. Gordin's work was interesting, though he seemed unduly influenced by the views of Muskens. Kaila (who had been in Heidelberg when I worked there in 1928) is apparently unable to give much time to research. Psychoanalysis and the related points of view are not favoured in the clinic.

Prof. Fabritius had been working on the effects of injecting separated leucocytes of schizophrenics subcutaneously into normal people, and he also told me of some studies on the cerebral spinal fluid, which had not been carried very far. He spoke critically of the work done by Brander, in Prof. Ylppo's Department, on premature children, and his extraordinary finding that the IQ of these children correlated with their birth weight. In Prof. Ylppo's Department there was apparently considerable interest in some of the psychiatric problems which children present.

I also saw Prof. Granit, who was good enough to show me his experiments on the eyes of decapitated frogs. It seemed that this was a field in which investigation into the effects of such drugs as mescaline, and also the changes that accompany visual hallucinations might be studied with profit; Granit agreed that there were possibilities, but the worker would obviously need some special training for a short time in his laboratory. It seemed also that his research into light and dark adaptation might be applied to a small corner of pharmacological investigation in psychiatry, but with far less profit than his work on the changes of retinal potential.

NORWAY[33]

Bergen

In Bergen I saw Dr Birkhaug. The bulk of his work is, of course, remote from psychiatry, centring around the relationship of immunity to allergy, in connection with tuberculosis. The exactness of his methods and especially the careful statistical checking were, however, illuminating and in striking contrast to some of the loose research in psychiatry which could be done with equal strictness perhaps. Some of

---

[33] See note 32 above for general Scandinavian trends. In Norway, a government-initiated inquiry into the conditions of life of the mentally ill in 1824 advocated opening four psychiatric houses, and led to a highly progressive Act in 1848 for the treatment and management of the mentally ill. The first psychiatric hospital, the Gaustad hospital in Oslo, opened in 1855, based on the Auxerre psychiatric hospital. Between 1855 and 1881 three more hospitals opened: Rotvold in Trondheim, Eeg in Kristiansand and Neevengarden in Bergen. The first psychiatric service began in 1917 and was part of general hospital Ulleval in Oslo; the second was the psychiatric service of the University of Oslo, built in 1926.

his work seemed applicable in principle to infections like anterior poliomyelitis and encephalitis lethargica, which are of importance for the psychiatrist. Of the alleged association of schizophrenia and tuberculosis he was a sceptical as most authorities; he knew the literature of it.

The social aspect of his work on tuberculosis and the success of his attempt to concentrate the preparation of BCG [*bacille Calmette-Guérin*] in one place were also interesting in relation to comparable problems in social psychiatry, especially the widespread employment of potentially dangerous therapeutic methods. The remarkably unhampered conditions under which he is able to work perhaps account in part for the critical thoroughness with which he is able to apply himself to a concrete scientific problem. He also showed me the leper hospital and two of the patients who had advanced anaesthesias and amputations.

Oslo

In Oslo I visited the University Clinic. Professor Vogt had recently been ill for three months, but he showed me round the clinic and discussed the lines along which it had developed. His interests seemed administrative, social and psychological. But it was clear that in spite of his special interest in problems of the family, sexual life, etc., he was no great appreciator of psychoanalysis, (though in theory, like many people, more sympathetic to Freud's intelligent system and sincere work than to the obscure or superficial views of some of the related schools). Like other people in Norway he deplored the way in which Harald Schjelderup's enthusiasm for psychoanalysis had swamped his earlier studies and work. On the other hand, Prof. Vogt was not much interested in somatic studies, such as Langfeld had been pursuing in his clinic.

Langfeld told me of his own inquiry into the prognosis, not only of schizophrenics, which he has published, but also of manic-depressives and obsessionals. He is proposing to work on the vegetative nervous system; one got the impression that in these somatic investigations his brother, the professor of physiology, was prompting him. So far as his clinical investigations are concerned, he seemed not sufficiently acquainted with the literature, in spite of considerable effort. I also met his brother, who mentioned the objections that had recently been made by him and others to Gjessing's conclusions. It is surprising that there is so very little contact between Gjessing and the physiologists at the university.

The university clinic is still incomplete and is intended for the treatment of neurotics, and the observation, only, of psychotics. Like others who have in the last 20 years developed a clinic on these lines, i.e. voluntary admission, open doors, etc. Prof. Vogt, when speaking of his experiences and hopes in detail, showed that he had worked his way independently along the same road as others were following; the problems are clearly very much the same, impose the same self-discipline on the doctors concerned, and cause the same surprise in each country when it is demonstrated, for instance, that a large measure of freedom can obtain in a voluntary clinic without any considerable risk. Likewise he had aimed at a children's department. The impossibility of having enough doctors to carry out detailed psychotherapy, the unwisdom of keeping patients for more than a year at the most, the uselessness of treating drug addicts in the clinic, and other points familiar for example at the Maudsley Hospital, came up in his conversation; his conclusions as to what is best were remarkably similar to those arrived at in London.

The problem of following up the cases after they have left the clinic is made difficult for him by the fact that they come from all over the country. For those who belong to the Commune of Oslo, Dr Lofthuis maintains a general supervision, and has a social worker to help him; he also had until lately been responsible for the recognition of defective children, etc.

The laboratories of the clinic did not seem to be in very active use. The psychological laboratory was empty, and in the chemical laboratories only routine work was going on. Langfeld, however, was doing blood sugar responses to insulin intravenously, in order to investigate why schizophrenics sometimes require such large doses before they exhibit the effects of hyperglycaemia. He did not, however, seem to know some of the recent work, e.g. that of Himsworth on sugar metabolism, and, as one so frequently found in the various countries, had been accustomed to rely on the German literature and had only latterly begun to read the English and American journals.

The buildings and equipment of the clinic seemed good, except for the occupational therapy [*sic*], which follow the old pattern of skilled carpentry, gardening and other useful or pleasant tasks, probably limited to the few who feel like it or are particularly trained for it. Recreational therapy, gymnastics, etc., are not organised. Making allowance, however, for the habits and outlook of the Norwegians, the arrangements probably work better than a more rigid system would. As elsewhere in Norway, much of the laboratory work is done by medical students waiting their turn to get on with their clinical studies. Apart from Langfeld, I heard only of one assistant – a young cand. med. – who was doing research (on histopathology under Prosector Jansen at the university). The clinic seemed on the whole good, but not enterprising, active or original.

The relationship between the clinic and the two neighbouring mental hospitals – Dikemark and Gaustad – is friendly but, I gathered not intimate. The result, however, of the present relationship between the psychiatric clinic and the Oslo mental hospital is that the clinic mainly keeps the manic-depressive cases, whereas the schizophrenics, and other prognostically less favourable forms, are passed on; consequently Gjessing rarely receives at his mental hospital typical affective cases such as he would like to study along the lines he has employed for cyclical schizophrenia. As far as the doctors are concerned, there seems to be some interchange; but for the University career, the essential MD examination, which is so rigorous, puts many mental hospital doctors entirely out of the running.

There seems no doubt that Prof. Vogt has had a great influence on the direction psychiatry has been taking in Norway, and that his broad-mindedness, philosophical interests and personality have not only been of general benefit, but have led particularly to a concern with the social and therapeutic side of the subject.

There were several people whom I was unable to see because they were away at a congress – Ödegaard, Monrad-Krohn, Jensen and others. I had also thought of seeing Lingjaerde, but he was away up in the north of Norway at Bødin, and most of the people I met had a low opinion of his unusually painstaking investigations into liver-function in schizophrenia. Apparently he interpreted as abnormal much that occurs in normal people, e.g. bile products in the urine.

I saw Prof. Mohr who told me about his Drosophila work. He also introduced me to Keonesland, an assistant of Jensen's, who was working on the effects of carbon-monoxide on the brain, in the manner of Alfred Meyer, and following the tracts in the brain affected by cortical lesions. Prof. Kristine Bonnevie discussed some of the questions arising out of her work on finger prints. I was surprised to find that she did not know of the English work, particularly that of Percy Stocks, on the finger prints of twins, and that she had not used palm prints at all to confirm her diagnosis of monozygosity in twins whom she had reported; on the other hand, it is extraordinary that workers in England have never adopted her method of denoting finger print patterns, so generally used elsewhere now. She also told me how the study of anomalies of digital development in some mice had demonstrated that during a brief stage of development the CSF was forced out under the skin and travelled round, interfering also with eye development. It occurred to me that the mysterious association of polydactylism with eye anomalies in the Lawrence-Meon-Biedl syndrome might be worth looking at from this point of view, though such an explanation would probably be impossible to apply because of the nature of the eye change. She told me of her studies on transplantation and of the work on anencephaly; she also showed me her preparations in celloidin. The relevance of her studies in comparative pathoembryology – as it may be called – to some of the problems of neurology, seemed fairly clear, though not to those of psychiatry.

Professor Langfeld told me of the work being done in his laboratory on calcium metabolism and vitamins, but it appeared that these were mostly limited investigations done by candidates for a doctorate, and that he would have preferred to have had more say in the choice of subject of the investigations, instead of merely advising and superintending these young men, who would leave the laboratory as soon as the investigation was complete.

Prof. Langfeld seemed extremely critical in his outlook, perhaps more critical than productive; his strictures on the physiological work of Lingjaerde and other psychiatrists, who had submitted MD theses – which came under his notice – were no doubt justified, but sharp.

I spent a day at Dikemark with Gjessing. Of his approximately 800 patients belonging to the city of Oslo, the majority were regarded by him as schizophrenics. There were some seniles and arteriosclerotics, but GPIs are lacking because they are filtered off by the General Hospital, and therefore the only ones he gets are those that have been unsuccessfully treated with malaria, etc.; and the recurrent affective conditions are drained off by the psychiatric clinics. He has succeeded in getting much support from the Commune for his research, as well as for building, and his new block for occupational therapy, etc., is admirably arranged for his purpose. The level of general organization was high; treatment was individualised, and, presumably because of good nursing and structural facilities, they have been able to dispense with sedative drugs during the daytime for the last four to five years. It was of interest that in spite of admirable arrangements and the pleasant surroundings of his hospital, Gjessing found it difficult to induce his former patients, who had been discharged "recovered", to come back for a few days for further metabolic study, because their relatives or the patients themselves did not like the idea. Consequently, Gjessing was anxious to have a small clinic or separate ward in Oslo for this purpose; evidently it takes much more than general hospital conditions to make people, even in Norway, regard the mental hospital as they would a general hospital. Possibly the difficulty is enhanced in Gjessing's case by his not having a social worker; Lofthuis, I gather, has nurses who act as social workers, and he keeps in touch with the patients, as does Saethre also, in some cases.

Gjessing's senior women nurses had, I was told, done three years general training before they came to him, and the level of nursing attained seemed well up to, or above, the standard of the average English mental hospital. Some of his male nurses were, like his laboratory workers, medical students obliged to mark time. From his point of view it is, of course, a great advantage to be able to pick out men particularly interested and competent in physiology for his work, and it has probably also the advantage of directing able students into the psychiatric field when later on they qualify, but of course the system is hard on the students themselves. It is a pity that, apart from a few women medical students who do psychiatric nursing during the long vacation, no advantage is taken in England, as far as I know, of the briefer opportunity available here during the holidays for encouraging some interest and detailed study in psychiatry.

In spite of his large staff Gjessing finds it impossible to carry out his detailed metabolic researches on more than three cases at once, and in view of the length of time during which he carried on an investigation and the strictness of dietary control, his researches would be impracticable in a psychiatric clinic. It was indeed on the method, rather than on the outcome of the research, that he laid most stress, insisting on the value of continuous observations over a long period. The thoroughness of his initial overhaul of the cases, both for general purposes and in order to determine suitability for the metabolic research, was impressive, and, as growing out from his earlier views as to the toxic origin of much mental disorder, indicated how the thorough prosecution of even a false scent proved, in the long run, more fruitful than dull or half-hearted research along more travelled roads; his combination of a speculative and even imaginative optimism with fairly severe self-criticism and, I gathered, receptiveness to criticism from outside was noteworthy. The two chief difficulties about accepting his work as it stands are presumably (1) the uncertainty as to whether the cases he has studied are mainly schizophrenic, as he suggests, and (2) the possibility that the metabolic changes he observes are dependent on the great change in muscular activity that occurs when the patient passes out of his stupor or into it. As to the former, he told me that he had found a pyknic habit of body among the immediate relatives, and the data I learned about the clinical picture in the patients I saw suggested that there was a large affective component (as witness the predominance of paranoid delusions, the cyclical course, the "facultative" stupor, and the striking manic conduct of a patient who was shown to me as schizophrenic) which fitted in with this view. This is not to dispute that there were also many schizophrenic features in the patients.

As to the dietary point (upon which Prof. Langfeld was inclined to lay much stress) one must accept Gjessing's statement that the food taken remains consistent in both phases, but as it is a diet adequate for resting conditions, it is understandable, as his critics say, that the nitrogenous output might increase with a catatonic excitement; he said that experts he had recently consulted, while abroad, had agreed with him that it was inadvisable to vary the diet according to the clinical state, but I could not see why he should not make his standard diet bigger. From his point of view the question is not an important one, because he believes there is no evidence that exercise would account for the alteration of nitrogen output, and the fact that the nitrogenous substances are turned out two days before the excitement comes on cannot be explained easily. Langfield's other criticisms e.g. of the view that there can be a storage of toxic nitrogenous substances, during the stuporose phase, in some indeterminate storehouse, probably the liver, and of Gjessing's view that the condition is a toxic diencephalosis, are less important, since Gjessing puts these forward only as speculations.

His earlier interest in focal sepsis leads him to search patients thoroughly for sources of infection, but no longer with the excess of zeal which prevailed during the Cotton phase, as one may call it. Gjessing holds, however, that many of the variations in the clinical picture are complications due to infection, and that with thorough "defocalisation", clear-cut swings in the clinical state are enabled sometimes to appear, where formerly they were muddled. Gjessing had also been using insulin treatment for some of his long-standing patients; he had given heroic doses, the largest I had ever heard of (even up to 800 units), and believed that it effected considerable social improvement in their state; he was proposing to combine it with thyroid treatment afterwards.

It seems a great pity that the researches he has done, which for exactitude and completeness are probably unequalled, could not be carried out on any manic-depressive cases, recognised by him as such. It would clear up some important ambiguities in his work. He has such a remarkable turnover each year that it is difficult to escape the conclusion that a number of manic-depressive patients, or what would be diagnosed as such in other countries, go into his statistics as schizophrenics. If that is not so, then his "defocalisation", and other measures of treatment, make nearly half his schizophrenics capable of returning to ordinary life – a better result than most people with a similar unselected material can report. It was regrettably impossible, the day I was there to get statistics of the frequency of the different disorders in the hospital. Another difficulty is that he cannot, for obvious reasons, demonstrate in the blood of his patients any particular toxic nitrogenous substances, though he believes that of the total nitrogenous substances only a small proportion can be toxic, and that in this sense it may be a quite unmeasurable, qualitative rather than quantitative, effect. There is no evidence that the metabolic happenings he observes are the cause, so to speak, of the stupor or excitement, they may well be concomitants and are, no doubt, none the less valuable for that. If his view that there are toxic nitrogenous substances, as indicated by variations in nitrogen output, is correct, one might ask about the findings in other diseases in which there is nitrogen retention. He also mentioned that he was anxious to find a tolerance test for protein, but had not been able to. I put this point to Theorell in Stockholm, and he considered, as Gjessing had been told by others, that the only thing one could do would be to work through the amino-acids one by one, obviously a huge task. Gjessing did not know of Prof. London's method of studying the changes that occurred in the liver and kidneys, which I thought might throw light on the problem.

Report

The doctor who was in charge of the female side of the hospital was working on folliculin, and had a good medical student assisting him. His results showed such close concord of folliculin output, presence or absence of menstruation, and effect of treatment by injecting a Norwegian gonadal hormone, as to be almost too good to be true.

SWEDEN[34]

Uppsala

First I went to Prof. Dahlberg's Institute. Unfortunately he was away but Dr Sjövall showed me the work that was going on. The inquiry that was being made into the factors bearing on the course of manic-depressive psychosis was a social, rather than a genetic study, so far as one could judge. The psychiatric problems raised by such an inquiry, which Sjövall was undertaking, had not been thought out; Dahlberg, however, had been there so short a time that the research had not got properly under way. An inquiry into the heredity of mental deficiency was evidently also in its initial stages. Sjövall said they were investigating fertility in the course of the latter investigation, but since still-births were not being included in the recorded number of siblings, there seemed a possibility of error. Later I saw Prof. Dahlberg in Copenhagen; he was good enough to explain to me the limited scope of the proposed investigations, which are only a beginning. He will obviously need the co-operation of an abler psychiatrist than seems available at present, if the psychiatric side of his research is to be done satisfactorily; he is himself (on some points perhaps unduly, and on others insufficiently) aware of the pitfalls.

I visited Prof. Svedberg's Institute, where he and Dr Tiselius kindly showed me the ultracentrifuge, as well as the cataphoresis method, for determining globulin fractions. Apparently the application of the methods to the study of the cerebro-spinal fluid, for example, has not yet come about.

I saw Prof. Jacobowsky at the mental hospital. He is very quick in his mind, but seems more interested in the administrative and vaguer social issues than in the details of psychiatry. Some of his opinions seemed more like impressions than conclusions. His staff did not seem particularly interested in research, except for the woman parasitologist in the laboratory, and the first assistant, Wahlström, who has been investigating for years the toxicity of the blood in schizophrenia, with on the whole negative results. The clinical material was extraordinarily interesting, and the general layout of the hospital good; occupational therapy was, as one nearly always found in Scandinavia, excellent. I was struck here, and at Beckumberga, by the low rate of charge for patients who have private rooms; it scarcely covers the per capita maintenance.

Prof. Jacobowsky was responsible for only a proportion of the beds in the mental hospital; another senior physician, in charge of 450 beds and also of the extra-mural

---

[34] See note 32 above for Scandinavian trends. The Order of the Seraphins was in charge of the hospital system in Sweden until 1876; these psychiatric hospitals were finally administered by medical services from 1877. It was only in 1851 that the State became involved. In 1929 a Swedish law included regulation for the admission and release of patients from psychiatric establishments.

arrangements, took me on his round among the 70 patients placed out in family care. They are visited by a nurse once a week, and come to the hospital for their baths, etc. The cost of upkeep is approximately 2 kronor a day, i.e. heavier, I gathered, than it would be in Belgium or Switzerland. If, however, the patients work for the people in whose houses they live, less may be paid. Some of the patients who were regarded as incapable of work in family care would almost certainly have been working if still in the mental hospital. A high proportion of the people placed out seemed to be defectives; this was in keeping with the Gheel experience, and should probably modify some of the opinions expressed by Pollock and others about the wide scope of colony and family-care treatment. In the Uppsala arrangement, it looked as though the number of people in family care, and the people selected for it, depended a good deal upon how much pressure there was on the mental hospital beds. Family care is regarded more as the intermediate stage between the mental hospital and ordinary life, than as a permanent arrangement for the patient. The system was fairly recent and was being built up slowly, so that in the Uppsala district they have not as yet had difficulty in getting enough guardians, apart from the initial prejudice – now somewhat overcome. In one house where the house-wife was a young woman of the urban type with children of her own, and two difficult patients (a suicidal involutional and an aggressive senile), I asked why she stood it, and learned that she was in fact just going to give up looking after patients. Dr Hojer, however, told me that one of the reasons why guardians can be found is that there are so many childless people who care to earn a little more money thus.

Prof. Bergmark showed me the medical clinic, including some interesting neurological cases. I also met Dr Waldenstrom who told me of his study in porphyria; it occurred to me that the different responses of people to large doses of sulphonal might be attributable to there being always a particular metabolic disturbance in those who develop pellagra-like symptoms and methaemoglobinaemia, and that this metabolic disturbance might be characteristic of their illness, so far as the mental hospital cases are concerned. I also met Dr Lindquist, who mentioned his work on vitamin deficiency. Dr Waldenstrom showed me a striking case of alcaptonuria.

Stockholm

Prof. Wigert was apologetic about the structural arrangements of his clinic, which is, as he says, an old mental hospital, but it has plenty of ground and did not strike me as deplorable, though the laboratory space is small. There are 260 patients, of whom the majority are "under voluntary treatment", but this is different from what passes by the same name in England, in as much as these Swedish patients cannot leave until the doctor consents; if they protest, they may, I gathered, write to a board composed of two psychiatrists, as well as a lawyer and a layman, on which Prof. Wigert sits. A small group of patients had been admitted without any formalities, i.e. they were comparable to English voluntary patients, but they were exceptional cases. Prof. Wigert has the inconvenience of being unable to get rid of some chronic cases already in the clinic; he has only a small turnover of cases, with a hundred or so beds which he may do what he likes with. There is much pressure on his beds, but the new arrangements proposed will probably enable him to run the clinic on more satisfactory lines. Prof. Wigert was enthusiastic, in his jovial volatile way, about the apparatus for doing electro-encephalograms, which had just been installed. It seemed an excellent set-up, and Dr Frey and the non-psychiatrist, specially responsible for it, were both very keen. I gathered that Zoltermann, who worked with Adrian, had had nothing to do with the arrangement, which had been put almost entirely in the hands of Ehrenswert.

They are also doing insulin and cardiazol treatment, though they cannot do more than about four cases at a time. The clinic is mainly an inpatient one; little psychotherapy is practised. The polyclinic is open two nights a week, and deals with about 30 patients each time; clearly when there are 10 or 15 new cases at a session, they cannot receive much individual attention. The new scheme provides for separate doctors to deal with the out-patients, so that the continuity now ensured by Rylander and Frey will be impossible.

In Hammerstein's laboratory (who was himself in hospital with a gastric ulcer) I saw Hugo Theorell. He told me of the work going on into the effectiveness of anti-anaemic principle; he and his associates were not working, however, on the changes that particularly affect the central nervous system. His chief interest, viz. the determination of the chemical structure of cytochromes, did not seem in any way applicable to clinical problems at present. He had, however, given much advice and help to Izikowitz whom I saw later. Theorell said, when we were discussing Gjessing's work and allied matters, that he supposed it might be better to try producing psychotic pictures by amino-acids, etc., than to attempt an analytical study of psychotics' metabolism. He also mentioned his grounds for being dubious about Verzar's views.

Prof. Antoni has some interesting neurological material in his wards, and it seemed that the cooperation between him and Dr Lyssolm, and probably also with Prof. Olivecrona, made for a very thorough organisation. He had several cases of aphasia, due to areas of softening, in people under 45 without syphilitic or vascular changes. Rather surprisingly, in his GPI ward he was not using tryparsamide because he thought it too dangerous. I saw him do two cisternal punctures for encephalography, and a combined cisternal and lumbar puncture for the photographic registration of the two pressures and the respiration by his assistant Lagergren. The latter had devised an ingenious and accurate method. Another assistant was about to study the oscillation arterial blood pressure in conditions of neuralgia and other disturbances. I was also told of the work that was being done on chronaxy in relation to Peer Wolfahrt's finding that one kind of muscle fibre predominated in the embryos of young people and was to be found in increased proportion in dystrophies.

Dr Höjer explained to me the administrative plans. I gathered that he had spent three or four years in psychiatry and was, therefore, well acquainted with the problems. Evidently the big towns – Stockholm, Gothenburg, and Malmö and one other – were being treated somewhat differently from the country districts, where more responsibility for mental care is to be put upon the county authorities. There were also the four institutions (including the one at Malmö) in which neurotic and psychotic patients remain, for roughly two months, in charge of physicians who are mainly internists with a few years' psychiatric training, the treatments being more along medical, occupational, and social than psychological lines. The purpose of the institutions was not so much to supply psychotherapy, as to be a means of ensuring that those receiving health insurance because of neurosis should be observed and treated. Apparently alcoholic cases are becoming less common in the big towns; Prof. Antoni said the same. In as much as the patient who is ordered to go to one of these places ceases to receive his insurance if he refuses, they differ from anything that exists in England. There is of course a fairly high proportion of relapses, though, I gathered, few patients are re-admitted more than three or four times.

Outside the town, which contains only a minority of the population of Sweden, the doctors are largely socialised, i.e. public officials. From what Dr Höjer said, it seemed that the private practitioners in those parts were rather less competent than the district doctor; in essentials the position was rather like what Bela Johan had described in Hungary, though presumably the standard is very different. These doctors correspond to medical officers of health, and have a trained nurse-social worker, who reports the cases requiring investigation; it is for these specialised investigations that physicians with three years training in a specialty, e.g. psychiatry, are recognised. Some of these are, at present, the doctors in local mental hospitals, as was the case, I suppose, with the doctor at Uppsala who had shown me the family care. On the whole Höjer did not seem disposed to staff the public psychiatric services in question with people engaged in mental hospital work, but said that a lot of these matters had not yet been decided, and were affected by the customary claims and dissensions, e.g. between paediatricians and psychiatrists in regard to children. He did not contemplate their embarking on any particular scheme of psychotherapy because of the obvious economic objections and the present uncertainty as to results. I surmised that there was not the same demand by the public for psychological treatment as has been aroused in some other countries in Western Europe or in America.

In Sweden, as in the other Scandinavian countries, none of the people holding authoritative positions had much esteem for psycho-analysis. Certainly the psychoanalysts have not gained any footing in the University clinics or in the public services. I was able to discuss with two of Dr Höjer's assistants, legal and administrative aspects, corresponding to the activities of the Board of Control in England, and the working of their law concerning sterilisation and alcoholism. There is also a department for the supervision of defectives, but attempts are being made to unify the two departments. Everyone emphasised the pressure on the mental hospital beds in Sweden.

I also saw Dr Izikowitz, who still works at the laboratory in Wigert's clinic, although now without any post there. Apparently he is hampered somewhat by lack of facilities and monetary support, having to provide some of this himself, but his investigations seemed extraordinarily painstaking and thorough. He had not been able to confirm Georgi's findings about cholesterine in manic-depressive psychosis. His chief interest for the last nine years has, however, been in estimating the albumin and globulin proportions in the cerebro-spinal fluid, in GPI. He had been studying the differences in this respect between pre- and post-malaria cases for their prognostic significance, and thought that a relationship had been established. Among his other interesting ideas was his attempt at providing prophylaxis against malaria, for those going to the tropics, by inoculating them artificially, as one would a GPI, and then giving sufficient quinine to kill the infection. His association with Theorell has clearly been to his advantage in working out reliable methods. I did not get the impression that he had any close contact with Prof. Wigert.

I visited Prof. Kinberg in the prison and saw him with his chief assistant. His department is quite independent of the Public Health Department, and is a section of the Department of Justice. He is enthusiastic rather than critical. The patients who are referred to him are persons not allowed out on bail, i.e. mainly criminal cases; the people with minor offences are referred to one of a group of approved psychiatrists. Prof. Kinberg has assistants whom he calls social workers, but they do no visiting; their training has been in general, not in psychiatric, social work in Stockholm. The psychological testing is done by these social workers. The histories, moreover, are not got by a questionnaire circulated to the relations; it may be amplified later by the social workers. The forensic side of the psychiatric work is emphasised in the fact that all the psychiatrist's interviews with patients and their relatives are recorded by a stenographer, sometimes through the medium of a small microphone, of which the patient is unaware. Psychological tests are detailed and include some from van Lennep in Utrecht. Crime seems to be on a small scale in Sweden, judging by the number of people in prison; the number of women seemed especially small. Prof. Kinberg, however, sees two or three new cases there a week, and his reports are usually acted upon by the judge according to the recommendations included in them.

I also saw Dr Ramer, who is in charge of the child guidance clinic. It is run by the state, and is held in the building in which orphans and other children for whom the state becomes responsible are dealt with. The clinic is held daily and is conducted by two almost full-time doctors; it has been in existence for four years, and all children in the state schools, who show either abnormalities of conduct, learning difficulties, or delinquency are referred to it. The two psychiatrists have trained social workers and psychologists, and much of the work is done on general child guidance lines, the case sheet being prepared by social workers who visit the home, and psychological tests being done before the child is seen by the doctor. The treatment is mainly social and educational, little time being given to direct or intensive psychotherapy. There is no psychoanalysis. As it is a state clinic they are not able to select their material, the greater part of which consists of behaviour problems. I gathered that the arrangements for defective and backward children are – for the severer defects – residential schools; for those with mild deficiency, special non-residential schools of which there are ten in Stockholm; special classes for intellectually handicapped children, held in certain of the ordinary state schools, but conducted by specially trained teachers; and finally, children with such defects as word blindness or high frequency deafness are referred to a psychological institute.

I did not discover that there was any active work in neuro-pathology going on, apart from that done by a somewhat junior pathologist (Dr Ringert) whom I met, who is engaged on a study of the minute structure of cerebral tumours. I visited Prof. Liljestrand who discussed the difficulties of applying pharmacological methods of research to psychiatry. I gathered that he was less interested in the synthetic or analytic-chemical side of pharmacology than in what might be termed its physiology. He told me of the work he had been doing on the effects of alcoholism, and I was able also to discuss with Dr Bernhard the special investigations the latter was making into this problem. Dr Bernhard showed me his conditioned reflex chamber in which he had just been beginning some work designed to have a bearing on problems of child psychology. Although he is located in the children's clinic, and had spent some time with Prof. Krasnogorsky, I gathered that he would prefer to work mainly with dogs, for the customary reasons. As had been the case with Prof. Pick and Prof. Supniewski, Prof. Liljestrand had very little that was precise or of immediate applicability to say about the possibilities of pharmacological research in psychiatry; but like them, he believed the field would be large and promising.

Dr Lyssolm showed me his X-ray department, which seemed extraordinarily good. The care with which he traced out the outlines and located the abnormalities visible in his diagrams of the brain, together with his careful recording system, indicated how far he combined technical excellence with a research thoroughness and caution. He told me of the investigation that he was now making into the abnormalities to be demonstrated by encephalogram in the patients at the nearby mental hospital, Beckumberga, and added that he proposed to have the results analysed with Dahlberg's co-operation. I was shown round Beckumberga by one of the assistant physicians. The buildings, which are new, seemed well designed, but in the disturbed ward, in spite of the various improvements introduced into the building, the noisy patient, who tears off her clothes and rushes about, seemed as much in evidence as elsewhere. The relatively low rate of charge for the pleasant private rooms was again striking. Although the hospital is well staffed, I did not gather that the neurotic patients received much individual treatment of a psychological kind. I was told of the routine investigation Dr S W Wolfahrt had been making into the physical anomalies of the patients admitted; its excellence seemed to lie in its thoroughness and regularity rather than in a wide range of anomalies looked for.

DENMARK[35]

Copenhagen

I first visited Tage Kemp: Prof. Thomsen, who is in the same building, was ill when I was there. Dr Kemp told me of his endocrine work, but indicated that he was rather marking time until his new laboratories were available. He told me of the limited genetic investigations he had been engaged on, but I gathered that he had not gone any further with social investigations, such as that reported in his monograph on prostitution. He seemed in touch with psychiatric activities in Sweden and Denmark, though not at the moment personally engaged in any co-operative work on psychiatry.

I visited Dr Sturup at the Psychiatric Clinic. Prof. Helweg had not then been appointed to the chair. Dr Sturup's interests, on the research side, seemed in the field of neuro-physiology and pathology rather than in psychiatry, he was, however, arranging to go to Switzerland so that he might introduce into the clinic insulin treatment, having already been working a little with cardiazol. Later on I met Dr Erik

---

[35] See note 32 above for Scandinavian trends. The first psychiatric hospital of the State of Denmark opened in 1820; during the remainder of the nineteenth century other psychiatric hospitals were built: Aarhus (1852), Oringe (1857), Saint-Jean (1860), Viborg (1977) and Middalfort (1888). A department of nervous illness was established at the municipal hospital in Copenhagen in 1875. Denmark was a pioneer in the treatment of "mental defectives", with a law adopted in 1934.

Report

Stromgren several times. He told me about his genetic and anthropometric inquiries on the island of Bornholm. I was impressed with the critical thoroughness with which he had been taking advantage of such an extraordinarily good opportunity for studying the incidence and genetic relationships of mental disorder in a limited population. He seemed to have an all round interest in medical psychiatry, including that of children, which is not always found in people who can pursue an exact investigation such as he had made, at so early a stage in their psychiatric education. I gathered that he will for another year be engaged in completing his training in general medicine. The requirements for specialising in psychiatry, as in other subjects in Denmark, seemed to be well adapted towards getting men who would not be one-sided or likely to make psychological medicine remote from general medicine. On the other hand, the impossibility of the senior assistant of the professor remaining for more than two to three years in this position, would appear to damage the continuity of teaching and research in the clinic; although it is to the advantage of the mental hospitals that their superintendents should be recruited in this way, it does not conduce to the university psychiatric clinic being as prolific as it might be in research. Presumably the matter turns on whether in the mental hospitals there are adequate facilities for a superintendent, who is keen to do research and not to be swamped by administrative routine.

I spent one afternoon with Dr Mogens Fog. He showed me his apparatus for studying the factors determining change in the size of the cerebral vessels. The investigations are obviously well devised and controlled, so that the results would be very reliable. It was arranged that I should go again, but my illness prevented this. Dr Fog also took me to his other laboratory where he was studying, with a dermatologist (Dr Christiansen), the variations of the skin temperature in the hand. In this, as in his other research, the technical and physiological pitfalls in what might superficially be regarded as a straightforward problem, came out clearly in his discussion with me on the precautions that had to be taken in working out and interpreting the experiments. He also introduced me to Dr Busch, the manifestly energetic neuro-surgeon, whose interest in histopathological problems Fog had managed to revive, with happy results for collaboration. Dr Busch showed me a number of his preparations.

During my illness there I also met a number of the physicians of the Rigshospital, who told me of their work, e.g. Prof. Warburg, Dr Preben Plum who had been making an extremely thorough investigation into agranulocytosis, Dr Kirk, who works on liver-function, Dr Nielsen who has been studying digitalis effects (in conjunction with the physiologist at Lund) and others.

GENERAL IMPRESSIONS

There are some very general impressions (especially as regards psychiatry), which can be gathered together at the end. It is not possible to summarise the good things I saw and learnt: they were, of course, the best part of my journey, but they were spread over many fields, and were mostly connected with individuals rather than with systems and organisations; moreover, they were on the whole more often in other branches than in psychiatric research or practice, which did not seem in a rapidly progressive stage of development anywhere. My general impressions may therefore seem rather misleadingly weighted towards the side of depreciation. Most of the good things will have been mentioned in the earlier, more detailed part of the report.

Psychiatry seemed everywhere rather a stagnant subject: there is much research activity but this does not advance practice or understanding, because of either conflicting results, weak technique, idea-less repetition, excess of speculation, or – probably most important of all – failure to see problems that are at once fruitful and attackable. Certainly the fruits of psychiatric research seem very meagre in relation to its volume; it is depressingly less alive and (intellectually, if not practically,) less exciting than research in some other branches of medicine and in the restricted biological sciences such as animal genetics. It was very rare to find any worker on psychiatric problems – Gjessing was one of the few exceptions – who was enthusiastic and absorbed in his investigation because of the unexpected or unknown details he was finding out: yet there were many such people to be found in physiology, say, or even in internal medicine (e.g. Snapper). Insulin and cardiazol had, in consequence, a rather disproportionate value given them in most clinics: they stirred the waters dramatically, and were esteemed for that.

Nowhere was there evidence of any characteristic psychiatric method of research developing. This or that method, worked out in other disciplines, was applied with little modification to psychiatric problems: often this was done with only superficial knowledge of the limitations of the method, by a psychiatrist who "wanted to try it". But even where the investigation was carried out competently by a man well trained in the subject from which it was borrowed, the application of the method seldom led to its being transformed in order to cope with the problems peculiar to psychiatry. This borrowing of methods is of course what happens in all branches of medicine, but it seems that generally, and apart from empirical research, each such study has, when it is fruitful, led to the development of some peculiar features in the method, adapted to the new problem. In psychiatry psycho-analysis would seem to be the only such characteristic mode of attack devised during this century; and perhaps malarial treatment of GPI, though this might equally well, I suppose, have been introduced in the treatment of a somatic disorder without any mental features. Insulin (and cardiazol) represent another of these half-empirical somatic procedures: providing an impetus to research and therapeutic effort which was everywhere needed, but probably more so in European than in the English-speaking countries, where schizophrenia had not latterly been regarded with such fatalistic resignation as in the German school of psychiatry, still influenced by Kraepelin's conception of dementia praecox. It did not seem either that in psychiatry, even in Russia, there was that pushing of an idea to extremes which, whether the idea be partly right or mainly wrong, generally leads to the discovery of something new; that is, so long as it is done with the usual accompaniment of opposition, criticism and enforced modification by experience.

Most of the research, as far as it consists in fructifying psychiatry from outside, is unfortunately separated from the centres where the original studies "outside" are being actively pursued: quite often it is begun by the psychiatrist with only a reading knowledge of what it is about and how it is done. There is extraordinarily little evidence of the "outsiders", at work in some growing science, asking or managing to get to grips themselves with the problem of psychiatry, which their research might elucidate.

Many of the people of this sort whom I met professed an interest in research into mental disorder, and even a keen desire to look at its problems and see what they could make of it, but ignorance of clinical psychiatry, limited time, administrative and other factors seemed almost always to be in the way. No doubt psychiatry, even where it was located in a general hospital as in Amsterdam, often remained rather out of the main stream of medicine, a division apart from the rest. Nevertheless, it looked as though in this and most of the other respects which entailed collaboration or fertilisation from without, conditions were appreciably better now than they had been and were improving steadily. Interest in the problems of psychiatry on the part of other physicians of ability seemed to be more hindered now by distrust of its vagueness, and of the excessive claims and obscure speculations of the psychopathologists and psycho-analysts than by any traditional prejudice.

Research in psychiatry seemed in most places poorly organised, when compared with neurology or physiology. It was bad when directed by a clinical psychiatrist who spent half his time in private practice, as nearly all the professors do, and much worse when directed by a laboratory man (even though full-time) who was not in daily contact with clinical psychiatric work. In the former instance it tended to be hand-to-mouth, slapdash or uncritical, short-sighted and excessively influenced by fashions and practical exigencies, bulky rather than valuable: in the latter (which was much less common) it commonly seemed to be departing from rather than approaching the problems of psychiatry; sometimes confusing the issues or leaving them in deeper shade, through ignorance of the many-sided phenomena of mental disorder and the fallacies and real questions they may give rise to.

In nearly all countries, moreover, the financial deterrents to entering on a career of research seemed harmful to the development of psychiatry. Those who go into private practice, as the majority must, are forced in the richer countries to direct their interests into psychotherapy, without being able to study its problems dispassionately, and in the poorer ones to aim at some prestige-giving academic status which is less a by-product of ability and enthusiasm than a means towards earning a living. Nevertheless, academic status and a record of having done some research have so much more to do with any advancement in a psychiatric or other medical career abroad than they have in England that the general level of training and experience in what may be called the hack-work of research – making a prescribed investigation painstakingly or at any rate industriously, working through the literature of a problem and summarising it with discrimination, using advice and criticism and learning one's limitations – was higher among the general run of psychiatric aspirants than it is with us. Particularly in the Scandinavian countries the rigorous demands of the MD qualification raised the standard of work in the university clinics and institutes, and indirectly throughout the country. I find it difficult to generalise, however, because of the enormous differences between countries, e.g. between Hungary and Holland; Sweden and Czechoslovakia; or even adjacent ones like Russia, Poland and Finland. Political factors and jobbery were, however, rapidly altering the state of affairs in the dictator or semi-dictator ruled countries: clearly the future professors and hospital directors were going to "get by" with less to their scientific credit than their predecessors had to show.

Almost everywhere I found a greater interest and activity on the physical than on the psychological or sociological side of psychiatric inquiry. This was, of course, less noticeable in Switzerland and the Scandinavian countries, but even in them psychological investigations tended to be rigorously kept in hand and to follow safe rather than speculative lines: (psychotherapy, moreover, was either for the most part reserved for private practice or was a matter of common-sense adjustment of social and emotional problems). Social work was very much a practical matter (deliberate sociological research was very exceptional, though the need and opportunities cried out) and got worse as one went further East and the countries were poorer. There was, however, in some countries a contrast between their impressive buildings and laboratory equipment on the one hand, and, on the other, the low standard of hospital care and of social concern or provision for the patients who were outside an institution. In short, all that in England or the USA is linked up with the psychiatric nurse and the social worker seemed to call for much improvement in most of the countries I visited – in all indeed but a few western ones. The neglect was not so often due to economic stringency, I believe, as they made out.

In some places the predominance of neurology and the extravagances of some psychotherapists seemed to have had almost an equal share in delaying the development of the social and psychological side of psychiatry. On the other hand there were few places where the social side was wholly neglected: certainly the influence of current modes of thought in the world, or in individual countries, was strongly evident in the practical development of social psychiatry (on broad rather than individual lines) and the study of inheritance, whereas individualised psychological work was on the whole little regarded, whether as research or treatment. Other factors were of course also responsible for the shift of emphasis.

The wave of therapeutic interest, which followed the introduction of insulin and cardiazol, was working out less well in many places than one would have hoped: certainly in a few countries the work was being well done and its range extended, but, in many, little clinical acumen was displayed in assessing the outcome of treatment, the research possibilities were ignored, and there was the risk that, as with psychotherapy, over-enthusiasm might in time provoke an excessive disillusionment. The standard of clinical work and knowledge was perceptibly lower in psychiatry than in neurology: people had often a very detailed knowledge of the literature and difficulties of some tiny problem they had worked on for a dissertation or article, but had a poor grasp of clinical psychiatry as a whole; partly, I think, because they had not time to examine all their cases thoroughly, and because they were unduly satisfied with text-book accounts and needlessly conversant with bygone controversies, in which, let us say, Kraepelin's error, and still another had shown three years later that they were all a little right and a little wrong: names of people and of categories and quarrels usurped the place of immediate experience. All the schools of psychiatry except the French seemed to have been derivative, looking to Germany for their nourishment. Now, however, mainly for political reasons, and because of the great drop in the standard of German scientific work, this seemed to have changed: and there was no country that I visited (even including Italy and Russia), where it did not occur that many of the people I met were eager to establish or strengthen their contacts with corresponding workers in the

English-speaking countries: they would spontaneously raise this matter (at first, and again in Russia, rather to my surprise), ask about the opportunities of getting their articles published in the journals, even beg for lists of people here interested in their line of work, with whom they could get in touch, and often wanted advice about English and American books and journals which they might get for their libraries: I do not think that this was only from politeness, or in hopes of a nearer approach to the countries in which more money is provided for the endowment of research than in their own. Whereas for physiology and clinical neurology in England and North America their respect is of long standing, in psychiatry there had been an evident contempt or indifference towards all but German, Austrian and Swiss work: this attitude seems to be changing fairly rapidly. The attitude of other doctors towards psychiatry is changing too.

The level of the general practice of psychiatry in hospitals and out-patient work was, of course, closely dependent in each country on the moral and economic position. There were also the political factors, already alluded to, and particularised in the earlier passages dealing with some countries, e.g. Russia and Austria. There was the tendency in "totalitarian" countries to reward spectacular work, whether sound or not, and to favour lavish building and equipment; also to promote party-men, to damp down scientific criticism, and to hamper or exclude some able people who should have had influential positions and good opportunities to work; even sometimes, to modify theory for irrelevant reasons, (e.g. in genetics of insanity and defect, aetiology of neuroses). An indirect and less obvious effect, which will possibly through propaganda and one-sided education be eliminated in the next generation, is the personal distress and unhappiness, apart from any material difficulties of their own, which some of the best productive workers feel while living under a tyranny or a threat, so that they cannot pursue their work with a free and single mind: I did not get the impression that those who told me they fret thus were neurotics or seeming to rationalise laziness and scientific sterility. In all countries individual economic problems of course troubled research workers and practitioners.

As I have said, psychiatry was not among the more stimulating and active branches of medical or biological work that I had the opportunity of learning about abroad. Although many countries have still much obvious leeway to make up in psychiatry, if they are to attain the standard that now prevails in a few, there are no immediate signs that I could see of a great advance in the subject, in any of its aspects, having yet got under way anywhere: nothing comparable to what has happened in pure genetics, biochemistry or even internal medicine during this century. But there is certainly an attack along a wide front, made with very widely varying enterprise and vigour in different places: and the results obtained in research so far correspond to the skill shown in using and adapting borrowed weapons; those achieved in clinical practice are more intrinsic, as it were – more dependent on what are as yet peculiarly psychiatric points of view (as has, I suppose, been evident in the advance of psychiatry, especially on the therapeutic and social side, in the USA for instance), and of course also on the opportunities of demands that come from the community and depend largely on its general cultural and economic level.

Biographical Register

Adrian, Edgar Douglas (1889–1977), began lecturing on the nervous system at Cambridge University in 1919, and was made Fellow of the Royal Society in 1923. In 1925 he began investigating the sense organs by electrical methods, and in 1929 was elected Foulerton Professor of the Royal Society. In 1937 he succeeded Sir Joseph Barcroft as professor of physiology at the University of Cambridge, a post which he held until 1951, when he became Master of Trinity College, Cambridge. Adrian pioneered the study of nerve impulses and electrical discharges in nerve fibres, which led to his being credited with providing a new quantitative basis of nervous behaviour. He also studied impulses caused by stimuli likely to cause pain, as well as the electrical activity of the brain. His work opened up new fields of investigation in the study of epilepsy and other lesions of the brain. For his work on the functions of neurones Adrian was awarded, jointly with Sir Charles Sherrington, the Nobel Prize for Physiology or Medicine for 1932. Among Adrian's numerous publications are *The basis of sensation* (1927) and *The physical background of perception* (1947).

Allers, Rudolf (1883–1963), worked from 1918 to 1938 at the Medical School of the University of Vienna, moving from physiology towards psychiatry in the late 1920s. He emigrated to the USA in 1938, where he taught philosophy for a decade at the Catholic University of America. He then became professor of philosophy at Georgetown University, and in 1955 was a Fulbright lecturer in Paris, Toulouse, Geneva and Vienna, becoming professor emeritus at Georgetown University in 1957. His books include *The psychology of character* (1931), *Sex psychology in education* (1937) and *Existentialism and psychiatry* (1961).

Ancel, Albert-Paul (1873–1961), was professor of embryology at Strasbourg University from 1919 onwards. He was a pioneer in sexual endocrinology, and received the Prix du Prince de Monaco in 1937.

Angyal, Lajor (?–?), worked on schizophrenia and insulin shock in Budapest, and contributed to the clarification of the effect mechanisms of chlorpromazine and imipramine.

Antoni, Nils Ragnar Eugene (1887–?), was professor of neurology at the Karolinska Institute at Stockholm University from 1931; and later director of the University Clinic.

Astachoff: could be **Nicolai Astachoff** (1875–1941), who was a full professor at the Leningrad Institute for Medical Education between 1921 and 1928, and in 1929 became professor for dental health. Until his death he held the chair in stomatology at the Leningrad Institute for Medical Education.

Biographical Register

Bach: could be **A N Bach**, a physiological chemist who went to Geneva after the Russian Revolution, and worked on albuminosis in 1937. Lewis refers to him as the "late" Prof. Bach, however, so it is possible he is referring to another person.

Baruk, Henri (1897–1999), found with Henk de Jong that mescaline could freeze laboratory animals into cataleptic positions (H H de Jong, 'Die experimentelle Katatonie', *Zentralblatt für die Gesamte Neurologie und Psychiatrie*, 1932, **139**: 468 ff.; and H H de Jong and H Baruk, *La catatonie expérimentale par la bublocapnine* (1930)). Baruk was a candidate for the professorship of psychiatry at the University of Paris psychiatry department in the Hôpital Sainte-Anne in 1946, but it was given to Jean Delay. Baruk's work in the 1950s focused on the phenothiazines' ability to induce catalepsy.

Bastianelli: it seems that Lewis is talking about **Giuseppe Bastianelli** (1862–1959), the Italian surgeon, and that the brother he mentions is **Raffaele Bastianelli** (1863–1961), professor of surgery and director of the Surgical Clinic in Rome, a pioneer of neurosurgery.

Bechterev, Vladimir Michaelovitsch (1857–1927), was chief exponent and founder of the school of psychiatry built up around Pavlov's work. After studying abroad under Émile DuBois-Reymond, Wilhelm Wundt, Paul Flechsig and Jean Martin Charcot, Bechterev established a psychophysiological laboratory in Kazan University. From 1893 he worked in St Petersburg on the neuropathology and anatomy of the nervous system.

Benedek, László (1887–Second World War), was made professor of neurology and psychiatry at Debrecen University in 1921; and professor of neurology and psychiatry and director of the University Hospital for Neurology and Psychiatry at Budapest University from 1936 onwards. He did lasting work in the field of organic brain syndromes and on Korsakov's syndrome.

Bergmark, Gustaf (1881–?), was made professor of internal medicine at Uppsala University from 1921 onwards.

Berlucchi: this could be **Carlo Berlicchi** (1897–?) who was titular professor at Parma University 1935–6; and was full professor of mental and nervous diseases from 1936 onwards.

Bersot, H (?–1955), was director of the Clinique Bellevue at Landeron (Neuchâtel) at the time of Lewis's visit.

Bertrand, Ivan (1893–?), a Belgian neuropathologist, was in charge of the histopathological laboratory at La Salpêtrière when Lewis visited Paris. His name is associated with the Guillain-Bertrand-Lereboullet syndrome, one of the choreiform syndromes.

Berze, Josef (1866–1957), was associate professor of psychiatry at the University of Vienna in 1921. In 1912 he was made director of the Lower Austria Provincial Asylum at Klosterneuburg in 1912; and of the Provincial Asylum in Steinhof in 1919, where he stayed until 1928.

Besta, Carlo (1876–1940), was a consultant neurologist in the S. Ambrogio military hospital in Milan in 1914, and his experiences led him to set up a neurosurgical hospital in Guastalla. After the war, Besta taught in Messina and then was made chair of the neuropsychiatric clinic in Milan.

Beule, Fritz de (1880–1949), was professor of surgical pathology at Ghent in 1919. From 1924 until his death he was director of the University Surgical Clinic there.

Binswanger, Herbert (1900–1975), was lecturer in psychiatry and first assistant in the Burghölzli Psychiatric Hospital at Zurich University. He published *Die Psychosen und Möglichkeiten ihrer Interpretation* in 1949.

Binswanger, Ludwig (1881–1966), was born into a family well-established in medicine and psychiatry. He studied under Carl Jung and interned under Eugen Bleuler at Zurich University, sharing their interest in schizophrenia. He became adept at insight-oriented therapy after visiting Sigmund Freud in Vienna in 1907, and after the death of his father Robert Binswanger, he took over the running of the Bellevue Clinic in Kreuzlingen in 1911 (the clinic had been founded in 1857 by Ludwig's grandfather). Binswanger maintained a close friendship with Freud until the latter's death. In the early 1920s, Binswanger became interested in the work of Edmund Husserl, Martin Heidegger and Martin Buber, turning increasingly towards an existential rather than a Freudian perspective; he is sometimes called the first existential therapist. In 1942 he published his major work *Grundformen und Erkenntnis menschlichen Daseins*. In 1956 Binswanger retired from Bellevue but continued to publish until his death.

Binswanger, Otto (1852–1929), was made associate professor of psychiatry and director of the Jena Canton Asylum in 1882; in 1891 he was made professor in psychiatry at Jena University.

Birkhaug, Konrad Elias (1892–?), was a bacteriologist who was associate professor at Rochester University from 1928 until 1934; between 1932 and 1934 he visited the Pasteur Institute in Paris investigating tuberculosis. In 1939 he was based at the Michelsens Institute in Bergen.

Bleuler, Eugen (1857–1939), was director of the Rheinau nursing home near Zurich from 1886 to 1898; and was appointed professor of psychiatry and director of the Burghölzli Psychiatric Hospital at Zurich University, where he served from 1898 to 1927 (succeeding Auguste-Henri Forel). He introduced the term "schizophrenia" in 1908 to describe – and shift the conception of – the disease known as dementia praecox. Bleuler questioned the view of schizophrenia as necessarily caused by irreversible organic deterioration of the brain, holding that it could have psychological causes, and also denied that schizophrenia always led to dementia. The term schizophrenia denoted the "splitting" of the different psychic functions which Bleuler held to be one of the disease's most important characteristics. He emphasised associative disturbances rather than dementia, and introduced two concepts fundamental to the analysis of schizophrenia: autism, denoting the loss of contact with reality, often through fantasy; and ambivalence, denoting the existence of mutually exclusive contradictions within the psyche. Bleuler urged practitioners to seek to understand and interpret the way patients express themselves. He also argued that instead of tying the individual to a cosmos of conventional meanings, obligations and expectations, language serves to provide a shortcut to wish-fulfilments and to spin out a web of private fantasies.

Bleuler was one of the first psychiatrists to apply psychoanalytical methods in his research. An early proponent of Freud's theories, and a long-standing member of the Vienna Psychoanalytic Society, he attempted to show how the mechanisms Freud found in neurotic patients could also be recognised in psychotic patients. He found intrapsychic complexes, as described by Freud, at the root of schizophrenic symptomatology and searched for a theory by which this symptomatology could be related to organic causes. In Bleuler's concept of schizophrenia two strands of psychiatric thinking met – a Kraepelin-inspired nosological framework indicative of a scientific psychiatry and by no means uncontroversial Freudian concepts. The difficulty of reconciling these strands is in part what led Bleuler to widen the symptomatology of schizophrenia, positing schizophrenic disturbances, differing in quantity rather than quality, as part of the panorama of everyday human experience. Latent schizophrenia was also acceptable to Bleuler. This had unforeseen consequences, in that the notion got hijacked by politically-motivated eugenicist discourse in the 1933 German sterilisation law for patients with hereditary diseases. Over the years, Bleuler moved away from Freud and emphasised the hereditary and organic basis of schizophrenia, having incurred much dissent from academic psychiatry. He also published works on hypnotism, subcortical aphasia, moral idiocy, and the physiology of ventricology. He was one of the editors of the *Jahrbuch für psychoanalytische Forschung*. His textbook, *Lehrbuch der Psychiatrie* (1916) is considered a classic, and his work on schizophrenia was published as *Dementia Praecox: oder, Gruppe der Schizophrenien* in 1911.

Bleuler, Manfred (1903–1994), became lecturer at the University of Basel in 1941, specialising in schizophrenia. From 1942 until 1969 he was director of the Burghölzli Psychiatric Hospital at Zurich University. In 1972 he published *Die schizophrenen Geistesstörungen im Lichte langjähriger Kranken- und Familiengeschichten* (Stuttgart, Thieme), a landmark study that appeared to challenge Eugen Bleuler's later move towards belief in the inexorability of schizophrenic deterioration. It was translated into English in 1978 as *The schizophrenic disorders: long-term patient and family studies* (New Haven, Yale University Press). Of 208 patients discharged from one hospital twenty years earlier, 20% were fully recovered and another 30% were greatly improved. Within a few years, other researchers replicated his findings.

Bogaert, Ludo van (1897–1989), gave his name to Van Bogaert's encephalitis, a rare, chronic and progressive encephalitis in children and adolescents. In 1933 he became director of the Clinical Services and Pathological Laboratory at the newly-established Bunge Research Institute in Antwerp, leading the neurological studies there. The Institute expanded after the war but then closed and since 1964 has housed the Centre of Medical Genetics.

Bonnevie, Kristine Elisabeth Heuch (1872–1948), became the first female member of the Norwegian Academy of Science and Letters in 1911, and in 1912 became the first female professor in Norway when she was appointed professor of zoology at the Kongelige Frederiks Universitet (now the University of Oslo) and director of the Zoological Laboratory until 1938. In 1908 she published work which contributed to modern concepts of the structure of chromosomes. In 1916, with three other professors, Bonnevie established a University Institute for Research on Heredity, which she directed until her retirement.

Biographical Register

Bouin, Paul (1870–1962), was professor of histology at Strasbourg University from 1919 onwards, and a pioneer of reproductive physiology. His publications include *Éléments d'histologie* between 1929–32 (2 volumes).

Bouman, Klaas Hermann Beerta (1874–1947), was a doctor from 1905 until 1916 at the Wilhemina Gasthuis in Amsterdam. In 1912 he was lecturer in psychiatry and in 1915 professor of psychiatry and neurology at Amsterdam University.

Boutdendyck, van: possibly **Buijtendijk, Frederick Jakobus Johanes** (1887–1974), who was professor of general physiology at Amsterdam and in 1925 professor of physiology at Gröningen. In 1946 he took up the chair of theoretical psychology at the University of Utrecht, and was considered the leader of the Dutch phenomenological school.

Bovet, Pierre (1878–1965), founded the Institut Jean-Jacques Rousseau in Geneva with Eduard Claparède in 1912, and was its director from its inception until 1944. In 1925 Bovet founded the Bureau International de l'Éducation, also in Geneva, of which Jean Piaget was director.

Bronner, Volf Moiseevich (1876–1938), was made professor at the Moscow State Venereological Institute in 1923, where he remained as its director until his death. Daniel O'Brien told Lewis that Bronner was a representative of the Committee on Foreign Relations of the Narkomzdrav (Ministry of Health), and had published *La Lutte contre la prostitution en URSS* in 1936.[1]

Brouwer, Bernard (1881–1949), was professor in neurology at Amsterdam University from 1923 and became one of the leading neurologists in Holland. Brouwer became rector of the Wilhemina Gasthuis in Amsterdam at the beginning of the German occupation, but resigned in 1946, when he succeeded Cornelius Kappers as director of the Central Institute of Brain Research, where he worked until his death.

Brunswik, Egon (1903–1955), was an assistant in Karl Bühler's Psychological Institute; he established the first psychological laboratory in Turkey while a visiting lecturer in Ankara during 1931–2; and became lecturer at the University of Vienna in 1934. In 1935–6 Brunswik received a Rockefeller fellowship that enabled him to visit the University of California, encouraged by his meeting Edward C Tolman, chairman of the department of psychology at the University, who had visited Vienna in 1933. He became assistant professor of psychology at Berkeley in 1937, and full professor in 1947.

Bühler, Charlotte (1893–1974), see **Bühler, Karl**

Bühler, Karl (1879–1963), was made associate professor in Münich in 1913 (where he had followed Oswald Kulpe as assistant). In 1916 he married **Charlotte Bühler** (1893–1974); they went to Vienna in 1922, he as professor of psychology, and she as associate professor, where they remained until 1938. After visiting posts in the USA, and declining an offer of a professorship at Radcliffe College in 1930, Karl Bühler was invited to be professor at the Roman Catholic Fordham University, but

---

[1] Letter from D P O'Brien, Rockefeller Foundation, to Aubrey Lewis, 23 February 1937, p. 8; held by the Lewis family.

the offer was withdrawn when it was found out that the Bühlers had married in a Protestant ceremony. Charlotte Bühler was a pioneer in developmental psychology. She became assistant professor at the newly founded Psychological Institute in Vienna, and later associate professor in 1929. Prolific and popular, she worked on the neglected field of psychology of the young and developmental psychology. Karl became a representative of action- or goal-oriented psychology of the Würzburg school; he achieved renown in the psychology of language, working also on the psychology of perception, developmental psychology and the psychological study of children. After Karl's imprisonment by the Nazis in 1938 and subsequent release, the Bühlers emigrated to the States where they had difficulty finding teaching work. They eventually found positions in Minnesota; Karl taught a little at Clark University and Charlotte at City College New York, but these posts were temporary. Charlotte moved into clinical psychiatry at Minneapolis General Hospital, and eventually the Bühlers moved to California, where Charlotte worked at Los Angeles County General Hospital. Karl became a clinical psychologist at Los Angeles Cedars of Lebanon Hospital, and opened a private clinical practice in Hollywood.

Buscaino, Vito Maria (1887–?), was professor of psychiatry and neurology and director of the Psychiatric and Neurological Clinic at Catania University from 1927 onwards (he was still based there in 1939).

Campbell, Charles Macfie (1876–1943), a student of Adolf Meyer, was later director of the Boston Psychopathic Hospital. He was professor of psychiatry at Harvard and a proponent of the application of psychoanalytic techniques to psychotic illness.

Carp, Eugène Antoine Désiré Emile (1895–?), was professor of psychiatry at Leiden University from 1930 onwards.

Cerletti, Ugo (1877–1963), finished his medical studies in Rome at the laboratory of Giovanni Mingazzini, the chair of neuropathology and director of the psychiatric hospital. After further studies in Heidelberg under Franz Nissl, director of the Laboratory of Clinical Psychiatry, where Emil Kraepelin was professor, Cerletti became assistant at the Psychiatric Clinic in Rome in 1901. He stayed there until the First World War, becoming director of the Anatomo-pathological Department, and working during this time with Kraepelin at the University Clinic in Munich. After the First World War he had several academic psychiatric postings, and in the early 1930s became director of the Neuropsychiatric Clinic in Genoa, where he researched epilepsy. In 1935 he became professor of psychiatry in Rome, and chief of the Clinic for Nervous and Mental Diseases of the University of Rome. In 1936 he worked with his assistants Ferdinando Accornero, Lucio Bini and Lamberto Longhi; Bini realised that one could apply electric shocks to dogs via their temples, which was far less risky than administering such shocks orally and rectally, as previously done. In 1937, Bini spoke on this matter at Max Müller's conference at Münsingen on therapies in schizophrenia, suggesting that the technique might be applicable to humans. He was keen to try it on patients, though the risks were considerable, and invented a machine which enabled shocks to be administered in a fraction of a second. On 18 April 1938 the first electro-shock therapy was given to patients. Results showed that ECT, while not a cure for schizophrenia, did alleviate symptoms of psychotic illness and allow psychotics to function normally. Cerletti then mobilised a vast research project on the method; it became clear that the best results came about when applied to the manic-depressive psychoses rather than schizophrenia. Electro-shock became widely used after the Second World War; technical improvements introduced by others as of 1955 led to its application spreading further. From the 1960s onwards, however, it became implicated in anti-psychiatry protests amidst concerns that it was being excessively and inappropriately used.

Chiari, Hans (1851–1916), was a pathologist who worked in Prague until 1906 when he was appointed professor of pathological anatomy in Strasbourg, where he remained until his death.

Chorobski, Jerzy (?–?), was, according to Daniel O'Brien, a former Rockefeller Fellow working with Professor Orzechowski, the professor of neurology and psychiatry at Warsaw.[2]

Claparède, Eduard (1873–1940), was professor at the Science Faculty in Geneva from 1928, and the founder with Pierre Bovet in 1912 of the Jean-Jacques Rousseau Institute, around which the "Geneva School" – which included Jean Piaget – developed. The institute later became the Institute for Educational Sciences.

Claude, Henri Charles Jules (1869–1945), was professor of psychiatry at the Paris Faculty in 1922 until 1939. In the 1930s he was director of the Clinic of Mental Diseases at Hôpital Sainte-Anne. He introduced the biological therapies of Julius Wagner-Jauregg, Manfred Sakel and Ladislas von Meduna into France; encouraged the founding of the Groupe de l'Évolution Psychiatrique; and ensured that psychiatry became a compulsory part of the French medical curriculum. He opened the door to psychoanalysis in his clinic and was editor of *L'Encéphale*. Claude's syndrome is a mid-brain syndrome with oculo-motor paresis and hemiataxia (*Revue Neurologique*, 1912). His many publications include *Précis de pathologie générale*, with Jean Camus (1909), *Psychiatrie médico-légale* (1932); *Éléments de criminologie psychiatrique* (1936); *Les états anxieux* (1938).

Dahlberg: this could be **Nathaniel Dahlberg**, born in 1874. Daniel O'Brien describes Dahlberg as the director of the Institute of Race Biology in Uppsala.[3]

Davidenkoff, see **Davidenkov, Sergey Nikolaevich**

Davidenkov, Sergey Nikolaevich (1880–1961), held from 1920 to 1925 the chair of neurological diseases at the University of Baku. In 1925 he became principal consultant in charge of the Neurological Department for Professional Diseases in the Institute "V. A. Obuha" in Moscow. In 1932 he was appointed professor of neurological disease at the State Institute of Postgraduate Education for Doctors "S. M. Kirova" in Leningrad.

---

[2] Letter from D P O'Brien, Rockefeller Foundation, to Aubrey Lewis, 23 February 1937, p. 7; held by the Lewis family.
[3] Ibid., p. 10.

Biographical Register

Dechaume: there is an **M Dechaume** (1897–?) who was a forensic pathologist at Paris University, and wrote a book in 1937 with L Dérobert called *L'Expertise en stomatologie*.

de Sanctis, Sante (1862–1935), was professor of experimental psychology at the Medical Faculty in Rome from 1905 until his directorship of the Neuropsychiatric Clinic upon Giovanni Mingazzini's death. In 1930 he was nominated president of the Italian League of Hygiene and Mental Prophylaxis. In 1930 he also took over the directorship of the Clinic of Nervous and Mental Diseases in Rome (Mingazzini had fused the institutes of psychiatry and neurology in 1919).

de Vecchi, Bindo (1877–1936), became professor of pathological anatomy at Perugia from 1920 to 1923; he taught this subject at Sassari and Catania between 1923 and 1924; in 1925 he took up the chair of pathological anatomy at Florence University. He became rector of the university in 1930.

D'Hollander, Fernand (1878–1952), was professor of psychiatry at Louvain from 1920 until 1950; he was director of the Psychiatric Institute from 1926 onwards and wrote *Manuel de psychiatrie* in 1942.

di Tullio, Benigno (?–?), wrote *La criminalità come problema medico-sociale* (1951).

Divry, Paul (1889–1967), was professor of psychiatry and neurology and director of the Psychiatric and Neurological Clinic at Liège University from 1925 onwards. An eponym associated with him is the van Bogaert-Divry syndrome, a familial syndrome characterised by angiomatosis of skin and cerebral meninges with progressive demyelinisation of white matter, hemianopsia and cutis marmorata. In 1925 he worked at the Dispensaire d'Hygiène Mentale in Liège.

Dumas, Georges (1866–1946), was professor of experimental psychology at the Sorbonne in 1913, and taught until 1942 as a psychologist and professor at the Laboratory of Psychology of the Psychiatric Clinic at the Hôpital Sainte-Anne in Paris. He was founder of the Société de Psychologie de Paris and founded with Pierre Janet the *Journal de Psychologie Normale et Pathologique*. His publications include *Traité de psychologie* (1923).

Durig, Arnold (1872–1961), was professor of physiology and director of the Physiological Institute at Vienna University from 1918 onwards. He published on muscular physiology, metabolism, sport and work physiology.

Economo, Constantin von (1876–1931), was a student of Julius Wagner-Jauregg and became a professor of psychiatry and neurology from 1921 in Vienna. He discovered the chewing, swallowing and sleep centres in the brain (*Über den Schlaf*, 1925), did lasting work on encephalitis lethargica and promoted the collection and study of outstanding brains. In 1931, he founded the Institute for Brain Research in the Clinic for Psychiatry and Nervous Diseases in Vienna.

Eppinger, Hans (1879–1946), was professor of medicine and director of the Medical Clinic at Vienna University from 1933 onwards, although he was called to Moscow in 1936 when Stalin fell ill; after 1945 he worked as a doctor for the Soviet high command.

Biographical Register

Epstein, Emil (1875–1951), was lecturer in General Pathology at Vienna University and director of the Franz Josef Hospital Sero-diagnostic Institute.

Essen, van: possibly **Jan van Essen** (?–?), who in 1918 is described as a physiotherapist in Amsterdam.

Ey, Henri (1900–1977), was chief doctor of the psychiatric hospitals in Paris in 1933; and while he presided over the Syndicate of Doctors of Psychiatric Hospitals, doctors in these hospitals gained a status equal to that of other hospital doctors. His actions also ensured a more discriminate use of obligatory internment of the mentally ill. He collaborated with Maurice Merleau-Ponty, Paul Ricoeur, Jean Hippolyte, and was involved with Jacques Lacan's École Française de Psychanalyse, known as the École Freudienne de Paris. Ey organised the first World Congress of Psychiatry in Paris in 1950.

Fabritius, Harald August (1877–?), was made professor at Helsingfors University in 1925. He was president of the Helsinki Psychiatric Congress in 1929.

Federn, Paul (1871–1950), was a doctor and psychoanalyst, who, having studied medicine in Vienna, worked in Vienna's General Hospital, advocating psychoanalysis as a medical treatment. He emigrated in 1938; from 1946 he worked as a training analyst in New York. He published *Zur Psychologie der Revolution: die vaterlose Gesellschaft* (1919), and *Ego psychology and the psychoses* was published posthumously (1952). He committed suicide in 1950.

Fessard, Alfred (?–?), became Professor Henri Piéron's collaborator in 1932; in 1936 he was joint director of the École des Hautes Études, and in that year published *Recherches sur l'activité rythmique des nerfs isolés*. Fessard was made professor of general neurophysiology at the Collège de France in 1949, a post created for him.

Fog, Mogens (1904–?), was based at the Municipal State Hospital in Copenhagen, at the laboratory of medical physiology; and then was professor and medical superintendent in the Department for Nervous Diseases at the State Hospital in Copenhagen.

Forel, Auguste-Henri (1848–1931), was appointed professor of psychiatry at the University of Zurich Medical School in 1879, as well as director of the Burghölzli Psychiatric Hospital at the University of Zurich (until 1898), which he helped make a renowned institution. Forel undertook work on the neuron theory which, together with Wilhelm His and Fridtjof Nansen, led to the modern neuron theory. In 1889, Forel founded the Asile d'Ellikon, an institute at Zurich for the medical treatment of alcoholism, and he had considerable influence on reforms in psychiatry and the penal code. He was interested in hypnotism and was involved in social reform as well as in sexual health.

Forel, O-L (?–?), was at Prangins, near Nyon in Switzerland, in 1931.

Fragnito, Onofrio (1871–1959), was professor of neuropathology and director of the Neuropathological Clinic at Naples University from 1927 onwards.

Freud, Anna (1895–1982), was the youngest daughter of Sigmund Freud. She trained as a primary school teacher and in psychoanalysis, becoming a member of the Vienna Psychoanalytic Society in 1922. During her early years in Vienna, she initiated the application of psychoanalysis to the treatment of children, and then to education and child rearing. She was general secretary of the International Psychoanalytic Association between 1927 and 1934, and in 1935 became director of the Vienna Psychoanalytical Training Institute. In 1938 she emigrated with Sigmund Freud to London, where the conflict between her views and methods and those of Melanie Klein threatened to split the British Psychoanalytical Society. Anna Freud established, during the war years, the Hampstead War Nurseries, and after the war founded the Hampstead Child Therapy Course and Clinic, of which she was director. She lectured widely throughout Europe and the United States and in 1973 was made honorary president of the International Psychoanalytic Association. A prolific writer in her own right, she also collaborated with James Strachey in the preparation of the standard edition of the *Complete psychological works of Sigmund Freud*, and was also an editor of *The Psychoanalytic Study of the Child*.

Friedheim, Ernst (1899–1989), specialised in microbiology, cell biology and physical chemistry before becoming professor at the Medical Faculty in Geneva in 1931. He was a pioneer of the chemotherapy of parasitical diseases, publishing work on the treatment of sleeping sickness.

Gamper, Eduard (1887–1938), was made associate professor at the University of Innsbruck; in 1930 he was made professor of psychiatry and neurology at the German University in Prague, where he stayed until his death.

Gannushkin, P B (?–?), was director of the Psychiatric Clinic in Moscow and considered the leading figure in Soviet psychiatry until his death. He was a strong supporter of the organisation of psychiatric services and wards in general hospitals. Daniel O'Brien wrote to Lewis that he had done important work on schizophrenia.[4] *Psychopathological symptomatology* was published in 1933.

Gaucher: this could be **Philippe Charles Ernest Gaucher** (1854–1918) who became head of the Charité laboratory in 1885, physician of the Paris Hospitals in 1886 and *agrégé* of the Faculty in 1892. In 1902 he was appointed clinical professor of cutaneous and syphilitic diseases. He worked on, amongst other things, the treatment of diphtheria, chronic autointoxication, and skin disease.

Gehuchten, Paul van (1893–?), was professor of neurology at the University of Louvain in 1936. His father, Arthur van Gehuchten (1861–1941) was chair of neurology at Louvain.

Gemelli, Agostino (1878–1959), was made professor of applied psychology and rector at the Sacred Heart University in Milan in 1924, which he had founded in 1921 and where he had opened a psychological laboratory. In 1937 he was made director of the Centre of Studies of Research in Medical Aeronautics of the Air Ministry in 1937. In 1920 he founded, with Federico Kiesow, the *Archivio Italiano di Psicologia*. In 1936 he was made president of the Accademia Pontificale delle Scienze.

Georgi, F (1893–1965), worked in Freiburg, Frankfurt, Heidelberg and Breslau before returning to Switzerland in 1933, where he worked in Bern and at Yverdon until 1946.

---

[4] Letter from D P O'Brien, Rockefeller Foundation, to Aubrey Lewis, 23 February 1937, p. 8; held by the Lewis family.

At Yverdon he was head of the psychiatric clinic; in 1946 he was made chief assistant at the Psychiatric University Clinic in Basel. He was made professor of neurology there in 1955.

Gerstmann, Josef (1887–1969), was professor of neurology and psychiatry in Vienna in 1938 when Alan Gregg of the Rockefeller Foundation visited him; his specialty was brain pathology. Gregg suggests that at the time of his visit Gerstmann was considering applying for American citizenship.[5]

Gersuni might be **Grigorij Viktorovic Gersuni** (1905–1992), a physiologist.

Gilarowsky might be **Giljarovsky, Vasilik Alekseevic** (1875–1958), a professor of psychiatry, who is possibly the person who published, with Z A Solevava and A I Vinokurova, *Problems of psycho-neurology of children and adolescents* in 1936.

Ginglinger, Albert (1899–1956), was an intern at Strasbourg in 1924; he became an *agrégé* in 1946, and succeeded Raymond Keller as chair of the Gynaecological Clinic in 1953.

Gjessing, Rolv Ragnvaldsson (1887–?), became director and chief psychiatrist at the Dikemark Asylum in Oslo in 1929. He was president of the Norwegian Psychiatric Society from 1932.

Gorter, Evert (1881–1954), was lecturer in paediatrics at Leiden University, then professor of paediatrics at Ghent University and chief physician at the Paediatric Clinic.

Granit, Ragnar Arthur (1900–?), became a lecturer in physiology at Helsinki University from 1929 onwards, was a research fellow at the University of Philadelphia from 1929 to 1931; became professor of physiology at Dorpat University in 1932; received a fellowship at Exeter College, Oxford, in 1934 and according to Daniel O'Brien, was "recently appointed" head of physiology in Helsingfors.[6]

Grünthal (?–?), was a displaced German who worked in the neuropathology department of Jakob Klaesi's university psychiatric service at Waldau-Bern.[7] He directed the Institute of Cerebral Anatomo-Pathology there and was known for his work on senile dementia and Korsakoff's syndrome.

Guillain, Georges Charles (1876–1961), was awarded the professorship of neurology at the Clinic for Nervous Diseases in the Faculty of Medicine in Paris in 1923, and he held the post until his retirement in 1943. His publications include *Études neurologiques* (1922–39).

Guiraud, Paul (?–?)), was, in 1950, chief doctor at the Hôpital Sainte-Anne in Paris.

Gurevitsch could be one of the following:
Gurevic, Ansel Lejrzerovic (1900?–?), the owner of a bacteriological laboratory.
Gurevic, Michail Osipovic (1878–1953), a professor of psychiatry.
Gurevic, Nikolaj Illic (1871–1960), a professor of surgery.

---

[5] Alan Gregg officer's diary, 29 June 1938, RG 12.1, box 21, RFA, RAC.

[6] Letter from D P O'Brien, Rockefeller Foundation, to Aubrey Lewis, 23 February 1937, p. 9; held by the Lewis family.

[7] Ibid., p. 4.

Biographical Register

Hadorn, Walter (1898–1986), was director of the Department of Internal Medicine at Tiefenau Hospital in Bern from 1933.

Hammerstein, see **Hammersten, Einar**

Hammersten, Einar (1889–1968), was professor of chemistry and pharmacy at the Karolinska Institute in Stockholm from 1928 to 1957.

Hartmann, Heinz (1894–1970), was a psychoanalyst associated with the Psychiatric Clinic at the University of Vienna who was one of the last to receive a training analysis from Sigmund Freud, and who, after emigrating to the USA, became known as the "American prime minister of analysis". He, Ernst Kris and Rudolf Löwenstein were key figures in ego psychology in the 1950s and 1960s, through whose work psychoanalysis entered academic medicine and psychology.

Haskoveç, see **Haškovec, Ladislav**

Haškovec, Ladislav (1866–1944), became professor of nervous diseases at the Psychiatric Clinic in Prague in 1919, and held the neurological chair at the Czech University in Prague until his emeritus professorship in 1936. A pioneer of neurology in Czechoslovakia, he was the first to establish it separately from internal medicine, and opened the first neurological clinic in the University in 1926. In 1935 he was vice-president of the Second International Neurologists' Congress in London.

Hasselt, Sjierd Folkert Willem van (1868–1934).

Herlitzka, Amadeo (1872–1949), was made professor of physiology at Turin University from 1910; he was exiled in 1940 to Argentina, and resumed his chair in Turin in 1946.

Hess, Walter Rudolf (1881–1973), was made director of the Physiological Institute at Zurich in 1917, a post he kept until 1951. In 1931 he set up the Jungfraujoch International Research Institute, and received the Nobel Prize in Medicine or Physiology in 1949 for his work on the central coordination of the vegetative organs.

Heuyer, Georges (1884–1977), was, in 1930, in charge of the service at the Hospital for Sick Children at the Sancelmoz Sanatorium in Haute-Savoie. He was a pioneer of child psychiatry, and much involved in legal psychiatry.

Heymans, Corneille (1892–1968), was professor of pharmacology and pharmacodynamics at Ghent University from 1922. He became director of the Jean-François Heymans Institute of Pharmacology and Therapeutics at the same university, J F Heymans being his father. He received the 1938 Nobel Prize for Physiology or Medicine for his investigations into breathing control.

Hill, Archibald Vivian (1886–1977), became university lecturer at Cambridge in physical chemistry in 1914, and was then appointed Brackenburg Professor of Physiology at Manchester University in 1920. From 1923 until 1925 he was Jodrell Professor of Physiology at University College London, and was in charge of the Biophysics Laboratory there until 1952. His many publications include *Muscular activity* (1926) and *Muscular movement in man* (1927).

Hoff, Hans (1897–1969), was made Otto Pötzl's assistant at the Psychiatric-Neurological Clinic in Vienna in 1928. In 1936 he became director of the Neurological

Biographical Register

Division of the Vienna Policlinic, and in 1938 emigrated to Baghdad as professor of neurology and psychiatry at the Royal Medical School. From 1942 he was assistant professor at the Neurological Institute of Columbia University in New York. In 1950 he returned to Vienna University as professor of neurology.

Hojer, Joan Axel (1890–?), was made assistant professor of experimental pathology at the Karolinska Institute in Stockholm in 1925; then assistant professor of hygiene at Lund University in 1927. In 1930 he was medical officer of health in Malmö in 1930; and director of the General State Medical Board from 1935.

Horst, van der: an **L van der Horst** was director of the Valerius Clinic of Psychiatry in Amsterdam. This is possibly the person who pioneered the field of medical psychology based on the Gröningen school, dealing with the investigation of temperaments and character-types, very much under the influence of the German school of Kretschmer.

Ivanov-Smolensky, Anatoly Georgievich (1895–?), is described by Daniel O'Brien as being in charge of the psychiatric clinic in Leningrad,[8] and is credited with extending conditioned reflex theory.

Jackson, John Hughlings (1835–1911), became interested in neurology while a staff member at the National Hospital, Queen Square, in London, where he studied seizures and elaborated principles that explained paroxysmal seizures. He also postulated evolutionary levels of the sensory-motor mechanisms. He exerted a considerable influence on neurology, psychiatry and psychology.

Jacobowsky, probably **Jacobovsky** (?–?), who was professor of psychiatry at Uppsala.

Jaksch von Wartenhorst, Rudolf Ritter (1855–1947), was a lecturer from 1884 in medical pathology and therapy at the University of Vienna. In 1887 he became associate professor of children's medicine and director of the University Children's Clinic in Graz; he was made professor of internal medicine and director of the Children's Clinic at the German University in Prague in 1889, becoming emeritus professor in 1925.

Jensen, Edmund Zeuthen (1861–1950).

Jong, de (?–?), Daniel O'Brien describes him as head of laboratories at the Neurological Clinic in Amsterdam where Bernard Brouwer was the director.[9]

Kalinowski, see **Kalinowsky, Lothar**

Kalinowsky, Lothar (1899–?), left Germany in 1933 for Italy; in Rome he witnessed the early ECT experiments on patients at Ugo Cerletti's clinic, and in 1939 introduced the method to the Hôpital Sainte-Anne in Paris. In July 1939 he came to England and helped Sanderson McGregor establish the use of ECT at the Netherne Hospital at Coulsdon. In 1940, Kalinowsky went to the New York State Psychiatric Institute, where he also introduced ECT, and helped insert the method into academic psychiatry as a whole.

---

[8] Letter from D P O'Brien, Rockefeller Foundation, to Aubrey Lewis, 23 February 1937, p. 9; held by the Lewis family.
[9] Ibid., p. 12.

Biographical Register

Kappers, Cornelius Ubbo Ariëns (1877–1946), was director of the Central Institute for Brain Research in Amsterdam from 1908 until his death, and was associate professor of brain research and comparative neurology at the University of Amsterdam from 1929. His publications include *The comparative anatomy of the nervous system of vertebrates, including man*, with G C Huber and E C Crosby (1936).

Katzenstein, Erich (1893–?), was first assistant at the Neurological Polyclinic in Zurich and then vice-director of the Neurological Polyclinic and Lecturer at the Medico-Pedagogical Seminary in Zurich.

Kauders, Otto (1893–1949), was made associate professor of psychiatry and neurology at Graz University in 1935; he emigrated to the United States in 1939, resuming his post in Graz in 1945. In 1946 he was made professor and director of the Neurological-Psychiatric University Clinic in Vienna.

Kemp, Tage (?–?), was lecturer in pathological physiology and director of the Institute of Human Genetics in Copenhagen.

Kiesow, Federico (1858–1940), of Polish origin, went to Turin in 1894, where in 1906 he was appointed to one of the first three chairs in psychology at the Turin Faculty of Letters, and helped diffuse Wilhelm Wundt's ideas through Italy.

Kinberg, Olof (1873–1960), a forensic psychiatrist at the Langbro Asylum from 1921 to 1927 and a lecturer from 1921 to 1939 in legal psychiatry at the Karolinska Institute, Stockholm. From 1934 to 1937 he was director of the Institute for Criminology in Stockholm.

Klaesi, Jakob (1883–?), was professor at Zurich University from 1932, and professor at Bern University from 1933; then he was professor of psychiatry and director of the Asylum at Waldau from 1936 onwards. While staff physician in 1920 in charge of the female ward at Zurich University's psychiatric hospital, the Burghölzli, he began to use a combination of two barbiturates of the Swiss drug firm Hoffman-La Roche marketed as Somnifen, with the aim of curing schizophrenia with prolonged narcosis. Klaesi's results seemed successful, offering the prospect of a cure; and the concept of addressing the brain with profound narcosis gained ground. German doctors used it in the early 1930s to help withdraw addicted patients from morphine. Klaesi's therapy was considered the first treatment which brought about at least transitory improvement in functional psychoses. Several patients, however, collapsed, and some died. A few years later, Max Müller at Münsingen exposed the mortality rate of Somnifen; deep sleep therapy was still used with other, safer, barbiturates, however, especially as a way of making patients accessible to psychotherapy.

Klein, Melanie (1882–1960), trained in Budapest and Berlin before moving to England in 1926. Her ideas challenged Anna Freud's work on children and were influential especially in England and South America. She emphasised pre-Oedipal layers of personality development, holding that Freud neglected the mother's nurturing role in child development. While she was supported by several senior figures in psychoanalytic circles, many of her views met with opposition, and fierce conceptual battles raged in British psychoanalysis. Klein set up a school of child analysis and clashed with Anna Freud on whether children should be treated psychoanalytically in a different manner from adults; Klein urged that the same technique should be applied, and that play material was the exact equivalent of verbal free associations. After their arrival in London in 1938, Klein became more explicitly separate from the Freuds and was considered by many to be deviationist. In 1943 Ernest Jones organised the 'Controversial Discussions' for debate between Kleinians and their opponents. There followed a division of the British Psychoanalytic Society into Group A, which included the Kleinians and the "middle group" (non-aligned), and Group B, which included Anna Freud and her followers. Klein continued to be highly active and to publish until her death.

Knaus, Hermann (1892–1970), was made professor at the University Women's Clinic in Graz in 1930, and then professor of gynaecology and obstetrics at the German University in Prague from 1934 until 1935, when he was made the director of the University Women's Clinic, where he stayed until 1945. In 1950 he was made head of the gynaecological obstetrics section of the State Hospital in Wien-Lainz. His name is associated with the Knaus-Ogino contraception method, outlined in 1933. After the introduction of synthetic contraception, Knaus was amongst the first to take a stand against the Pill. As an advisor to Pope Paul VI he had a decisive influence in the rejection of the Pill throughout the Catholic Church, while under Pius XX the Knaus-Ogino method had already been endorsed.

Konorski, Jerzy (?–?), worked with Ivan Pavlov in Leningrad from 1931 to 1933, and from 1940 to 1945 he worked at the Primate Research Centre in Sukhumi in the Caucasus. It seems that the Soviet response to Konorski's *Conditioned reflexes and neuron organisations* in 1948 was not favourable; the label of "revisionist" was removed from his work after Stalin's death, however.

Koupalov, see **Kupalov, Pyotr Stepanovich**

Krasnogorsky, Nikolai (1871–1960), was a pupil of Ivan Pavlov, and applied the conditional reflex method to the study of children; his later work focused on language formation in children.

Krayenbuhl, Hugo Alfred (1902–?), ran a neurosurgery department in Zurich at the time of Lewis's visit. Later in his career, he was director of the University Children's Clinic in Zurich.

Kris, Ernst (1900–1957), was an art historian based at the History of Art Museum in Vienna from 1922; he became acquainted with Sigmund Freud, and had training analysis with Helene Deutsch, becoming a member of the Vienna Psychoanalytic Association in 1930. With Robert Wälder he was editor-in-chief of the psychoanalytic magazine *Imago*. He emigrated to London in 1938, and then lived in New York from 1940, as professor at the New School for Social Research, becoming a child psychologist at Yale University from 1951. He became known as one of the triumvirate, with Heinz Hartmann and Otto Löwenstein, reigning over ego psychology in the 1950s and 1960s.

Kroll, M B (?–?), was director of the Neurological Clinic in Moscow at the time of Lewis's visit.

Kronfeld, Arthur (1886–1941), led, as of 1926, a psychotherapeutic practice in Berlin and in 1928 he founded, with E Kretschmer, the *Allgemeine Artzliche Gesellschaft für*

Psychotherapie. He was the first lecturer in psychotherapy at the Charité in Berlin in 1933. He emigrated in 1935 to Switzerland, but was called to Moscow in 1936 and became leader of the section for experimental therapy at the P B Gannushkin Psychiatric Research Institute, where the treatment of schizophrenia was his focus. During the German winter offensive of 1941 he and his wife took their own lives. His publications include *Sexualpsychopathologie* (1923) and *Die gegenwäertigen Probleme der Lehre von der Schizophrenie* (1936).

Kupalov, Pyotr Stepanovich (1888–?), was professor of physiology at the Leningrad Medical Institute in the late 1930s. Kupalov continued his teacher Ivan Pavlov's line of work at the Institute of Experimental Medicine in Leningrad.

Lagache, Daniel (1903–1972), had worked under Paul Guiraud and Georges Heuyer, and in 1955 became professor at the Sorbonne, as well as president of the French Psychoanalytic Society.

Laignel-Lavastine, Paul-Marie Maxime (1874–1953), was made *Chef de Clinique* at the Laënnec hospital in Paris in 1919. In 1924 he went to La Pitié, and from 1931–9 held the chair of history of medicine at the Paris Faculty. In 1939 he received the chair of the Clinique des Maladies Mentales, succeeding Henri Claude. He retired from clinical work in 1943. Laignel-Lavastine was also well known for his work in legal medicine and criminology, as well as for his writings in the history of medicine.

Lapicque, Louis (1866–1952), was head of the Department of General Physiology at the Natural Science Faculty in Paris. He linked the intensity of a stimulation and the length of its application into a general law of the nervous system and muscular excitation; chronaxy is the minimum interval of time necessary to electrically stimulate a muscle or nerve fibre, using twice the minimum current needed to elicit a threshold response. Lapicque was director of the Institut Marey from 1936 to 1941.

Laruelle (?–?), ran, according to Daniel O'Brien, the Centre Neurologique de Bruxelles. The research emphasis, states O'Brien, was on brain architectonics, with interesting work being done on degenerative tracts in the central nervous system.[10]

Lépine, Jean (1876–1967), was made professor of neurology and psychiatry at Lyons University in 1911.

Leriche, René (1879–1955), was professor of the surgical clinic at the Faculty of Medicine in Strasbourg from 1927. He was chair of medicine at the Collège de France in 1937 and continued to practise in Strasbourg.

Levi, Giuseppe (1872–1965), became professor in anatomy at Turin University from 1919, after having been at Sassari and Palermo Universities. He was director of the Anatomical Institute in Turin when Lewis visited.

Levit, Solomon Grigorjevich (1894–?), was chief of the Department of Genetics at the Maxim Gorky Medico-Genetical Research Institute in Moscow from 1928 onwards, and director of the Institute from 1930 onwards. Levit was expelled from the Communist Party in 1936, accused of holding pro-Nazi biological views.

---

[10] Letter from D P O'Brien, Rockefeller Foundation, to Aubrey Lewis, 23 February 1937, p. 3; held by the Lewis family.

Biographical Register

Levitt, see **Levit, Solomon Grigorjevich**

L'hermitte see **Lhermitte, Jacques Jean**

Lhermitte, Jacques Jean (1877–1959), was professor of psychiatry at Paris in 1922. He was a doctor at the Hospice Paul-Brousse from at least the time Lewis met him until the 1960s and head of the Foundation Dejerine.

Liljestrand, Göran (1886–1968), was professor of pharmacology and director of pharmacology at the Karolinska Institute in Stockholm from 1927 onwards.

Löewenstein, see **Löwenstein, Otto**

Lombroso, Ugo (1877–1952), was made professor and director of the Physiological Institute at Palermo University in 1926. At the time of Lewis's visit he was professor and director of the Institute of Physiology at Genoa University.

London, Efim Semenovich (1869–1939), became professor for pathological anatomy at the University, the Veterinary Institute and the Institute of Further Education in Leningrad in 1919. He also worked at the Leningrad University Institute for Experimental Medicine (in the section on the pathophysiology of metabolism), and was made chair of biochemistry at the Institute for Medical Education in Leningrad.

Löwenstein, Otto (1889–1965), became professor of neurology and psychiatry at Bonn in 1931. He founded the first Child Psychiatry Clinic in 1926 in the Rhein County Asylum in 1926, of which he was director until his emigration to Switzerland in 1933. From then until 1938 he was consulting physician at the Clinique La Metairie, in Nyon. In 1939 Löwenstein went to the United States and became professor in neurology at New York University, teaching there until 1947, and until 1962 at Columbia University as research professor in ophthalmology. His specialty was the physiology and pathology of eye pupil movements, which he urged as having an indicatory function for diseases of the central nervous system. His publications include *Die Störungen des Lichtreflexes der Pupille bei den lütischen Erkrankungen des Zentralnervensystems* in 1935.

Lugaro, Ernesto (1870–1940), was head of the Psychiatric Clinic in Turin in 1911, and in 1927 of the Neurological Clinic. He was editor of the *Rivista di patologia nervosa e mentale* from its foundation, and was professor of psychiatry at Turin at the time of Lewis's trip.

Luria, Alexander Romanovich (1902–1977), established the Kazan Psychoanalytic Association while still a student. His early research sought to establish methods for assessing Freudian ideas about abnormalities of thought and the effects of fatigue on mental processes. In 1923 he won a position at the Institute of Psychology in Moscow, where he developed a psychodiagnostic technique called the "combined motor method" for diagnosing individual subjects' thought processes. The book describing these studies was not published in Russian until 2002; it was associated with psychoanalytic theorizing disapproved of during the Soviet period. In 1935 Luria met L S Vygotsky and together with him and A N Leontiev, Luria sought to establish a "cultural", "historical" psychology. In the late 1930s, however, Luria entered medical school and worked on aphasia – largely to remove himself from public view during Stalin's purges. During the Second World War he researched brain function and brain lesions. After the

Biographical Register

war he continued in neuropsychology, although he was removed for several years from the Institute of Neurosurgery due to anti-semitic repression. Resuming in the 1950s, he pursued work in this field until his death.

Lutz, Jakob (1903–?), after studies in the USA in 1937 and 1938, was made lecturer in psychiatry and neurology at Zurich University. He was head doctor of the Psychiatric Policlinic for Children and Adolescents and of the Children's Department in Stephansburg.

Lysholm, Erik (1891–?), was lecturer and assistant professor in Radiology at Stockholm University from 1931 onwards. He published several works on neurological and general radiology. In 1939 he was based at the Serafimer Hospital in Stockholm.

Lyssolm, see **Lysholm, Erik**

Maier, Hans Wolfgang (1882–1945), was first assistant at the Psychiatric Clinic in Zurich between 1910 and 1927; he became professor, succeeding Eugen Bleuler, and director of the Burghölzli Psychiatric Hospital at Zurich University from 1927 onwards. He retired in 1941. At the time of Lewis's visit, Maier was, according to Daniel O'Brien, interested in the insulin treatment of schizophrenia and the use of sleep therapy.[11] Maier is credited with opening the first *maisons d'observation* for children at the Burghölzli Psychiatric Hospital, Zurich, in 1920, which eventually extended beyond Switzerland.

Marburg, Otto (1874–1948), was made professor of neurology and director of the Vienna Neurological Institute in 1919. After the Anschluss of Austria in 1938, he emigrated to New York where he was professor at the College of Physicians and Surgeons of Columbia University.

Margaria, Rodolfo (1901–?), was made professor of physiology at Pavia University a few months before Lewis's visit, having been professor at Ferrara previously. In 1950 he was professor of human physiology at the University of Milan.

Meduna, Ladislas von (1896–1964), pioneered the use of camphor, and then cardiazol, as a means of producing seizures which would abate symptoms of schizophrenia, publishing his findings in 1935. Eventually it was felt that the techniques were unreliable in producing fits, also causing too much anxiety in patients. In the 1930s and 1940s cardiazol was much used in the United States but eventually more or less discarded. Meduna trained in neuropathology in 1923–6 at Budapest's Interacademic Institute for Brain Research, and then followed his chief Karl Schaffer to the university psychiatry department. In 1939 Meduna went to Chicago, becoming professor at Loloya University and then at the University of Illinois Medical School, where he worked on carbon-dioxide therapy.

Meyer, Adolf (1866–1950), studied in Zurich, and then Paris, Edinburgh, London and Vienna before going to the United States in 1892, where he worked in psychology and neurology in Chicago. From 1895 to 1902 he was lecturer at Clark University in Worcester, Massachusetts; from 1902 to 1909 he was director of the Pathology

---

[11] Letter from D P O'Brien, Rockefeller Foundation, to Aubrey Lewis, 23 February 1937, p. 4; held by the Lewis family.

Institute of State Hospitals in New York and professor of psychiatry from 1904 until 1909 at Cornell University Medical School. From 1910 onwards he was professor at Johns Hopkins University in Baltimore and chief psychiatrist of the Johns Hopkins Hospital. Meyer was a highly influential figure in American psychiatry, advocating a unified vision of psychiatry – "psychobiology" – in which psyche and soma are different dimensions of the same entity. Rather than seeing mental illness as a structural defect in a specific location, he saw mental illness as the diminution of an individual's ability to function, with important social aspects to this process, resulting in "maladjustement" or "maladaptation", rather than "insanity". He thereby helped foster the notion of a psychiatry that extended into everyday life concerns, by blurring the boundaries between normality and abnormality, and psychosis and neurosis. He strongly desired that the study and treatment of mental illness attain the status and legitimacy of general medicine, and argued for the full integration of mental institutions into the emerging university medical schools and hospitals. Meyer held that the so-called functional psychoses (schizophrenia, manic-depression) were reaction patterns of the central nervous system and represented the interplay of three causal factors – heredity, physical disease and emotional development. There was no particular treatment considered *a priori* appropriate for the improvement of a patient's condition. Meyer's vision heralded the possibility of a single profession of psychiatry, out of the splintered collection of practitioners – asylum-based physicians (the alienists), private-practice neurologists and general practitioners.

Meyer, Hans Horst (1853–1939), was professor of pharmacology and history of medicine in the University of Dorpat in 1881. He taught at Vienna University from 1904 to 1924, where he was rector from 1917 until 1918.

Meyerhof, Otto Fritz (1884–1951), was asked in 1929 to head the newly founded Kaiser Wilhelm Institute for Medical Research at Heidelberg; he emigrated in 1938, becoming director of Research until 1940 at the Institut de Biologie physico-chimique at Paris. In 1940 he emigrated, becoming research professor of physiological chemistry at the University of Pennsylvania. Meyerhof was awarded, together with A V Hill, the Nobel Prize for Physiology or Medicine for 1922, for his discovery of the fixed relationship between the consumption of oxygen and the metabolism of lactic acid in the muscle.

Meyerhoff, see **Meyerhof, Otto Fritz**

Meynert, Theodor (1833–1892), was made prosector of the Vienna Asylum in 1866, and in 1870 was appointed director of the Psychiatric Clinic and associate professor of psychiatry. In 1873 he became professor of nervous diseases. He was also a member of the Supreme Committee of Experts for the Ministry of Health. His research on brain anatomy and function established the anatomy of the cerebral cortex; a proponent of the brain as the basis of mental illness, he published *Psychiatrie: Klinik der Erkrankungen des Vorderhirns begründet auf dessen Bau, Leistungen und Ernährung* in 1884, translated into English as *Psychiatry: clinical treatise on diseases of the fore-brain* in 1885.

Minkowski, Eugène (1885–1972), is considered, together with Ludwig Binswanger, the founder of phenomenological psychiatry; Jacques Lacan considered him the introducer of the notion of structure in French psychiatry. Based mostly in France, he participated in the creation in 1925 of L'Évolution Psychiatrique, which fostered interaction between phenomenology, psychoanalysis and psychiatry. In the 1950s his ideas gained influence in the United States and R D Laing quotes Minkowski in *The divided self*. Minkowski never occupied a significant post, and experienced suspicion and hostility from the French. Post-war, however, Henri Claude opened doors to him at *L'Encéphale*.

Minkowski, Mieczyslaw (1884–1972), was made associate professor at Zurich University in 1928; he was then director at the Institute for Anatomy of the Brain and Polyclinic for Nervous Diseases and was made head of the Zurich Association of Psychiatry and Neurology. He was also vice-president of the Swiss Neurological Association.

Minor: Lewis writes of a **Victor Minor**; there is a **Lazar Salamowitch Minor** (1855–1942), a Russian neurologist who was, according to Daniel O'Brien, at the Institute of Experimental Medicine in Moscow, and "interested in diagnostic tests for lesions of the central nervous system, but especially in studies of the neuro-physiology of perspiration".[12] He is associated with Minor's disease, a syndrome characterised by haemorrhage into the spinal cord and sudden onset of back pain with paraparesis or paraplegia.

Miskolczy, Dezsö (?–?), was a former fellow of the Rockefeller Foundation, who directed the Institute of Psychiatry and Neurology at the University of Szeged. He worked on the histological correlations of schizophrenia. In 1968 he was professor at the Postdoctoral Studies Institute in Budapest.

Mohr, Otto Lous (1886–?), was chief physician at the Biological Station in Oslo University in 1916; at Columbia University in New York between 1918 and 1919, he was made professor of medicine at Oslo University in 1919. In 1920 he was at the Marine Biological Laboratory at Stanford University. In 1934 he was dean of the Medical Faculty at Oslo University. At the time of Lewis's visit he was working on genetics with Kristine Bonnevie in Lund.

Mollaret, Pierre (1898–?), was, when Lewis visited, a doctor at the Hôpitaux de Paris, professor at the Paris Faculty of Medicine and head of Laboratories at the Institut Pasteur.

Monakow, Constantin von (1853–1930), was of Russian origin, but his father was expatriated from Russia to Switzerland; von Monakow studied in Zurich, where he later founded an Institute of Cerebral Anatomy and a neurological policlinic in 1887 and became professor of neurology in 1894. In 1897 he published *Gehirnpathologie* and a treatise on cerebral localisation. He studied philosophy, psychology and political and social sciences, and elaborated a vast system incorporating biology and neurology into a philosophical vision inspired by the "creative evolution" of Bergson. *Introduction*

---

[12] Letter from D P O'Brien, Rockefeller Foundation, to Aubrey Lewis, 23 February 1937, p. 8; held by the Lewis family.

biologique à l'étude de la neurologie et de la psychopathologie was published with R Mourgue in 1928. Monakow helped found the Swiss Neurological Society.

Monnier, L M (?–?), is described by Daniel O'Brien as assistant to Professor Lapicque at the Department of General Physiology at the Paris Natural Science Faculty, working on nerve action studies.[13] In 1964 Monnier was professor of general physiology at the Sorbonne.

Monrad-Krohn, Georg Herman (1884–1964), held various posts in the State Hospital in Oslo, in London at the Middlesex Hospital; the National Hospital for Nervous Diseases, Queen Square; the Maida Vale Hospital for Epilepsy and Nervous Diseases; the LCC Mental Hospital in Bexley; the Bethlem Royal Hospital; and in Paris at La Salpêtrière. He was professor of medicine at Oslo University and chief physician at Oslo University Clinic of Neurology as well as consulting physician at the Norwegian State Epileptic Institute.

Montassut, this may well be **Marcel Montassut** (b. 1897) who was a doctor at the Hôpital Henri-Rousselle, Paris, under Henri Claude, in the late 1930s.

Morselli, Enrico (1852–1929), was director of the asylum in Macerata and of the psychiatric clinic at the University of Turin in Genoa. He founded the *Rivista sperimentale di freniatria*; the *Rivista di filosofia scientifica* and the *Rivista di patologia nervosa e mentale*.

Morsier, Georges de (1894–?), was a Swiss neurologist associated with, amongst other conditions, de Morsier's syndrome I, a diencephalic lesion appearing in the first decade of life and accompanied by a variety of behavioural, psychomotor and sensory disorders, as well as signs of precocious sexual development.

Mosinger, Michel (1901–?), was professor at the medical faculties of Marseilles and Coimbra universities in 1946.

Müller, H J, see **Muller, Hermann Joseph**

Muller, Hermann Joseph (1890–1967), became associate professor at Texas University in Austin in 1920, and then professor in 1925. From 1918 his studies of mutation led to his formulation of the chief principles of spontaneous gene mutation and chromosome change as now recognized; in 1927, working with drosophilia, he proved that X-rays are mutagenic, a discovery that became the basis of radiation genetics and for which Muller was awarded the Nobel Prize for Physiology or Medicine in 1946, nineteen years later. In 1932 he worked for a year in Oscar Vogt's Institute in Berlin, and at the request of N I Vavilov, he then went to the Institute of Genetics of the Academy of Sciences of the USSR as senior geneticist, first in Leningrad, later (1934–7) in Moscow. With the rise of the Lysenko anti-genetics movement, he moved to the Institute of Animal Genetics at Edinburgh University (1937–40); from 1940 to 1945 he was at Amherst College where he was professor and where he completed a large-scale experiment showing the relationship of ageing to spontaneous mutations. In 1945 he went to Indiana University's Zoology Department, from where in 1964 he went to the Institute for Advanced Learning in the Medical Sciences in California.

[13] Letter from D P O'Brien, Rockefeller Foundation, to Aubrey Lewis, 23 February 1937, p. 1; held by the Lewis family.

Biographical Register

Müller, Max (1894–1980), worked with Eugen Bleuler in Zurich and then became head doctor and director of the Münsingen Aslyum from 1939. He imported insulin treatment of schizophrenia to Switzerland and was a pioneer of electro-shock but also made psychotherapy a component of psychiatric treatment. From 1954 to 1962 he was professor of psychiatry and head of the University Clinic Waldau bei Bern.

Muralt, Alexander von (1903–1990), was made professor in 1935 of the division of physiology at the University Institute in Bern. He was president of the governing body of the High Alpine Research Institute at Jungfraujoch (1937–73) and in 1942 founded the Swiss Foundation for Biological-Medical Grants. In 1952 he was founder of Swiss National Funds for the Promotion of Scientific Research.

Musatti, Cesare Luigi (1897–1989), was director and professor of experimental psychology at Padua and Urbino universities from 1928; in Padua he worked on Gestalt psychology and Freudian concepts, introducing psychoanalysis to university courses in 1933; due to the racial laws, however, he was suspended from teaching. During the war he directed a laboratory of industrial psychology within a company. In 1948 he returned to academic life as chair of psychiatry in Milan and from 1955 gave new life to the *Rivista di psicoanalisi* which had been suspended by fascist authorities in 1934.

Nielsen in Copenhagen could be any of the following:
Nielsen, Karl Rudolf Rasmus (1899–?), who was at Aalborg from 1935 at least until 1939.
Nielsen, Michael (1891–?), who was at Bispebjaerg Hospital and then the Obstetrics Department at the State Hospital in Copenhagen at least until 1933.
Nielsen, Niels Aage (1887–?), who was at the Aarhus Municipal Hospital at least until 1939.
Nielsen, Ove (1888–?), who was a specialist in surgery in Copenhagen from 1927 onwards and was still there in 1939.

Noyons, Adriaan Karel Marie (1878–?), was lecturer in physiology at Utrecht University in 1909; professor of experimental physiology at Leuven University from 1912 to 1927; and then held the same post at Utrecht University from 1927 onwards.

Nunberg, Hermann (1884–1970), studied in Zurich with Eugen Bleuler and Carl Jung, worked at the Zurich University's Burghölzli Psychiatric Hospital and at the Bern Psychiatric Hospital. He worked with Julius Wagner-Jauregg and Otto Pötzl in Vienna; and was a member of the Vienna Psychoanalytic Society from 1915, becoming a training analyst in 1925. In 1933 he went to the United States, where he was professor of clinical psychiatry at Temple University, Philadelphia. He had his own practice in New York from 1934.

Nyiro, Gyula (?–1966), was professor of psychiatry and director of the Psychiatric Clinic at the University of Budapest. He came to develop a structural dynamic psychiatry theory.

Oberholzer (?–?), was one of the founding members of the Swiss Psychoanalytic Society (founded in 1919).

Oberling, Charles (1895–?), became professor at the Faculty of Medicine in Paris in 1928 and professor at the Faculty of Medicine in Strasbourg in 1937. His publications include *Précis d'anatomie pathologique* (with G Roussy and R Leroux, 2 volumes) in 1933.

Ödegaard, see **Ødegård, Ørnulv**

Ødegård, Ørnulv (?–?), was at the Psychiatric Clinic of the University of Oslo from 1932 (where the chief physician was Ragnar Vogt), after having spent some time at the Henry Phipps Psychiatric Clinic in Baltimore. In 1956 he became professor of psychiatry at the University of Oslo and medical superintendent at Gaustad Mental Hospital until 1961; in 1963 he was at the Social Psychiatry Research Institute, Gaustad Hospital.

Olivecrona, Herbert (1891–?), was assistant surgeon-in-chief at the Serafim Hospital in Stockholm from 1925 to 1935 and director from 1935 onwards, as well as professor of neurological surgery at the Karolinska Institute from 1935 onwards.

Opalski (?–?), according to Daniel O'Brien, was a former Rockefeller Fellow working with Professor Orzechowski (the professor of psychiatry and neurology in Warsaw).[14]

Orbeli, Leon Abgarovich (1882–1958), became head of the department of physiology at the Institute of Physical Education in Leningrad in 1918, a post he held until 1957, as well as head of the First Leningrad Medical Institute from 1920 to 1931, and head of the Military Medical Academy from 1925 to 1950. From 1936 to 1950 he was director of the USSR Academy of Sciences' Pavlov Institute of Physiology and from 1939 to 1950 was director of the Institute of Evolutionary Physiology and Higher Nervous Activity of the USSR Academy of Medical Sciences. From 1942 to 1946 he was Vice-President of the Academy of Sciences. By the time Lewis visited him, he had shown that the autonomic nervous system has the same influence on skeletal as on heart muscles, demonstrating its manifold effects on metabolism throughout the body.

Orzechowski is most likely **Orzechowski, Kazimierz** (1878–?), professor of neurology at Warsaw University.

Osipov, Viktor Petrovich (1871–1947).

Ossipov, see **Osipov, Viktor Petrovich**

Pende, Nicola (1880–1970), was professor of special medical pathology and clinical methodology at Rome University from 1935. Pende had his own Biotypological-Orthogenic Institute, making films on physical fitness, and he did propaganda work for the fascist government in magazines and radio speeches.

Petrov, Nikolai Nikolaevich (1876–1964), became a professor at Warsaw in 1912, and in 1913 was at the Petersburg Institute for Medical Education. He later became professor of surgery and director, until 1946, of the Oncological Institute in Leningrad, which he founded in 1926. He also founded the Institute for Experimental Cancer Research at the All-Unions Institute for Experimental Medicine. He was editor of *Voprosy onkologii* and *Vestnik Khirurgi*. He was awarded the Order of Lenin, the Stalin Prize and the Lenin Prize.

---

[14] Letter from D P O'Brien, Rockefeller Foundation, to Aubrey Lewis, 23 February 1937, p. 7; held by the Lewis family.

Piaget, Jean (1896–1980), a pioneer of development psychology, became director of studies at the Jean-Jacques Rousseau Institute in Geneva in 1921 at the request of Eduard Claparède and Pierre Bovet. He held the chair in the history of scientific thinking at Geneva from 1929 to 1939; was director of the International Bureau of Education from 1929 to 1967 and director of the Institute of Educational Sciences at Geneva from 1932–71; he held the chair in psychology and sociology at Lausanne from 1938 to 1951; the chair of sociology at Geneva from 1939 to 1952, then that of genetics and experimental psychology from 1940 to 1971. In 1955, he created and then directed the International Centre for Genetic Epistemology until his death.

Pichler, Hans (1877–1949), was made professor of surgery at Vienna University in 1919, and became professor and head of the Vienna Dentistry University Institute in 1930.

Pick, Ernst (1872–1960), became assistant to Richard Paltauf at the Vienna Sero-therapeutic Institute from 1899 to 1911. In 1917 he was made professor, and from 1911 to 1924 was assistant to Horst Meyer, working on experimental pharmacology and toxicology. From 1924 to 1938 he was professor of pharmacology at Vienna University; after the Anschluss of Austria he emigrated to the United States, where from 1939 to 1960 he was professor at Columbia University and adviser to Merck, Sharp and Dohme.

Pienkowski, Stefan Kazimir (1885–?), was professor at Krakow University from 1932 onwards and director of the University Nervous Disease and Psychiatric Clinic.

Piéron, Henri (1881–1964), was a central figure in the Psychophysiology Laboratory at the Sorbonne and the Laboratory of the Sensory Physiology at the Collège de France. On Alfred Binet's death in 1911 he succeeded him as director of the Laboratory of Physiological Psychology. He organised the Institute of Psychology with the help of George Dumas. In 1923 he entered the Collège de France for the chair of physiology of sensation created for him. In 1926 he founded the Laboratory of Sensory Physiology. He was director of the National Institute for Professional Orientation established in 1928.

Podkopaev, Nikolai Aleksandrovich (1892–?) is described by Daniel O'Brien as being, along with Rosenthal, a physiologist at the Institute of Experimental Medicine in Leningrad and at the Academy of Sciences, using the Pavlovian method.[15]

Policard, Albert (1881–1972), was professor of histology in Lyons from 1919 onwards.

Ponzo, Mario (1882–?), succeeded Sante de Sanctis in 1931 as chair of experimental psychology at the Ateneo in Rome.

Pötzl, Otto (1877–1962), was Julius Wagner-Jauregg's successor as professor of psychiatry at Vienna University's Psychiatry Clinic in 1928, after having been professor of psychiatry and neurology at the German University in Prague in 1922. From 1945 he was director of the Clinic. His publications include *Die Aphasielehre vom Standpunkte der klinischen Psychiatrie* (1928).

---

[15] Letter from D P O'Brien, Rockefeller Foundation, to Aubrey Lewis, 23 February 1937, p. 9; held by the Lewis family.

Propper, N (?–?), is described by Daniel O'Brien as being in Professor M B Kroll's department (the neurological clinic in Moscow);[16] Propper had recently been to the United States to work with Fulton and had also worked with Adrian at Cambridge between 1935 and 1936. O'Brien calls him a "key man" who studied the pathogenesis of epilepsy.

Querido, Arie (1901–1983), got his MD from Harvard in 1932, having previously trained in physiology with W B Cannon in 1923–4 on a Rockefeller Fellowship. He was – at least in 1950 – director of public health and the hospitals of Amsterdam, at the Department of Public Health, City Health Service in Amsterdam.

Rademaker, Gijsbertus Godefriedus Johannes (1887–1947), was appointed professor of physiology at Leiden in 1928, and in 1946 took up the newly-created chair for neurology at Leiden. His work focused primarily on the physiology of muscle and the nervous system.

Ramer, Karl Torsten (1902–?), was chief doctor at the Children's Psychiatric and Neurological Clinic in Stockholm from 1933 onwards.

Révész, Géza (1878–1955), worked in empirical psychology, especially on sound, language and anxiety. At the time of Lewis's visit, he was interested in the psychopathology of the blind. He is described in *The contribution of Holland to the sciences: a symposium* (edited by A J Barnouw and B Landheer in 1943) as being the most important empirical psychologist working in Holland at the time.

Rey (?–?), was assistant at the Institut des Sciences de l'Éducation, and a lecturer at the University of Geneva.

Rittmeister could be **John Rittmeister** (1898–1943), who studied medicine and became interested in Jung, Bakunin and Marx. He had been a conscientious objector in the First World War and from 1929 was a psychoanalyst in Switzerland, where he looked after German emigrants. In 1938 he was chief doctor at the Waldhaus Clinic of Nervous Disease in Berlin; in 1939 he was head of the Policlinic of the German Institute for Psychological Research and Psychotherapy. He helped Jewish patients with emigration and resisted discrimination against homosexuals. Arrested in 1942, he was brought in front of the Reich War Court and sentenced to death.

Rosenthal could be **Rozental, Solomon Kondratevic** (1890–1955); the Rosenthal Lewis refers to is described by Daniel O'Brien as a pupil of Ivan Pavlov who spent a year with Joseph Barcroft, and who, along with Podkopaev, was a physiologist in Leningrad working at the Institute of Experimental Medicine and the Academy of Sciences.[17]

Rossi, Ottorino (1877–1936), was lecturer in nervous and mental diseases in Sassari in 1911 and in Pavia in 1925. He was professor of psychiatry and neurology there when Lewis visited.

Rotfeld, see **Rothfeld, Jakob**

---

[16] Letter from D P O'Brien, Rockefeller Foundation, to Aubrey Lewis, 23 February 1937, p. 8; held by the Lewis family.

[17] Ibid., p. 9.

Biographical Register

Rothfeld, Jakob (1883–?), was a research student at the Wagner-Jauregg Clinic, Obersteiner Institute and the Nonne Neurological Clinic in Hamburg until 1919; he was assistant and then deputy director of the Lvov Neurological and Psychological Clinic and from 1928 honorary professor at Lvov University.

Röthlin, Ernst (1888–1972), studied medicine, chemistry and physiology in Germany and Switzerland and between 1922 and 1956 led the pharmacological laboratory of Sandoz AG in Basel. He taught from 1934 as professor of pharmacology at the University of Basel and was a founder member of the Swiss Academy of Sciences and the International College of Neuropsychopharmacology.

Rotholin, see **Röthlin, Ernst**

Roussy, Gustave (1874–1948), who was Swiss, became a professor at the Paris Medical Faculty in 1910. In 1913 he was chief doctor at the Hospice Paul-Brousse, newly-founded in Villejuif, a post he resumed after the war. He pioneered studies of cancer; a centre within the hospital became the Institut du Cancer de Villejuif. In 1925 he became professor of pathological anatomy and was the doyen of the Faculty of Medicine in Paris in 1933. In 1937 he was named rector of the University of Paris. After his death the Institut du Cancer was renamed the Institut Gustave Roussy.

Rubénovitch: Daniel O'Brien wrote to Lewis about a **Peter Rubenovitch** who was an assistant to Henri Claude at the Hôpital Sainte-Anne.[18] There is, however, also a **Jacques Roubinovitch** (1862–1950) who became *Chef de Clinique* in psychiatry and a neuropsychiatric doctor at the Paris hospitals, La Salpêtrière and the Hospice Bicêtre; he was also doctor at the Henri-Rousselle psychiatric hospital. It is not clear which one Lewis is referring to.

Rüdin, Ernst (1874–1952), became professor in the University Psychiatric Clinic at Munich in 1915 and from 1917 was head of the Genealogical-Demographic Section of the German Psychiatric Research Institute. In the 1920s he was co-founder of the Society for Race Hygiene and co-editor of the *Archivs für Rassen- und Bevolkerungsbiologie*. Rüdin was the advocate of what was the precursor to Nazi "racial hygiene". He played a key role in the creation in 1933 of the Law on the Prevention of Offspring with Hereditary Diseases, which provided for compulsory sterilisation. He published *Strömungen im Art and Umfang der Sterilisastionspraxis* in 1937.

Rümke, Henricus Cornelis (1893–1967), was physician at the Valerius Clinic in Amsterdam until 1927; in 1928 he was chief physician at the Psycho-Neurological Clinic at Amsterdam University and from 1936 was professor of psychiatry at the University.

Rylander, Gösta (1903–?), was a hospital practitioner at the Urological and Psychiatric Clinic in Stockholm. He was at St Eric Hospital from 1930 until 1934, then a doctor at the Psychiatric Clinic of Stockholm University and then chief at the Psychiatric Policlinic of the Serafimer Hospital.

Saethre, see **Säthre, Haakon**

---

[18] Letter from D P O'Brien, Rockefeller Foundation, to Aubrey Lewis, 23 February 1937, p. 1. held by the Lewis family.

Biographical Register

Säthre, Haakon (1891–?), was chief doctor at the Psychiatry Department at Ullevaal Hospital from 1933 and then became a specialist in psychiatry at Oslo University.

Sakel, Manfred (1900–1957), discovered, in the late 1920s in Berlin, that recovering morphine addicts had less compulsion for morphine once they came round from coma brought about by insulin shock. In 1933 he went to the Vienna University Psychiatric Clinic under Otto Pötzl, where he began systematically testing the possibility that insulin shock could cure schizophrenia. (It seems that Sakel was not initially aware of previous efforts to treat psychosis with insulin.) In 1936 he went to the USA to treat a wealthy private patient, and stayed on, first as staff member of the New York State Psychiatric Hospital, then in a private practice in Manhattan. Insulin-coma therapy was not adopted uniformly, but was popular in Switzerland and in the Anglo-Saxon world. Max Müller organised a world conference on new therapies for schizophrenia in 1937 and Münsingen became the destination for insulin treatment. Ultimately, however, it was discovered that insulin did not differ in its long-term success rate from barbiturate sleep therapy.

Schaffer, Karoly (?–?), while professor at Budapest University, established a laboratory for research in cerebral pathology.

Scherer, Hans Joachim (1906–1945), was a pioneer in glioma research. A political refugee in Antwerp between 1934 and 1941, he was the first to distinguish primary and secondary glioblastomas. His name is associated with the van Bogaert-Scherer-Epstein syndrome, a familial disorder of metabolism.

Schubert, Gustav (1897–1976), became a lecturer at the German University in Prague in 1928 and in 1943 became professor of physiology there. In 1945 he went to Vienna and until 1950 was professor of physiology at the Veterinary School. From 1950 to 1968 he worked in the Medical Faculty at the University of Vienna.

Snapper, Isidore (1889–1973), was at the Medical University Clinic in Amsterdam from 1919 as professor for propaedeutics and general pathology.

Speranskii, Aleksei Dmitrievich (1887–1958), was professor of pathology and physiology at the Institute of Experimental Medicine in Moscow. He did research on, amongst other topics, the physiology of cerebrospinal fluid.

Staehelin, John Eugen (1891–1969), was assistant and senior doctor at Zurich University's Burghölzli Psychiatric Hospital under Eugen Bleuler from 1919 to 1929; he became director of the Psychiatric Clinic and the Friedmatt Nursing Home in Basel in 1929; from 1929 to 1959 he was professor of psychiatry at Basel University, where he was rector in 1938.

Steck (?–?), undertook work on correlations between constitutional types and the complications of cranial trauma. In 1941 he opened the Grangette Clinic in the Cery asylum, Lausanne, designed initially to receive cranio-cerebral traumatisms, but whose activity subsequently enlarged.

Stern, Lina Solomonovna (1878–1968), was a distinguished Soviet physiologist who pioneered the chemical investigation of physiological processes, most notably in the brain and central nervous system. The author of more than 400 works on medical

Biographical Register

and physiological topics, Stern was the first to describe the blood-brain barrier which protects the nerves and spinal fluid from harmful substances in the blood. Stern studied in Geneva, where she became professor of physiology until 1925 when she emigrated to the Soviet Union and was naturalised as a Soviet citizen. She worked at the Moscow Medical Institute on chemical foundations of physiological functions of the nervous system, eventually taking over its directorship. She was the first woman to be admitted to the Academy of Sciences in the Soviet Union. In 1943 she received the Stalin Prize for Scientific Research, but five years later a government purge found her guilty of "rootless cosmopolitanism", a code phrase generally used to stigmatise Jews. Stern was forced to resign from all academic positions. After Stalin's death in 1953 Stern was "rehabilitated" and restored to a position of honour in the Soviet Union, where she remained until her death.

Strömgren, Erik (1909–?), was professor of psychiatry at Copenhagen at the time of Lewis's visit, and worked in genetics.

Svedberg, Theodor (1884–?), was lecturer at the University of Uppsala in 1922. In 1944 he was professor of physical chemistry there. During the 1920s, Svedberg's work on the determination of particle size distribution in solutions of high-molecular organic substances ultimately led to construction of the ultracentrifuge, with which he and Robin Fahraeus, in a famous experiment in 1924, centrifuged haemoglobin. The ultracentrifuge became a tool for characterising and determining the molecular weight of biochemically important substances. Svedberg went on to develop equipment such as the ultramicroscope, the electron microscope and the cyclotron.

Szent-Györgyi von Nagyrapolt, Albert (1893–1986), won the 1937 Nobel Prize for isolating vitamin C. He also discovered flavone or vitamin P, effective against purpura; the protein actin; and vitamin B_2. Later in his life he explored the origins of cancer. He had received Rockefeller sponsorship to study in Cambridge and in the USA, but in the late 1920s, at the request of the Hungarian minister of education, took the chair of medical chemistry at the University of Szeged. In 1947 he emigrated to the United States.

Szondi, Leopold (1893–1986), was professor of psychopathology at the College for Remedial Education in Budapest in 1927. After being imprisoned for some months in the Bergen-Belsen concentration camp, he fled to Switzerland, where he worked in the psychiatric clinic in Prangins. In 1946 he went to Zurich and in 1959 founded the International Research Community for *Schicksalspsychologie* – "fate analysis". This stipulated that the various kinds of instincts may be determined by analysing photographs of the mentally ill, psychopaths and neurotics.

Szondy, see **Szondi, Leopold**

Tamburini, Augusto (1848–1919), became director of the asylum in Reggio Emilia in 1877, where he introduced many reforms, and which became the principal training site for psychiatrists. He was one of the first Italian psychiatrists to work on aphasia, and became renowned for his *Sulla genesi delle allucinazioni* (1880). In 1905 he took over the chair in psychiatry at Rome previously held by Ezio Sciamanna.

Biographical Register

Tanzi, Eugenio (1856–1934), worked under Augusto Tamburini in Reggio Emilia, became professor of psychiatry in Caglioni in 1893 and in 1895 succeeded to Tamburini's post where he remained until the end of his career. In 1896 he founded the *Rivista di patologia nervosa e mentale*, and in 1905 published the *Trattato delle malattie mentali*, of Kraepelinian inspiration. Along with Augusto Tamburini, he did significant work on hallucinations.

Terni (?–?), is described by Daniel O'Brien as being in charge of the department of histology and embryology at Padua University, and as having done interesting work on tissue cultures of the nervous system.[19]

Theorell, Axel Hugo Teodor (1903–1982), was a Swedish biochemist, awarded the 1955 Nobel Prize for Physiology or Medicine for his contribution to the study of oxidation enzymes. Theorell's work constituted the first detailed description of enzyme activity in which the mechanisms and interaction of "coenzymes" and "apoenzymes" were clearly outlined. Theorell studied medicine at the Karolinska Institute in Stockholm, but polio forced him to abandon practice as a physician and he became a professor and researcher at the University of Uppsala, where he undertook his biochemical studies. In 1937, Theorell took over as director of the Nobel Institute for Biochemistry, a department of the Karolinska Institute. Theorell was also the first to isolate a pure crystalline form of myoglobin, a red-coloured variety of haemoglobin found in muscle fibres. His other notable achievements include the invention of a blood test for drunkenness.

Thomsen, Oluf (1878–1940), was the driving force behind the Institute of Human Genetics in Copenhagen and had been working on blood groupings from the hereditary stand-point, according to Daniel O'Brien.[20]

Tiebout, Petronella Hendrica Catherine (1899–1968), is described by Daniel O'Brien as being at the Neuro-Psychiatric Dispensary of the Office of Hygiene in Amsterdam.[21]

Tschermak-Seysenegg, Armin von (1870–1952), became professor at the College of Veterinary Surgery in Vienna from 1906 until 1913 and was then at the German University in Prague, where he became an emeritus professor in 1939.

Vermeylen (?–?), was, in 1936, professor of psychiatry in Brussels, according to Daniel O'Brien.[22]

Verzár, Fritz (1886–1979), a physiologist in Basel at the time of Lewis's visit, was professor of physiology in Debreczen between 1913 and 1918. He called to Basel in 1930 as professor of physiology and director of the Physiological Institute and became dean of the Medical Faculty there in 1937.

Vincent, Clois (1879–1947), was based at the Hôpital de la Pitié next to La Salpêtrière in Paris, running the clinic in neuro-surgery and neurology.

---

[19] Letter from D P O'Brien, Rockefeller Foundation, to Aubrey Lewis, 23 February 1937, p. 6. held by the Lewis family.
[20] Ibid., p. 11.
[21] Ibid., p. 12.
[22] Ibid., p. 3.

Biographical Register

Vogt, Ragnar (1870–?), became director of the Gaustad Asylum, Oslo, in 1911 until 1914, was director of the Psychiatric Clinic in Oslo from 1926 and was professor of psychiatry at Oslo when Lewis visited.

Waals, Hermanus Gijsbertus van der (1894–1974), was head clinician in Amsterdam with Klaas H B Bouman. He was one of the founders of the psychoanalytic institute there and was a training analyst for many years. In 1956 he went to Topeka, Kansas, where he was superintendent of the C F Menninger Memorial Hospital.

Wagner-Jauregg, Julius (1857–1940), was head of the Vienna University Psychiatric Clinic from 1893 to 1928 and pioneered fever therapy for the treatment of neurosyphilitic psychosis. Initially injecting tuberculin, he went on to induce malarial fevers in patients. Wagner-Jauregg received the Nobel Prize for Physiology or Medicine in 1927. It eventually became obvious, however, that fever cures were no panacea; moreover, they were dangerous, expensive and cumbersome. His publications include *Verhütung und Behandlung progressiven Paralyse durch Impfmalaria* (1931) and *Mechanismus der Wirkung der Infektions- und Fiebertherapie* (1935).

Waldenstrom, Johann Henning (1877–1972), received his doctorate from Stockholm University in 1910, and became lecturer in orthopaedic surgery at the Karolinska Institute in Stockholm before going to Uppsala, where he worked on the relation of pernicious anaemia to the nervous system.[23]

Wälder, Robert (1900–1967), was a lay analyst who became a member of the Vienna Psychoanalytic Society in 1924, when he began publishing his own psychoanalytic work. From 1925 he taught at the Society's training institute and was the Society's librarian from 1928. Wälder was editor, with Ernst Kris, of *Imago* from 1932 until 1938. That year he emigrated to the United States, teaching and lecturing in Boston and New York, eventually becoming professor of psychoanalysis in the psychiatry department of Jefferson Medical College in Philadelphia.

Walthard, Max (1867–1933), became professor in obstetrics and gynaecology at Bern University in 1903 and then professor at Frankfurt am Main, before going to Zurich University.

Warburg, Erik Johan (1892–?), was possibly chief doctor at the State Hospital in Copenhagen when Lewis visited; by 1939 at least he was professor of internal medicine at Copenhagen University and chief doctor at the State Hospital.

Wigert, Viktor Hjalmar Hugo (1880–1942), was made professor of psychiatry at Lund University in 1923 and went to the Karolinska Institute in Stockholm in 1929.

Wolff, Etienne (?–?), was, in 1936, assistant at the Institute of Embryology and Teratology of the Medical Faculty at Strasbourg University.

Ylppo, see **Ylppoe, Arvo**

Ylppoe, Arvo (1887–1992), became lecturer at the University of Helsingfors in 1919; in 1921 he was associate professor and in 1925 professor of children's medicine.

---

[23] Letter from D P O'Brien, Rockefeller Foundation, to Aubrey Lewis, 23 February 1937, p. 10; held by the Lewis family.

Zalla (?–?), was professor of psychiatry and neurology at Florence.

Ziedses des Plantes, Bernard George (1902–?), Daniel O'Brien describes him as having done work on x-raying the head at the psychiatry department in Utrecht.[24]

---

[24] Letter from D P O'Brien, Rockefeller Foundation, to Aubrey Lewis, 23 February 1937, p. 12; held by the Lewis family.

Index

The letters *br* stand for Biographical Register, *n* indicates a note.

abortion 61
  Hungary 113
  therapeutic 78, 91
Abraham, Karl 90*n*
Accornero, Ferdinando 153
Ackner, Brian 14
Addens (zoologist, Amsterdam) 69
Adler, Alfred 108*n*
Adrian, Edgar Douglas 148*br*
Alberti (Genoa) 98
alcoholism
  Belgium 61
  Germany 45
  Poland 114
  Russia 125–6
  Sweden 140, 141–2
  Switzerland 91, 92
Alexander, Franz 50, 52–3, 90*n*, 106*n*
Alexander (psychiatrist, Brussels) 71–2
alienists 12, 41, 42*n*, 46
Allers, Rudolf 111, 148*br*
Alzheimer, Alois 42, 66*n*
Alzheimer s disease 66
Amsterdam, Holland 59, 64–9
Ancel, Albert-Paul 82, 148*br*
Anderson, E W 23
Andrée (assistant, Brussels) 71
Angyal, Lajor 90, 108, 148*br*
animal experiments, Leningrad 124
Antoni, Nils Ragnar Eugene 139, 140, 148*br*
Antwerp, Belgium 73–4
art 93, 103, 111
Ashkenazy (Geneva) 85
Astachoff, Nicolai 148*br*
Astachoff, Prof. (Russia) 128, 148*br*
Austria 40, 108–13

Bach, A N 149*br*
Bach, Miss (Moscow) 116
Bach, Prof. (Moscow) 116, 149*br*
Balinski, I M 116*n*
Balint, Michael 106*n*
Bancroft, Joseph 96
Banissoni, Prof. (Rome) 101, 102
Bannisoni (Padua) 105
Barbour, R F 25

Barkas, Mary 6
Bartlett, F C 32
Baruk, Henry 81, 149*br*
Basle, Switzerland 94–5
Bastianelli, Giuseppe 149*br*
Bastianelli, Raffaele 149*br*
Bechterev, Vladimir Michaelovitsch 116*n*, 122, 149*br*
Beckumberga mental hospital, Stockholm 137, 142
Bel-Air Sanatorium, Bois-Bougy 85
Belgium 71–8
  Loi de la Défense Sociale 61, 72, 73
Belmont Hospital, Sutton 14, 26–7
Benedek, László 106, 107–8, 113, 149*br*
Bergen, Norway 131–2
Berger, Hans 64*n*
Berger Rhythm (EEG) 64, 82, 117
Bergmark, Gustaf 138, 149*br*
Beringer, Karl 10
Berlicchi, Carlo 149*br*
Berlucchi (Padua) 104, 105, 149*br*
Berne, Switzerland 87–8
Bernhard, Dr (Stockholm) 141–2
Bersot, H 86, 87, 149*br*
Bertrand, Ivan 80, 82, 149*br*
Berze, Josef 108*n*, 111, 149*br*
Besta, Carlo 97, 101, 149–50*br*
Bethlem Royal Hospital 10, 37
Beule, Fritz de 75, 150*br*
bi-polar effective disorder 13
Bini, Lucio 153
Binswanger, Herbert 92, 150*br*
Binswanger, Ludwig 84*n*, 150*br*
Binswanger, Otto 150*br*
Binswanger, Robert 150
Bion, Wilfrid 22
Birkhaug, Konrad Elias 131–2, 150*br*
Blacker, C P 12, 21, 27–8, 36
Bleuler, Eugen 42, 84*n*, 90*n*, 91, 94, 97, 150–1*br*
Bleuler, Manfred 90*n*, 95, 151*br*
Bloch, Sidney 45
Blonsky, Prof. (Russia) 119
Bogaert, Ludo van 73–4, 78, 151*br*
Bois-Bougy, Switzerland 84–5

Index

Bolus, Dr (Ministry of Pensions) 25
Bond, Hubert 7, 24
Bonhoeffer, Karl 10
Bonnevie, Kristine Elisabeth Heuch 134, 151*br*
Bouin, Paul 82, 152*br*
Bouman, Klaas Hermann Beerta 64, 65, 66, 69, 152*br*, 177
Bourguignon (Paris) 115
Boutdendyck, van (Amsterdam) 64, 152*br*
Bovet, Pierre 84, 152*br*, 154
Bowlby, John 22
Brain Institute, Leningrad 122–3
Brain Institute, Moscow 117
"brain mythology" 42
brain research
    Austria 109, 110, 111
    Belgium 71
    Hungary 106
    Norway 134
    Poland 114
    Russia 117, 122–3, 124–5
    Sweden 142
    Switzerland 88, 92–3, 94
Braines (Gurevitsch's assistant, Leningrad) 122, 129
Brander (Helsingfors) 131
Bremer (researcher, Brussels) 71
Brill, A A 90*n*
British Postgraduate Medical Federation 37
Bronner, Volf Moiseevich 128, 130, 152*br*
Brouwer, Bernard 69, 152*br*
Brown, Theodore M 49, 54*n*
Brunswik, Egon 111, 152*br*
Brussels, Belgium 71–3
Budapest, Hungary 107–8
    National Asylum 105*n*
Bühler, Charlotte 65, 152–3*br*
Bühler, Karl 64, 111, 152–3*br*
Buijtendijk, Frederick Jakobus Johanes 152*br*
Bunge Institute, Antwerp 73–4
Burghölzli Psychiatric Hospital, Zurich 84*n*, 90–1
Buscaino, Vito Maria 105, 153*br*
Busch, Dr (neurosurgeon, Copenhagen) 143
Busscher, de (neurologist, Ghent) 74–5
Buzzard, Farquhar, 25
Byloque, Ghent 74, 75

Campbell, Charles Macfie 8, 110, 153*br*
Campbell, T D 11–12
camptodactyly 93
Capgras, Joseph 79*n*
cardiazol 44, 62, 144
    Denmark 143
    for depression 13–14
    Hungary 107
    Italy 85–6, 89, 101
    Sweden 139
    Switzerland 85, 87, 107
Carp, Eugène Antoine Désiré Emile 68, 69, 153*br*
Carstairs, Morris 37
case histories *see* records
Catholic University laboratory, Milan 97
Cerletti, Ugo 44, 98, 101, 104, 153–4*br*
Chiari, Hans 109, 111, 154*br*
Chicago Institute for Psychoanalysis 50–4
    Rockefeller Foundation funding 51–2
children
    developmental studies 84, 86
    environmental influences 75–6
    psychological testing of 65
    psychometric testing 69
    psychopathic 85
    research into abnormal behaviour 61
    research into diet 110
    research on premature 131
    residential care 61, 85, 87
    school for abnormal, Milan 97
    twins, studies 98, 117–18, 127, 134
    see also delinquency; schizophrenia
children's clinics 61
    Belgium 71*n*, 72
    France 80
    Holland 64, 67–8, 69, 70
    Russia 117
    Sweden 141, 142
    Switzerland 61, 87, 92
Chorobski, Jerzy 115–16, 154*br*
Christiansen, Dr (dermatologist, Copenhagen) 143
chronaxie 83, 111, 139
Churchill, Winston 32
Claparède, Eduard 84, 152, 154*br*
Claude, Henri Charles Jules 80, 81, 154*br*
Clérambault, Gaétan de 79*n*
Clivio (neurosurgeon, Milan) 97, 101
Cobb, Stanley 52*n*, 53*n*
Combat Stress *see* Ex-Services Welfare Society
conditioned reflex studies 121, 122, 123, 124–5, 127
congenital mental deficiency 45
Conquest, Robert 15
continuous narcosis 85, 87, 92, 123
contraception 112–13
    Knaus-Ogino method 91
Copenhagen, Denmark 142–3
Cornil (Marseilles) 83
Cracow, Poland 113–15
Creak, Mildred 12, 27
Crichton-Miller, Hugh 13
Cripps, Stafford 32
Croce, Benedetto 105
Croix Rouge Centre, Brussels 72
Curran, Desmond 14, 25, 27
cyclothymia 44, 64
Czechoslovakia 111–13

Index

Dahlberg, Nathaniel 154*br*
Dahlberg, Prof. (Uppsala) 137, 142, 154*br*
Davidenkoff *see* Davidenkov, Sergey Nikolaevich
Davidenkov, Sergey Nikolaevich 127, 128, 154*br*
Davies, D L 32, 34, 37
Dawson, W S 6
de Lisi, Prof. (Genoa) 100–1, 104
de Sanctis, Sante 101, 104, 155*br*
de Vecchi, Bindo 96, 155*br*
Dechaume (Lyons) 83, 155*br*
Dechaume, M 155*br*
Delaville (the younger, Paris) 81
Delay, Jean 149
delinquency 61
  applications of psychiatry to 79
  juvenile, Russia 126, 130
Delmond (Paris) 81
dementia praecox 20, 52, 83, 109, 144
  see also schizophrenia
Deming, Julia 110
Demole (Hoffman-La Roche, Basle) 95
Denmark 59, 142–3
depression (melancholia) 13–14
  Austria 109
  insulin treatment 89
  photodyn treatment 71
  Russia 128
  see also cardiazol
Dérobert, L 154
Deutsch, Helene 162
Devine, Henry 7
D'Hollander, Fernand 73, 78, 155*br*
di Tullio, Benigno 98, 155*br*
Dide, M 80
diet
  for children 110
  in schizophrenia 135–6
digital anomalies 93, 135
Dikemark Hospital, Oslo 58, 133, 134
Dispensaire d'Hygiène Mentale, Brussels 71–2
Divry, Paul 73, 155*br*
Dohrn (Naples) 103
Donaggio (Pavia) 96, 97
Dumas, Georges 82, 155*br*
Durig, Arnold 111, 155*br*
dyes, research 85

Economo, Constantin von 109, 155*br*
Edsall, David L 46, 47, 48, 49
"effort syndrome" cases, Mill Hill 28–9
Ehrenswert (Stockholm) 139
Ehrlich, Paul 43*n*
electro-physiological research 64, 97, 122–3, 124
electro-convulsive therapy (ECT) 2, 13, 14, 33, 34, 105*n*, 153–4
electroencephalography 64*n*
encephalitis 96, 109

endocrinology
  research 112, 142
  treatments 128, 137
epilepsy
  experimental 109
  hereditary 44
  research 79*n*, 93, 109, 119, 128
  therapy-induced 85, 86
epileptiform convulsions 33
Eppinger, Hans 111, 155*br*
Epstein, Emil 111, 156*br*
Essen, Jan van 156*br*
Essen, van (Amsterdam) 64, 156*br*
eugenics 33, 36
  Germany 33, 90, 113*n*
  see also sterilisation
"L'évolution psychiatrique" group 79, 80
Ex-Services Welfare Society 8
Expert Committee on the Work of Psychiatrists and Psychologists in the Services 32
Ey, Henri 80, 156*br*
Eysenck, Hans 29

Fabinyi (Hungary) 105*n*
Fabritius, Harald August 130–1, 156*br*
family care schemes
  Sweden 138
  Switzerland 77–8, 84*n*, 87, 92
  see also Gheel
Federn, Paul 110, 156*br*
Feitelberg (Vienna) 110
Feitscher (child psychologist, Amsterdam) 65
Ferenczi, Sándor 105–6*n*
Ferrera, Gian 98
Fessard, Alfred 82, 156*br*
Filatov Hospital, Leningrad 122
finger tip patterns 90, 93, 134
Finland 130–1
Flexner, Simon 49
Florence, Italy 103
Fog, Mogens 143, 156*br*
folliculin 83, 137
Fondation Déjerine, Paris 79
Forel, Auguste-Henri 42, 84*n*, 90*n*, 91, 156*br*
Forel, O-L 89, 156*br*
forensic psychiatry 98, 101
Fosdick, Raymond 50, 52
Fragnito, Onofrio 103, 156*br*
France 40, 79–83
Freud, Anna 55, 110, 156–7*br*, 161, 162
Freud, Sigmund 11, 13, 34, 108*n*, 150, 151, 156, 159
Freudian approach *see* psychoanalysis
Freudians, French 80
Frey, Dr (Stockholm) 139
Friedheim, Ernst 85, 157*br*
Fulton, John F 34, 100*n*, 172

Galli, Padre (Milan) 97

Index

Gamper, Eduard 111–12, 157*br*
Gannushkin Institute 120, 129
Gannushkin, P B 157*br*
   clinic 120, 129
Gates, Frederick T 45*n*
Gaucher 94
   see also Gaucher, Philippe Charles Ernest
Gaucher, Philippe Charles Ernest 157*br*
Gaustad Hospital, Oslo 131*n*, 138
Gehuchten, Arthur van 157
Gehuchten, Paul van 73, 157*br*
Gemelli, Agostino 97, 104, 105, 157*br*
General Education Board 45*n*
general paralysis of the insane (GPI) 72, 79*n*, 99, 102, 139
   malaria treatment 81, 85, 129, 134, 144
   research 85, 102, 140
genetics 95, 98, 117, 143
   twin studies 98, 117–18, 127
Geneva, Switzerland 84, 85
Génil-Perrin, Dr (Hôpital Henri Rousselle, Paris) 81
Genoa, Italy 98–101
Genoa mental hospital 98–100
Georgi, F 85–6, 89, 90, 140, 157–8*br*
German University, Prague, clinic 111–12
Germany 40*n*
   psychiatry in 44–5, 57, 146–7
   see also eugenics; sterilisation
Gershonson (Moscow) 117
Gerstmann, Josef 104, 108, 111, 158*br*
Gersuni, Grigorij Viktorovic 158*br*
Gersuni (Leningrad) 121, 158*br*
Gheel, Belgium 75–8
   attitude of inhabitants 75–6
   Dimphne legend 75*n*
Ghent, Belgium 74–5
Gilarowsky (histopáthologist, Moscow) 119, 158*br*
Giljarovsky, Vasilik Alekseevic 158*br*
Gillespie, W H 27
Ginglinger, Albert 82, 158*br*
Gjessing, Rolv Ragnvaldsson 20, 132, 134–6, 144, 158*br*
Glaus (senior Oberarzte, Burghölzli) 91
Godlowski (assistant to Pienkowski, Cracow) 113, 114
Golgi, Camillo 95*n*
Golla, Frederick Lucian 19–20, 28
Gordin (assistant to Fabritius, Helsingfors) 131
Gormaghtigh, Prof. (Ghent) 75
Gorter, Evert 69, 70, 83
Granit, Ragnar Arthur 131, 158*br*
Gregg, Alan 15, 17–18, 47, 48, 56, 158
   and Chicago Institute for Psychoanalysis 50–4
   and definition of psychiatry 49–50
   importance of laboratory research 15
   and Maudsley Hospital 18, 40
   and psychoanalysis 53
   and Tavistock Clinic 25

Griffith-Boscawen, Arthur 3
Grünthal (neuropathologist, Waldau-Bern) 85, 88, 158*br*
Gudden, Bernard von 90*n*
Guillain, Georges Charles 80, 158*br*
Guiraud, Paul 80–1, 158*br*
Gurevic, Ansel Lejrzerovic 158*br*
Gurevic, Michail Osipovic 158*br*
Gurevic, Nikolaj Illic 158*br*
Gurevitsch (Leningrad) 122, 129, 158*br*
Gurolevsky (Moscow) 119
Guttman, Eric 18, 27, 28

Hadorn, Walter 90, 159*br*
hallucinations, research
   Finland 131
   Italy 103
   Russia 122
Hammerstein (Stockholm) 139
   see also Hammersten, Einar
Hammersten, Einar 159*br*
Harris, Arthur 14
Harris, J S 12, 21, 26
Hart, Bernard 7, 10, 16, 25
Hartmann, Heinz 110, 159*br*
Haskoveç *see* Haškovec, Ladislav
Haškovec, Ladislav 112, 159*br*
Hasselt, Sjierd Folkert Willem van 64, 159*br*
Head, Henry 9, 16
head injuries, research 92–3
Healy, William 8
Hellerstein, S G 119
Helsingfors, Finland 130–1
Helweg, Prof. (Copenhagen) 142
Henderson, D K 32
Herlitzka, Amadeo 97, 159*br*
Hermann (Lyons) 83
Hess, Walter Rudolf 93, 109, 159*br*
Heuyer, Georges 80, 159*br*
Heymans, Corneille 75, 159*br*
Hill, Archibald Vivian 96, 122, 159*br*
Hill, Dennis 22, 38
Hippolyte, Jean 156
His, Wilhelm 156
history-taking *see* records
Hitzig, Eduard 90*n*
Hoff, Hans 108–9, 111, 159–60*br*
Hoffman-La Roche, Basle 95
Hoffman-La-Roche, Fritz 95*n*
Hojer, Joan Axel 138, 139–40, 160*br*
Holland 64–70
Holmes, Gordon 9, 25
Hood, Alex 32
Hôpital Edouard Herriot, Lyons 83
Hôpital Henri Brousse, Paris 79
Hôpital Henri Rousselle, Paris 80, 81
Horder Committee, war pensions 8, 25–6
Horder, Mervyn, 2nd Baron Horder of Ashford 25, 32
Horst, L van der 160*br*

Index

Horst, van der (Amsterdam) 64, 65, 160*br*
hospitals, public and private 62
Huber, Hans 92*n*
Hubert, W H de B 13, 25
Hungary 105–8
  state of mental hospitals 107, 108
Huntington, George Sumner 92*n*
Huntington's chorea 44, 92
Hyssen, Prof. (Ghent) 74

Institut Jean-Jacques Rousseau, Geneva 84
Institute Bunge, Antwerp 73–4
Institute of Pathology, Prague 112
Institute of Psychiatry, London 17–21, 37
insulin 64, 100, 108, 144
  research 108, 133
  treatment 2, 13, 14, 33, 34, 43–4
    Austria 108, 109
    Holland 64
    Hungary 105*n*, 108
    Italy 96, 98, 100, 101
    Norway 136
    Russia 120, 123
    Sweden 139
    Switzerland 85–6, 87, 89–90
  see also cardiazol; depression
Isaacs, Rachel *see* Lewis, Rachel
Italy 95–105
Ivanov-Smolensky, Anatoly Georgievich 119, 123, 160*br*
Izikowitz, Dr (Stockholm) 139, 140–1

Jablonsky (Giuseppe Levi's assistant, Turin) 97
Jackson, John Hughlings 16, 100, 160*br*
Jacobovsky, Prof. 160*br*
Jacobowsky, Prof. (Uppsala) 137–8, 160*br*
Jaksch von Wartenhorst, Rudolf Ritter 112, 160*br*
James, G W B 32, 33
Jameson, William Wilson 32
Janet, Pierre 155
Jansen, Prosector (Oslo) 133
Jantschow (Szeged) 106
Jensen, Edmund Zeuthen 133, 160*br*
Johan, Bela 107, 140
Jones, Ernest 90*n*, 162
Jones, Frederick Wood 11
Jones, Maxwell 22, 27, 28, 29, 30–1
Jong, de (neurologist, Amsterdam) 69, 160*br*
Jong, Henk H de 149
Juba (histopathologist, Budapest) 108
Jung, Carl 90*n*, 91, 94

Kaila (Helsingfors) 131
Kalinowski (Rome) 101, 102
  see also Kalinowsky, Lothar
Kalinowsky, Lothar 160*br*
Kandinski, V C 116*n*

Kappers, Cornelius Ubbo Ariëns 66, 69, 97, 161*br*
Karanovitch (Narkomsdrav, Moscow) 121
Katt (Bouman's assistant, Amsterdam) 66
Katzenstein, Erich 90, 92–3, 161*br*
Kauders, Otto 109, 161*br*
Kemp, Tage 142, 161*br*
Keonesland (assistant to Jensen, Oslo) 134
Kern, Alfred 95*n*
Kernig, Vladimir Mikhailovich 116*n*
Keyser (Strasbourg) 82
Kiesow, Federico 157, 161*br*
Kinberg, Olof 61, 141, 161*br*
Kinnier Wilson's disease 100
Kirchner, Fräulein (technician, Hôpital Henri Brousse, Paris) 79
Kirk, Dr (Copenhagen) 143
Klaesi, Jakob 43, 87–8, 161*br*
  narcosis treatment 43
Klein (assistant to Gamper, Prague) 112
Klein, Melanie 94, 110, 156, 161–2*br*
Knaus, Hermann 112, 162*br*
Kojevnikov, A J 116*n*
Konorski, Jerzy 116, 162*br*
Korsakov, S S 116*n*
Koupalov *see* Kupalov, Pyotr Stepanovich
Kraepelin, Emil 16, 34, 37, 47, 66*n*, 85, 123, 144, 146
Krafft-Ebing, Richard von 108*n*
Kral (chief assistant to Gamper, Prague) 112
Krasnogorsky, Nikolai 122, 142, 162*br*
Krayenbuhl, Hugo Alfred 93, 94, 162*br*
Kretschmer, E 163
Kris, Ernst 110, 111, 159, 162*br*
Kroll, M B 118, 119, 120, 128, 162*br*
Kronfeld, Arthur 89, 120, 129, 162–3*br*
Kupalov, Pyotr Stepanovich 121, 163*br*

Lacan, Jacques 167
Ladame (Geneva) 85
Laforgue, Mme (Vienna) 110
Lagache, Daniel 81–2, 163*br*
Lagergren (Stockholm) 139
Lahy (Hôpital Henri Rouselle, Paris) 81
Laignel-Lavastine, Paul-Marie Maxime 80, 163*br*
Lambert; R A 52–3, 54
Landeron, Switzerland 86–7
Langfeld, Prof. (Oslo) 132, 133, 134, 135–6
Lapicque, Louis 79, 163*br*
Laruelle (neurologist, Brussels) 71, 163*br*
Lashley, K S 16, 125
Laszt (Versár's assistant, Basle) 94
Lausanne, Switzerland 85
Lawrence-Meon-Biedl syndrome 134
Lebas, Mme (secretary of Hôpital Henri Rouselle, Paris) 81
Leiden, Holland 69–70
Leningrad, Russia 121–30
Leontiev, A N 164

Index

Lepine (Marseilles) 83
  see also Lépine, Jean
Lépine, Jean 83
Leriche, René 82, 163*br*
Leroux, R 170
leucotomy 2, 13, 14, 33, 100*n*
  Moniz's method 100
Levi, Giuseppe 96, 97, 105, 163*br*
Levit, Solomon Grigorjevich 117–18, 163*br*
Levitt, Prof. *see* Levit, Solomon Grigorjevich
Lew, Auguste 71
Lewin, Kurt 111
Lewis, Aubrey
  anthropological research 8, 11–12
  clinical director at Mill Hill 14, 27, 28–9, 30–2
  death 38
  early life and career 8–12, 40*n*
  European trip and report 1, 39–41, 44, 55, 56
  influence as psychiatrist 37–8
  and the Maudsley 8–10
  personal style 34–7
  publications 31–2, 35
  relationship with Edward Mapother 21–2
  Rockefeller fellowships 8–10, 12, 40*n*, 57
  and Rockefeller Foundation 54–6
  and Tavistock Clinic 2, 24–5
  view of psychiatry 32–4
  visits to Germany 9, 10, 57
Lewis, George Solomon 10–11
Lewis, Hilda 22, 35
Lewis, Rachel 10–11
Ley, Rodolphe 71
L'hermitte *see* Lhermitte, Jacques Jean
Lhermitte, Jacques Jean 79, 164*br*
Liège, Belgium 73
Liljestrand, Göran 141, 142, 164*br*
Lindberg (Leningrad) 124
Lindquist, Dr (Uppsala) 138
Lingjaerde (Oslo) 133–4
Lippay (Vienna) 111
lithium 34
Löewenstein *see* Löwenstein, Otto
Lofthuis, Dr (Oslo) 133, 135
Lombroso, Cesare 95*n*, 98
Lombroso, Ugo 164*br*
London County Council
  funding of Tavistock Clinic 24
  and Maudsley Hospital 5, 20
London, Efim Semenovich 124, 128, 136, 164*br*
Longhi, Lamberto 153
Louvain, Belgium 73
Löwenstein, Otto 84–5, 162, 164*br*
Löwenstein, Rudolf 159
Lugaro, Ernesto 96, 97, 98, 164*br*
luminal 86
Luria, Alexander Romanovich 118, 119, 164–5*br*
Lutz, Jakob 92, 165*br*
Lyons, France 83

Lysholm, Erik 139, 142, 165*br*
Lyssolm *see* Lysholm, Erik

McDougall, William 16
McGregor, Sanderson 160
Maclay, W S 27, 28, 30
Maier, Hans Wolfgang 90, 92, 165*br*
malaria
  research, Sweden 85, 140
  see also general paralysis of the insane
manic-depression 14, 20, 43, 89, 123, 132, 136
  research, Sweden 137
  Russia 125
Mapother, Edward 4–6, 28, 44
  appointment to Maudsley 5
  and C P Blacker 27–8, 36
  death 27–8
  early career 7–8, 19
  and Horder Committee 25–6
  and Aubrey Lewis 21–2, 31, 38, 39–40
  psychiatric perspective 12, 13–14, 15–17
  and Rockefeller Foundation 15–16, 17–18, 21, 27, 54
  and William Sargant 21, 33
  and Tavistock Clinic 2, 13, 23–4
  trust fund 18–19
Marburg, Otto 109–10, 165*br*
Margaria, Rodolfo 95–6, 165*br*
Marseilles, France 83
Mason, Max 47, 52*n*
Massary, de (Hôpital Henri Brousse, Paris) 79
Massazza (physiologist and histologist, Genoa) 99
Masurkiewics, Prof. (Warsaw) 115
Maudsley Hospital 1, 3–6, 8–10, 37–8, 44
  clinics in north London 23
  closure 26–7, 28
  disorders treated 4–6
  funding 17–19, 20–1, 29, 37, 40–1, 54–6
  laboratories 19–21
  Medical School 37
  merger with Bethlem Royal Hospital 37
  patient accommodation 6
  patient population 22, 23
  psychiatric model 12–17
  psychiatric research 17–21
  reputation 18, 21, 28, 37–8, 57
  staff 6, 12, 22
  and Tavistock Clinic 23–5
  voluntary admission 5
May, Dr (Münsingen) 89
Mayer, Fräulein 97
Mayer-Gross, William 10, 18
Mayerhof, Otto Fritz 96, 166*br*
mechanical restraint 92
Medea, Prof. (neurologist, Milan) 97, 100
Meduna, Ladislas von 44, 107, 108, 110, 113, 154, 165*br*
Meile (Geneva) 84
melancholia *see* depression

Index

Merleau-Ponty, Maurice 156
mescaline 64, 114, 115, 122, 131
Meyer, Adolf 16, 18, 50, 109, 165–6*br*
   doctrine of psychobiology 10, 14–15, 46, 49
   influence on Aubrey Lewis 8–9, 34
   and university training for psychiatrists 46
Meyer, Hans Horst 85, 111, 166*br*
Meyerhof, Otto Fritz 96, 166*br*
Meyerhoff *see* Meyerhof, Otto Fritz
Meynert, Theodor 66*n*, 109, 166*br*
Michotte, Albert 65*n*
Milan, Italy 97
Military Academy, Leningrad 122
Mill Hill EMS Hospital 14, 27, 28–32
   funding from Rockefeller Foundation 29
Mingazzini, Giovanni 105, 155
Ministry of Pensions 4–5, 8, 25–6
Minkowski, Eugène 80, 81, 167*br*
Minkowski, Mieczylaw 92, 93, 167*br*
Minor, Lazar Salamowitch 167*br*
Minor, Victor 116
   see also Minor, Lazar Salamowitch
Minski, Louis 14, 23, 27
Mira, Emilio 27
Miskolczy, Dezsö 105–6, 107, 167*br*
Modena (Ancona) 86, 102
Mohr, Otto Lous 134, 167*br*
Mollaret, Pierre 80, 167*br*
Monakow, Constantin von 92, 93, 167–8*br*
mongoloid idiots 93
Moniz, Egas 34, 100*n*
Moniz method 100
Monnier, L M 79–80, 168*br*
Monrad-Krohn, Georg Herman 133, 168*br*
Montassut, Marcel 168*br*
Montassut (Paris) 81, 168*br*
Moodie, William 6
Morselli, Enrico 105, 168*br*
Morsier, Georges de 85, 168*br*
Moscow, Russia 116–21
Mosinger, Michel 83, 168*br*
Mott, Frederick 4, 5, 6, 12, 17, 19, 20, 28
Mourgue, R 168
Movement Psychanalytique Français 79*n*
movement research 84–5, 90, 114
Muller, Hermann Joseph 117, 168*br*
Müller, Max 43, 86, 89–90, 161, 169*br*
Müller, Prof. H *see* Muller, Hermann Joseph
Münsingen Asylum, Switzerland 89–90
Muralt, Alexander von 88, 169*br*
Musatti, Cesare Luigi 104–5, 169*br*
Muskens (Helsingfors) 131
Mysliçevek (Prague) 112

Nansen, Fridtjof 156
Naples, Italy 103
National Hospital for Epilepsy and Nervous Diseases, London 8, 9, 57
Nencki Institute, Warsaw 116
"nerve specialists" 42

"nervous illness" 42
neurasthenia *see* shell shock
neuro-fibril research 97, 104, 106
neurological clinics 96, 98, 112, 115
neurology 58, 60, 146
neurosis *vs* psychosis 13–14
neurosurgery
   Belgium 74–5
   France 82
   Hungary 106
   Italy 96, 97, 100
   Poland 115–16
neurosyphilis 43, 84
   see also general paralysis of the insane
neurotransmitter/neurotransmission research 79–80, 88, 114–15
Nevin, S 21
Nielsen, Dr (Copenhagen) 143, 169*br*
Nielsen, Karl Rudolf Rasmus 169*br*
Nielsen, Michael 169*br*
Nielsen, Niels Aage 169*br*
Nielsen, Ove 169*br*
Niemann, Albert 94*n*
Niemann-Pick disease 94
Nissl, Franz 42*n*, 66*n*
nominalism *vs* conceptualism 16
Norway 131–7
Novikova, Mlle (Leningrad) 122–3
Noyons, Adriaan Karel Marie 70, 169*br*
Nunberg, Hermann 110, 169*br*
nurses
   Belgium 78
   Holland 67
   Italy 96, 103
   Norway 135
   Poland 114
   as social workers 67, 126, 135
   Switzerland 87–8
   training 58, 62
nursing, Russia 130
Nyiro, Gyula 105*n*, 107, 169*br*

Oberholzer (psychoanalyst, Zurich) 93–4, 169*br*
Oberling, Charles 80, 169–70*br*
O'Brien, Daniel 18, 28, 51, 53, 119
   list of key people in Europe 55
occupational therapy 29, 87, 120, 126, 133, 137
Ödegaard *see* Ødegård, Ørnulv
Ødegård, Ørnulv 133, 170*br*
Oldham, A J 14
Olivecrona, Herbert 96, 139, 170*br*
Opalski (neurologist, Warsaw) 115, 170*br*
Orbeli, Leon Abgarovich 122, 124, 128, 129
Order of the Seraphins 137*n*
Ormondt, van (Leiden) 69
Orzechowski (Cracow) 114, 115, 170*br*
Orzechowski, Kazimierz 154, 170*br*
Osipov, Viktor Petrovich 122, 123, 128, 170*br*
Oslo, Norway 132–7
Osowsky, Prof. (Leningrad) 125–7

Index

Ossipov *see* Osipov, Viktor Petrovich

Padua, Italy 103–5
pain research 74, 119
Palmer, Harold 22, 25
Pancratoff (Leningrad) 124
Paris, France 79–82
Pastore, Dr (Milan) 97
pathology, research in comparative 73–4
Pavia, Italy 95–6
Pavlov, Ivan Petrovich 42, 121, 122, 123, 125, 127
Pearce, Richard M 17, 47, 49–50
Pende, Nicola 96, 97, 98, 102, 170*br*
pentetrazol 33
perception research 104
Petrie, A A W 6
Petrov, Nikolai Nikolaevich 123, 170*br*
Pferrsdorf (psychiatrist, Strasbourg) 82
pharmacological research 110–11, 114–15, 141–2
phonetics 97
photodyn 71
physostigmine 103, 106, 109
Piaget, Jean 84, 152, 154, 171*br*
Pichler, Hans 108, 171*br*
Pick, Arnold 42, 66*n*
Pick, Ernst 110, 111, 142, 171*br*
Pick, Ludwig 94*n*
Pick's disease 66, 106, 117
Pienkowski, Stefan Kazimir 113–14, 171*br*
Piéron, Henri 82, 156, 171*br*
Pighini (Padua) 97, 105
Piltz (Poland) 113–14
Pintus (Genoa) 101
Plum, Preben 143
Podkopaev, Nikolai Aleksandrovich 121, 171*br*
Poland 62, 113–16
Policard, Albert 83, 104
Polish Psychiatry Society 113*n*
political contexts 44–5, 60, 145, 147
    Austria 58
    Germany 44–5
    Hungary 112
    Italy 95*n*, 98, 100
    Poland 114
    Russia 38, 45, 118, 119, 128–9, 130
Ponzo, Mario 101, 102, 104, 105, 171*br*
Post, Felix 34
Pötzl, Otto 44*n*, 108, 171*br*
Prague, Czechoslovakia 111–13
Pressman, Jack 49, 50, 53–4
Prideaux, J F E 25
Prison de Forêt, Brussels 72
prisoners 71–2, 73, 79, 141
Propper, N 119, 172*br*
Psychiatric Clinic, Cracow 113–14
psychiatry
    in 1930s Europe 42–4, 56, 147
    in Britain 12, 15, 17, 42, 54, 57

definitions of 41–2, 49–50
development as a specialism 1–2, 43, 49–50, 53–4, 57, 58, 59–60
social *vs* physical treatment 13–14, 32
psychoanalysis 2, 33–4, 40, 42–3, 59–60, 144
    Austria 108*n*, 110
    Belgium 78
    Britain, Tavistock Clinic 13, 22, 23–5
    Finland 131
    France 80, 81–2
    Holland 65–6, 68
    Italy 104
    Norway 132
    Russia 120
    and scientific approach 47, 49–50
    Sweden 140
    Switzerland 84*n*, 93–4
    see also Chicago Institute for Psychoanalysis; psychotherapy
psychobiology 13, 14–15, 34, 46, 49
psychological assessment
    Britain, Mill Hill 29
    Holland 65, 69
    Italy 99, 102
    Russia 119, 127
    Sweden 141
    Switzerland 92, 94
psychological research 81–2, 97, 111, 122
psychological *vs* organic causes 12–13, 20
psychosis 20
    and neurosis 13, 14, 20
    senile 97
    treatments 43–4
    twin studies 117–18
    see also schizophrenia
psychotherapy 34, 43, 87, 89, 91, 114, 120, 146
    training 91, 93–4
    see also psychoanalysis

Querido, Arie 66, 67–8, 172*br*
Querido, Mrs (child psychiatrist, Amsterdam) 68

Raczyska (Szeged) 106
Rademaker, Gijsbertus Godefriedus Johannes 70, 104, 172*br*
Rado, Sandor 106*n*
Raemaekers, Dr (Gheel) 76
Ramer, Karl Torsten 141, 172*br*
Rapaport, David 106*n*
Raven, J C 29
records 13, 34, 90, 101
Reddaway, Peter 45
Rees, J R 23–4, 29, 32, 234
Reggio Emilia mental hospital 105
Reiss (Prague) 112
research 58–9, 60, 61, 62–3, 143–7
    Austria 108–12, 113
    Belgium 71, 72, 73–4, 75
    Britain 17–21, 30–1

Index

Denmark 142–3
France 79–82, 83
Holland 64–5, 69–70
Hungary 106, 108
Italy 95–6, 97–8, 99, 100–2, 103–4, 105
Norway 131–2, 133–6
Poland 114–15, 116
Russia 116–19, 121–3, 124–5, 127–8, 130
Sweden 139, 140–2
Switzerland 84–7, 88, 89, 90, 92–3, 94–5
Reumont, Mlle (Brussels) 71
Revesz *see* Révész, Géza
Révész, Géza 68, 172*br*
Revue Française de Psychanalyse 79*n*
Rey (Geneva) 84, 172*br*
Richardson, Air Vice-Marshal 25
Ricoeur, Paul 156
Rieti (Genoa) 98, 99, 101
Rigshospital, Copenhagen 62
Ringert, Dr (Stockholm) 141
Riquier, Prof. (Pavia) 96, 105
Rittmeister, John 172*br*
Rittmeister (Münsingen) 90, 93, 172*br*
Roberti (Florence) 103
Rockefeller, John D, Sr 45*n*
Rockefeller Foundation
   and development of psychiatry 15, 29, 45–56
   Division of Medical Sciences (previously Division of Medical Education) 47–8, 49–50
   and Maudsley Hospital 17–18, 20–1, 39–41, 54–6
   and psychiatry 15–16, 45–8
   and psychoanalysis 50–4
Rockefeller Institute of Medical Research 45*n*
Rockefeller Sanitary Commission 45*n*
Rohracher (Milan) 97
Rome, Italy 101–2
Rorschach, Hermann 92*n*, 94
Rorschach's test 92, 99
Rosenthal (Leningrad) 124–5, 172*br*
Rossi, Ottorino 96, 172*br*
Rossi (physicist, Padua) 104
Rössler (Vienna) 110
Rossolimo, Grigorii Ivanovich 99*n*, 116*n*
Rossolimo test 99
Rotfeld *see* Rothfeld, Jakob
Rothfeld, Jakob 114, 173*br*
Röthlin, Ernst 95, 173*br*
Rotholin *see* Röthlin, Ernst
Roubinovitch, Jacques 173*br*
Roussy, Gustave 80, 170, 173*br*
Royal Army Medical Corps 4, 7
Rozental, Solomon Kondratevic 172*br*
Rubénovitch (Paris) 81, 173*br*
Rubenovitch, Peter 173*br*
Rüdin, Ernst 95, 173*br*
Rümke, Henricus Cornelis 70, 173*br*
Russia 45, 116–30
   Academy of Sciences 45
   access to scientific literature 129
   Lewis's problems with meeting people 116, 118–19, 128, 129
   rayon service 121, 123
Rylander, Gösta 139, 173*br*

Saethre *see* Säthre, Haakon
Sakel, Manfred 43, 44*n*, 85, 89, 108*n*, 109, 154, 174*br*
Salmon, Thomas 15, 16
Salpêtrière, Paris 80
Salvarsan 43*n*
Sandiford, H A 32
Sandoz, Edouard 95*n*
Sandoz Ltd, Basle 95
Sargant, William 13–14, 20–1, 22, 27, 28, 33
Säthre, Haakon 135, 174*br*
Scandinavian countries 60, 61, 62, 130*n*
   see also individual countries
Schaffer, Karoly 106, 107, 174*br*
Scherer, Hans Joachim 73–4, 174*br*
Schiff, Paul 61, 79, 81
Schilder, Paul 108*n*
schizophrenia 13, 66, 110, 144, 150–1
   diagnosis 89, 90, 107, 109, 120, 121
   family cares schemes 92
   juvenile 92
   Klaesi's interest in 87, 88
   metabolic research 135–6
   recovery/"cure" 89, 90, 101
   recreational therapy 120
   research 20, 90, 92, 93, 133–6, 137, 139
   treatments 120, 122, 123
   and tuberculosis 73, 77–8, 132
   see also cardiazol; dementia praecox; finger tip patterns; insulin
Schjelderup, Harald 132
Schubert, Gustav 113, 174*br*
scientific approach 45–8, 49–50, 54–6
   see also research
Serejski, Mark 119, 120
servicemen
   "annexure scheme" for psychoneurotics 29
   leucotomies 33
   war pensions 4–5, 8, 25–6
shell shock 4–5, 7–8, 12–13, 15, 24–6
   at Mill Hill Hospital 28–32
Shepherd, Michael 34
Sherrington, Charles S 16, 42, 148
Shorter, Edward 42*n*
Simon, E D 119
Simonelli (Florence) 103
Simonet (Hôpital Henri Rouselle, Paris) 81
Sjövall, Dr (Uppsala) 137
Skrzypinska, Mme (assistant to Masurkiewics) 115
Slater, Eliot 16, 18, 20, 22, 27, 34, 35–6
sleep research 84, 93, 127
Smitt, Silvies 70
Snapper, Isidore 67, 68–9, 144, 174*br*

social care 61, 90–1, 130
  see also family care schemes
Social Psychiatry Research Unit 37
social work 146
social workers
  Belgium 72–3
  Holland 67, 68, 69
  Norway 135
  nurses as 67, 126, 135
  Sweden 141
  Switzerland 92
  training of 68, 72–3, 92
Sodoku 95
Solevava, Z A 158
Somnifen 43
Somogyi (Prague) 113
Soviet Union see Russia
Spearman, Charles 111
spectrophotometry 83
speech research 84, 112, 115
Speranskii, Aleksei Dmitrievich 119, 129, 174br
Speransky see Speranskii, Aleksei Dmitrievich
Staehelin, John Eugen 95, 174br
Stahl (Strasbourg) 82
statistics 30–1
  Italy 102
  Russia 121, 125, 126, 127
  Switzerland 86–7
Steck (Lausanne) 43n, 85, 174br
Stengel, Erwin 108, 110
Sterba (Vienna) 110
sterilisation
  Belgium 78
  Germany 33, 44, 90
  Hungary 113
  Poland 113n
  Switzerland 61, 90, 91, 95
  voluntary 33, 36
Stern, Alfred K 51, 52
Stern, Lina Solomonovna 116, 119, 128, 174–5br
Sternberg (Institute Gannushkin, Moscow) 120
Stockholm, Sweden 138–42
Stoessiger, Hilda see Lewis, Hilda
Stokes, A B 27, 28, 30
Storr, Anthony 35
Stransky, Erwin 108n
Strasbourg, France 82
Strömgren, Erik 142–3, 175br
Sturup, Dr (Copenhagen) 142–3
Supnieswski, Prof. (Pharmacological Institute, Cracow) 111, 114–15, 142
Sutherland, John 22
Svedberg, Theodor 137, 175br
Sweden 137–42
Swiss Society of Psychoanalysis 84n
Switzerland 40, 61, 84–95
syphilis see neurosyphilis
Szeged, Hungary 105–6

Szent-Györgyi von Nagyrapolt, Albert 106, 175br
Szondi, Leopold 108, 175br
Szondy see Szondi, Leopold

Tamburini, Augusto 95n, 105, 175br, 176
Tanzi, Eugenio 105, 176br
Tavistock Clinic 22
  foundation 13
  funding from LCC 24
  and Maudsley Hospital 23–5
  and University of London 23–4, 25, 52
Tennent, Thomas 14
Terni (histologist, Padua) 103–4, 105, 176br
thalamus, comparative studies 88
Theorell, Axel Hugo Teodor 136, 139, 140, 176br
Thomas (pathologist, Ghent) 75
Thomsen, Oluf 142, 176br
Thomson, Mathew 47n
Tiebout, Petronella Hendrica Catherine 68, 176br
Tiselius, Dr (Uppsala) 137
Tolman, Edward C 152br
tropical diseases hospital, Antwerp 74
Truffi (syphilologist, Padua) 104
trypanosomiasis, research 85
tryparsamide 95, 139
tryptophane 81
Tschermak-Seysenegg, Armin von 113, 176br
Tscherniakovsky (chemist, Paris) 81
tuberculosis and schizophrenia 73, 77–8, 132
Turin, Italy 97–8

Uktomsky, Prof. (Leningrad) 128
university clinics 58–9, 60
  Italy 96, 103
  Norway 132–3
University of London 17, 23–4, 25, 52
Uppsala, Sweden 137–8
USA
  teaching in psychiatry 45–6
  see also Chicago Institute for Psychoanalysis; Meyer, Adolf; Rockefeller Foundation
Utrecht, Holland 70

Vermeylen, Prof. (psychiatrist, Brussels) 71, 72, 78, 176br
Versár, Fritz 94, 96, 139, 176br
Vervaeck, Louis 61, 72
Vienna, Austria 108–11
Vincent, Clois 96, 176br
Vinokurova, A I 158
vitamins research 83, 86, 94, 95, 106, 134
vocational testing research 102
Vogt, Ragnar 132–3, 177br
Vygotsky, L S 164
Vyshinsky, Andrei 45

188

Index

Waals, Hermanus Gijsbertus van der 65, 177*br*
Wagner, Prof. (Leningrad) 122
Wagner-Jauregg, Julius 43, 108, 109, 111, 154, 177*br*
  fever therapy 43
Wahlström (Uppsala) 137
Waldenstrom, Johann Henning 138
Wälder, Robert 110, 162, 177*br*
Wäler (sociologist, Vienna) 111
Walker, Miss (matron at the Maudsley) 21
Walthard, Max 85, 177*br*
"war neuroses" *see* shell shock
war pensions 4–5, 8, 25–6
Warburg, Erik Johan 143, 177*br*
Warsaw, Poland 62, 115–16
Weinberg, Dr (Leningrad) 128
Wespi (policlinic, Zürich) 92
Westphal, Karl 66*n*
Wientjes (Amsterdam) 65
Wiersma (Leiden) 69
Wigert, Viktor Hjalmar Hugo 28, 138–9, 141, 177*br*
Wilhemina Gasthuis clinic, Amsterdam 65, 66

Wilson, Samuel Alexander Kinnier 100*n*
Wolfahrt, Peer 139
Wolff, Etienne 82, 177*br*
Wolff, Harold 53*n*
Wolfhart, S W 142
Wolters, A W P 32
Wood, Paul 28, 29
Wulf, de (superintendent of the Corbeeloo, Louvain) 74
Wyss, von (Zürich) 93

X-ray 70, 117, 142

Ylppo, Prof. *see* Ylppoe, Arvo
Ylppoe, Arvo 131, 177*br*
Yverdon private mental hospital, Switzerland 85–6

Zalla, Prof. (Florence) 103, 177*br*
Ziedses des Plantes, Bernard Georges 70, 178*br*
Zoltermann (Stockholm) 139
Zürich, Switzerland 90–4